T0322709

Knight Errant

LORD CRAVEN AND THE COURT
OF THE WINTER QUEEN

ROBIN HAIG

FONTHILL

Fonthill Media Limited
Fonthill Media LLC
www.fonthillmedia.com
office@fonthillmedia.com

First published in the United Kingdom
and the United States of America 2015

British Library Cataloguing in Publication Data:
A catalogue record for this book is available from the British Library

ISBN 978-1-78155-324-4

Typeset in 10pt on 13pt Sabon Lt Std
Printed and bound in Great Britain by CPI Group (UK) Ltd, Croydon, CR0 4YY

CONTENTS

Acknowledgements

The subject of this book has intrigued me for many years, but it has taken me far longer than I would have liked to complete it.

To begin with I would like to thank the staff of the London Library, British Library, and Bodleian Library for their help and patience. Maxwell Craven has been full of useful information about the various houses built by Lord Craven. And since my language skills are sadly lacking, I have instead relied on Nadine Akkerman, Nydia Pineda de Avila, Petra Bryce, and Simon Neal to produce excellent translations from French, German, and Latin.

Finally, I am grateful to the National Trust for permission to reproduce the painting of Lord Craven by Honthorst and also to Nicola Cornick for permission to reproduce her photograph of Ashdown House.

Introduction

Through all the story, she—mother of Rupert of the Rhine—rides conquering all hearts near her, reckless, spendthrift, somehow ineffably great; and lifting, in a desperate cause, all those hearts to ride with her, despising low ends, ignoble gains; to ride with her down and nobly over the last edge of the world.

Sir A. Quiller-Couch

[The] old Lord Craven having been the professed and valorous knight-errant, and perhaps something more, to the Queen of Bohemia.

Lord Chesterfield

A Paladin of Romance, Craven remains one of the noblest instances in history of a knightly, generous, unswerving devotion to a woman and her cause.

H. Schütz Wilson

I first heard of Elizabeth of Bohemia, the Winter Queen, on a visit to Ashdown House, a beautiful, jewel-like mansion hidden away in a wide valley high up in the Berkshire Downs. I well remember approaching the house in thick mist along a grassy valley, past huge glacial boulders embedded in the grass, through white gates and up a tree-lined drive. Out of the mist loomed a tall, stately but improbable-looking mansion, looking for all the world like a gigantic dolls' house, hidden quite unexpectedly in the valley. We entered, to find the interior dominated by an enormous staircase, taking up almost a quarter of the entire building and lined from top to bottom with portraits of the Winter Queen and her family, bequeathed by her to her faithful friend William, first Earl of Craven, who had devoted his life to her service, and had built Ashdown House as a memorial to her after her death.

Ever since that visit I have been intrigued by Elizabeth of Bohemia. In part, perhaps, because 'Bohemia' to me always conjured up images of an exotic, far-away land filled with sensitive, artistic souls. Then I began to read more about Elizabeth, known by some as the Winter Queen and by others as the Queen of Hearts, and about the romantic origins of Ashdown House, and I was doubly intrigued. The house, I learnt, had been built for Elizabeth by Lord Craven, who had devoted his entire life, and his vast fortune, to the service of that poignant, beautiful, and brave-hearted exile who became something of a cult figure throughout Protestant Europe after she and her husband were driven from the throne of Bohemia in 1620. They set up a small, impoverished court in exile in the Hague, and there Elizabeth lived for many years until she finally returned to England in 1661, the year before her death.

Elizabeth's courage in the face of adversity, her bravery in defying the forces of Catholicism, her charm, attractiveness, and humour made her a compelling figure. 'The charm of this woman still fascinates the imagination,' wrote Sir Arthur Quiller Couch in 1921,

> [...] almost as in her lifetime it won and compelled the souls of men to champion her sorrowful fortunes [...]. It would almost seem as though no gentleman could come within the aura but he knelt to Elizabeth of Bohemia her sworn knight; that either he followed thenceforth to the last extremity, proud only to serve, or, called away, he departed as one who had looked upon a vision which changed all the values of life, who had beheld a kingdom of the soul in which self and this world were well lost for a dream.[1]

In the same vein, the historian C. V. Wedgwood described Elizabeth as

> [...] one of those rare figures whose charm and personality have outlived the grave [...] they call forth sentiments of chivalry and devotion; they awaken pictures of a beauty, or a grace, or a nobility outside common experience [...] their world was not, by and large, nobler or more chivalrous than ours [a moot point, but then this was written in 1953], but they called forth devotion from their contemporaries, and we, living sometimes centuries later, can succumb to this same persuasive, ennobling charm.[2]

Craven lived in a romantic age imbued with the spirit of chivalry, and he shared the romantic devotion which led so many men to pledge themselves to serve the Winter Queen. There was the colourful Christian of Brunswick, who rode into battle with his banners emblazoned with the words 'Für Gott und für Sie' ('For God and for her') and wore her glove in his helmet, announcing that he would return it to her in Heidelberg. There were the gentlemen of the Middle Temple, who held a ceremony one Christmas in which they swore on their swords to live and die in her service. But of all the Winter Queen's many admirers, Lord Craven was certainly the most devoted. Wealthy, generous, and brave, he deserves to be better remembered, and this book attempts to do him justice. An account of his life is to a large extent a record of his devoted, even obsessive, service to the Queen of Bohemia and her family.

Craven was the son of a London merchant of enormous wealth. At the age of fifteen he left university to fight for the United Provinces in its war against the

Spanish Habsburgs. Shortly afterwards he met the exiled Queen of Bohemia, and in doing so discovered the cause to which he was to devote the rest of his life, and a large part of his fortune. Valiant, unstinting, and warm-hearted, this latter-day knight-errant threw everything he could into his efforts to recapture the Palatinate, risking his life and spending enormous sums in the process. Indeed in 1639, while hopes still remained of reconquering this territory, he pledged to spend the whole of his fortune in the service of the Palatine house. When Craven's estates were sequestered in 1653, they were valued at £250,000, making him one of the nine wealthiest peers in England. By that time, admittedly, he had inherited the majority of his brother John's estate, but even without this he was spectacularly wealthy; in fact, his income was comparable to that of a small German state. It is hard to think of a more recent comparison, but imagine, say, a Russian multi-millionaire émigré to England after the Revolution dedicating his entire fortune to the destruction of the Soviet Union out of devotion to a surviving grand duchess, and then in later life planning a scaled-down version of the Winter Palace in St Petersburg, together with one or two other houses sprouting onion domes, to remind her of her homeland.

Alas, all attempts to reconquer the Palatinate came to nothing, and in 1642 Craven came to live at Elizabeth's threadbare court in the Hague. He helped to support her financially, as well as contributing £50,000 towards the expenses of her nephew, the exiled Charles II. In 1653 Craven's estates were sequestered by the Commonwealth, but he managed to regain their possession after the Restoration in 1660.

When Charles II unchivalrously failed to offer accommodation to his aged aunt when she wished to return to her native land, Craven stepped in and put his own London mansion at Elizabeth's disposal. Practical as ever, he wasted no time in drawing up plans for a summer palace for his heroine at Hamstead Marshall, and to remind her of happier times he intended to build it in the style of Heidelberg Castle. Sadly, she died before construction had even begun, but he went ahead with it anyway, though in the event the building had no Heidelberg-like features whatsoever. At the same time, Craven started work on a Dutch-style house on his newly purchased Ashdown estate. Hamstead Marshall Park was destroyed in a fire in 1718, but Ashdown House still remains, a moving tribute in stone to Craven's lifelong devotion to Elizabeth of Bohemia.

The remainder of Craven's life—he was to live for another thirty-five years—was in a sense just a footnote to this one great theme. In fact, he remained as frenetically busy as ever, as Colonel of the Coldstream Guards, patron of a variety of colonial ventures, succourer of the people of London during the Great Plague of 1665, and tireless fighter against the Great Fire the following year. In 1688, loyal to the last, when the Prince of Orange mounted what was in effect a *coup d'état* and forcibly surrounded Whitehall Palace with his guards, Craven refused to give up his post until ordered to do so by James II. Deprived of his posts by the new King, he spent the last years of his life at Drury House, its walls covered by the family portraits of the Winter Queen which he had inherited.

In later years it was rumoured that Craven had been secretly married to the Queen of Bohemia, but this was a belief that almost certainly owed more to fancy than to fact. There are no contemporary references to such a marriage, although there was no shortage of scandalous gossip about mésalliances between, for example, Henrietta Maria and her courtier Lord Jermyn, or Anne of Austria and Cardinal Mazarin. The gossip at the Restoration court, on the contrary, was that Lord Craven was to be rewarded with the hand of the Winter Queen's eldest daughter, Princess Elizabeth. Whether there was anything to this particular strand of gossip we have no idea, but no such marriage ever took place. As early as 1724, however, Daniel Defoe repeated a story that Lord Craven had abandoned building work at Hamstead Marshall after his hopes of marrying the Queen of Bohemia had been dashed by her death. There was certainly no truth in this, since construction did not even start in earnest until after her death. But it became generally accepted that Craven might at least have been rather more than simply a disinterested friend to the Winter Queen. In 1763, Lord Chesterfield wrote of 'the old Lord Craven having been the professed and valorous knight-errant, and perhaps something more, to the Queen of Bohemia.'[3] It later became a general assumption that there had probably been a secret marriage between the two, or at least a romantic involvement of some kind, and people pointed to the strange allegorical painting by Lely, 'The Allegory of Love', which is said to depict Elizabeth of Bohemia crowning the Earl of Craven with a wreath, as beaming cherubs look on with approval. Neither of the principal figures, it has to be said, bear the slightest resemblance to the couple they are said to represent.

The truth is that letters between Craven and the Queen of Bohemia show an attitude on the one hand of respectful devotion, and on the other of polite and even distant formality. Elizabeth was used to being the object of ardent devotion; she accepted it as her due, and she never seems to have regarded Craven as very much more than a useful friend. We can be sure that Sophie, Elizabeth's youngest daughter, with her sharp tongue and her equivocal attitude to Craven, would have had something to say had she thought there was anything improper about his relationship with her mother. And it is certainly hard to believe that Elizabeth, always conscious of her rank, would ever have contemplated marriage with a commoner, let alone a mere merchant's son.

Sophie was often downright rude about her family's friend and benefactor, writing to her brother that Craven 'n'a pas trop le sens commun' and making graceless comments in her memoirs about his eccentricities and lack of education. Still, her memoirs are full of uncharitable if amusing comments about all and sundry. In England, sniffy courtiers turned up their noses at Craven's new money, while Pepys made pointed comments about his bawdy language and his chaotic chairing of meetings. He certainly had his flaws. But in terms of courage, munificence, constancy, and sheer goodness of heart, he has few equals. H. Schütz Wilson was close to the mark when he wrote of Craven as 'one of the noblest instances in history of a knightly, generous, unswerving devotion to a woman and her cause.'[4]

1

The Lady Elizabeth

For many years, a curious visitor strolling up Wych Street (now the Aldwych) and into Drury Lane in London might have paused and inspected a fresco painting on the wall of a small courtyard on the east side of the street. It depicted William, first Earl of Craven seated on a white horse in a mountainous landscape, clad in armour and holding a marshall's baton. Dating originally from the late seventeenth century and repainted many times over the years, the fresco was long considered one of the sights of London. It finally disappeared in the early nineteenth century with the demolition in 1809 of the adjacent Craven House, or Bohemia Palace as it sometimes exotically appeared on old maps. The London home of Lord Craven, the mansion earned its alternative name after it provided a temporary home for Elizabeth, Queen of Bohemia after her return from exile in the Hague in 1661. An old engraving of the fresco by Thomas Pennant, dating from 1791 (see plate 6), bears the following inscription:

> This nobleman was Son of Sir William Craven Lord Mayor of London, gained great reputation as a soldier under Henry Prince of Orange, and Gustavus Adolphus King of Sweden, and took the strong fortress of Crutznack in Germany by storm, which is one of the most extraordinary Actions recorded in the history of the Great Gustavus, who knighted him as he lay wounded before the said fortress.

The mountainous landscape in the background represented the Palatinate, the scenic German principality on the banks of the middle Rhine which was to become a familiar name in Britain in the years after 1613. On 14 February of that year, Princess Elizabeth, the charming and lively daughter of James I, married Frederick V, Prince Palatine of the Rhine, senior elector of the Holy Roman Empire and leader of the German Protestants. Lord Craven was one of the many thousands of Englishmen and Scotsmen who would cross the seas to fight in the terrible conflict precipitated by Frederick's rash acceptance of the Bohemian crown in 1619, which became known as the Thirty Years War.

Royal marriages were always diplomatic events of the greatest importance, and the union between Princess Elizabeth and the Prince Palatine was the fruit of years of calculated planning on both sides. For King James, the overriding consideration was that his daughter must marry a Protestant, and the Prince Palatine was the best available candidate. For the Palatinate, marriage to an English princess was a considerable diplomatic triumph. It would greatly increase the prestige of the state, as well as strengthen the Protestant cause in Germany.

At the time of their marriage, both Princess Elizabeth and her husband were sixteen years of age—Elizabeth was in fact just four days older than Frederick. She was a cheerful, vivacious, chestnut-haired girl, tall like her mother. Hugely popular both in Scotland, the land of her birth, and in England, the kingdom which her father had inherited in 1603, Elizabeth became known as 'The Pearl of Britain'. Addicted to riding, hunting, and the outdoor life, her vitality was inexhaustible, and she had inherited the sense of adventure of her grandmother, Mary Queen of Scots. Her godmother had been her namesake, Elizabeth I, and the people of England came to regard her as a worthy successor to the great Queen herself.

After travelling down from Edinburgh to London at the age of seven, Princess Elizabeth spent much of her childhood at Combe Abbey in Warwickshire, the home of her guardian, Lord Harrington. Originally a Cistercian monastery, Combe Abbey still contained cloisters and a belfry, but the Harringtons renovated it to provide a suitable residence for the young Princess. There she was brought up with good Protestant principles, spending as much of her time as possible riding and looking after a menagerie of dogs and monkeys, not to mention an aviary of birds which she kept on an island in the moat.

At Combe Elizabeth received an excellent education: languages, history, geography, theology, and music were all part of the curriculum. James required his children to send little notes to him in French, Latin, or Italian so that he could judge their linguistic progress, and by the age of twelve Elizabeth was fluent in several languages. The outside world rarely intruded on this rural idyll, although at the age of nine she had to be whisked away to safety in nearby Coventry after the discovery of a plot by Guy Fawkes's associates to seize her—they had planned to place her on the throne after assassinating her father and brother.

At twelve Elizabeth began to spend increasing amounts of time at court, and she was given her own apartments at Whitehall Palace. After the peace and quiet of the country, she fell in love with the colour and glamour of the court, and to her great excitement she was able to see much more of her adored older brother, Prince Henry. As she approached marriageable age, foreign ambassadors began to send home reports of her beauty and charm. There was speculation that she might marry the French dauphin, and the French ambassador observed her closely on her first public appearance. She was handsome, graceful, and well-nourished, he wrote, and moreover she spoke French fluently, much better than her brother.[1] However, James had decided that his daughter must marry a Protestant. The Swedish king, Gustavus Adolphus, was rejected because he was at war with Queen Anne's brother, the King of Denmark. The Duke of Savoy was rejected as being too lowly. That really only left one satisfactory candidate: the Elector Palatine.

To James, the Prince Palatine, or the Palsgrave as he was known in England, seemed an eminently suitable match; the Queen, however, was less happy. A Catholic herself, she had favoured a Spanish match and was bitterly disappointed when it fell through. Now she was faced with the prospect of her daughter becoming, not Queen of Spain, but the wife of a mere German princeling. Elizabeth, she said bitterly, would be known as 'Goody Palsgrave'. But despite her opposition, James got his way.

Queen Anne's scornful assessment of the Prince Palatine was hardly fair. Frederick's family, the Wittelsbachs, were of venerable lineage, of greater antiquity in fact than the Stuarts. Originally, the Counts Palatine of the Rhine had acted as the Palace Counts of the Holy Roman Emperor, an office which went back to the time of Charlemagne. They had become the leading princes of the empire, the senior of the four lay electors who since the fourteenth century had formed the college whose duty it was to elect a new emperor. In addition to the four lay electors— the King of Bohemia, the Count Palatine of the Rhine, the Duke of Saxony, and the Margrave of Brandenburg—the electoral college included three prestigious ecclesiastical members—the Archbishops of Mainz, Trier, and Cologne.

In the early seventeenth century, the Palatinate consisted of two separate areas. The larger of the two, the Lower Palatinate, straddled the middle Rhine, stretching from Alsace in the west to Würtemburg in the east. Its capital, Heidelberg, lay on the Neckar, a tributary on the east side of the Rhine. The smaller Upper Palatinate was a mountainous country further to the east, on the north bank of the Danube and bordering the Kingdom of Bohemia.

The marriage contract was signed in May 1612, and in the middle of October the young Palsgrave landed at Gravesend with a retinue of 150. A slim, handsome young man with dark hair and ardent black eyes, he made a good impression on the court, with his studied politeness and skilful horsemanship. The King certainly liked him, even if the Queen did not. Prince Henry warmed to him too and treated him like a brother. And, as was noted with general satisfaction, the couple themselves fell in love straight away. Weeks of lavish festivity followed, the court practically bankrupting itself on clothes, jewellery, masques, plays, entertainments, and feasting.

The happiness was soon marred when Prince Henry fell dangerously ill. For a while he had been suffering from headaches and dizziness, though recently he had been as active as ever, playing tennis and swimming in the Thames. At the end of October, it was announced that he had been taken ill with a fever. Just a few days later, on 6 November, he died. It was a tragedy for the nation, and an enormous shock for Elizabeth, who had idolised her elder brother. For a time, to the great alarm of the Palatine advisors, the King began to wonder whether he should not provide his daughter with a more high-born husband. After all, she was now second in line to the throne. But upon reflection he decided that the marriage should go ahead, and on 27 December the Princess and the Palsgrave were betrothed in the Banqueting House at Whitehall—not in Inigo Jones's fine structure, but its predecessor, which burnt down in 1619.

For the ceremony Frederick was dressed in a suit of purple velvet, and Elizabeth, in order to strike an even balance between joy and mourning, wore black satin with white feathers in her hair. The words of contract were spoken in French by the new Secretary of State, Sir Thomas Lake, whose atrocious French pronunciation caused the couple to break down into giggles until decorum was restored by the solemn nuptial benediction pronounced by the Archbishop of Canterbury. Queen Anne was pointedly not present, officially because of a sudden attack of gout.

Over the following weeks the young couple went hunting and attended endless banquets and plays. Elizabeth loved the theatre and had her own company of players, the Lady Elizabeth's Men: both they and the King's Men gave performances over the festive period. A tradition relates that Shakespeare's *The Tempest*, with its love story of an island princess, was rewritten and given its elaborate nuptial masque for production on the couple's betrothal night. Though there is no evidence to substantiate this, the pair certainly saw several of Shakespeare's plays during these weeks.

On 14 February 1613, St Valentine's Day, came the wedding itself. It took place in the Chapel Royal at Whitehall, 'in Royall sort adorned' for the occasion. This time Elizabeth wore a dress of cloth of silver, with on her head a gold crown dripping with pearls and diamonds. Elizabeth was in high spirits; one of the guests noticed that,

> While the Archbishop of Canterbury was solemnising the Marriage some Corruscations and Lightnings of Joy appear'd in her Countenance that express'd more than an ordinary smile, being almost elated to a Laughter.[2]

A week of revelry followed, full of tournaments, fireworks, and other festivities. The gentlemen of the Middle Temple and Lincoln's Inn produced a masque appropriately entitled *The Marriage of Thames and Rhine*. The Palsgrave took part in tilting displays in which his horsemanship was much admired, and he paid a visit to the University of Cambridge, where he was welcomed by erudite Latin poems, and sat stoically through a comedy which lasted 'between seven and eight hours'.[3]

James seemed in no hurry to part from his daughter, but on 10 April the royal couple at last left Whitehall on a barge destined for Greenwich, the first stage of their journey to the Palatinate. Towards the end of the month they boarded the *Prince Royal* lying at anchor at Margate, and their sizeable entourage embarked on a small fleet of accompanying vessels. All in all, the bridal train numbered almost 700. Two days later, the newly-weds were rowed ashore in Zeeland and greeted by Frederick's uncle, Prince Maurice of Orange. There were more presents, plays, and banquets, and yet more speeches, hunting, and sightseeing, before they resumed their journey. Frederick went ahead to prepare for his bride's arrival in Heidelberg, while Elizabeth travelled up the Rhine in style, on a sumptuously decorated barge.

On 17 July Elizabeth arrived in Heidelberg, her arrival prompting more celebrations and tournaments, after which the procession finally wound its way up to the castle, under a triumphal archway decorated with statues of past Palatine rulers who had married English princesses. The retinue stopped in the great courtyard, the Schlosshof. Heidelberg Castle today stands a sad ruin, its vast sandstone bulk dominating the city. Much of it was destroyed by the Spanish Army during the Thirty Years War. In 1613, the forbidding aspect of its exterior gave little indication of the splendid Renaissance buildings within. In anticipation of his marriage Frederick had constructed a ten-room 'English Wing' of astonishing lavishness, decorated with porphyry floors, gilt pillars, cornices studded with gems, fresco ceilings, and tapestry-hung walls. The finest room of all was the Silver Chamber, its white marble walls covered in silver decorations and brocade hangings of white and silver. Across the courtyard was the famous Palatine library.[4]

The couple took up residence in the newest part of the castle, the Otto Heinrichs Bau. One of Frederick's first improvements was to plan a new English garden for his bride, and to this end in June 1614 he appointed Solomon de Caus to improve the surroundings of the castle. The site was far from ideal, with steep slopes on all sides, and the work involved a prodigious amount of earth-moving. Eventually, however, what had once been steep mountainside was transformed into an extraordinary garden of parterres, grottoes, fountains, water organs, and speaking statues.

For Elizabeth life became an enjoyable round of parties, balls, and, especially, hunting. 'Madame,' wrote one of the courtiers, 'takes her pleasure in hunting and is become a second Diana of our shady Rhine-side woods.'[5] Elizabeth was a good shot and proficient in the use of the crossbow, to the surprise of the people of the Palatinate, who were more used to hunting deer with the lance.

Still only seventeen when she left England, Elizabeth soon found that she was pregnant. On 25 June 1613 William Trumball, the British resident in Brussels, wrote to Sir Ralph Winwood that

> Her Highness's Physicians do report that in all appearance she should be with Child. I pray God they prove true Prophets, and that with the New Year her Highness may be the joyful Mother of a fair Prince.[6]

News spread quickly, both in Heidelberg and in London, but Elizabeth refused to talk about the subject, continuing to ride as energetically as ever and not really believing that she was pregnant at all. But on 2 January 1614, to her great surprise, she gave birth to a healthy son, whom she referred to as her 'black baby' because of his resemblance to her swarthy-featured husband. They christened him Frederick Henry.

Elizabeth's daughter, Sophie, was later to complain that her mother lavished more affection on her animals than on her children. She may have been exaggerating, but Elizabeth certainly loved animals. In Heidelberg she soon built up a whole menagerie with the help of friends such as Sir Dudley Carleton, English Ambassador in the Hague, who sent her a present of monkeys. English visitors to Heidelberg sent back enthusiastic reports of the young couple. 'My lady your gracious daughter,' wrote Sir Henry Wotton, 'retaineth still her former virginal verdure in her complexion and features, though she be now the mother of one of the sweetest children that I think the world can yield.'

Eager to please and fearful of offending, it soon became apparent that Elizabeth was strikingly inept at managing a household. One by one her servants left, the amiable courtier Sir George Goring explaining their departures thus:

> [...] for some she likes not, others not the countrie. She hath not one with her who is able upon any occasion to advise for the best. Some inferiors have will but want wit, others wit but noe will, and a third kind voyed of both.[7]

Her steward, Colonel Hans Meinhard von Schomberg, complained of her lack of firmness. A few months after her arrival, he expressed his concern in a letter to James:

> Madame allows herself to be led by anybody, and for fear of giving offence to someone, is almost afraid of speaking to anybody. This makes some of her people assume a little more authority than they should do.[8]

She found it difficult to say no to anyone. 'Every day people beg of Madame,' Schomberg grumbled the following year, 'and, right or wrong, she cannot refuse.' The result was that she was already £1,500 in debt. Schomberg left Heidelberg, vexed by the impossible situation he was in, but returned soon enough, captivated by the charms of Ann Dudley, Elizabeth's childhood friend who was now one of her maids of honour. Financial discipline, however, had not improved. Elizabeth was too irresolute and overly generous. Schomberg's solution was to give his mistress a list of simple hints for running a household.

> Never grant anything at the first request, but answer to all, 'I will consider, I will think of it [...].' Your highness should never be teased into countermanding an order [...] prevent gossiping between servants of all grades.[9]

Schomberg also had words of advice for Frederick, who suffered from periods of depression which had begun to alarm Elizabeth. He should not look morose and preoccupied in public. Public appearances were an important part of his job, after all, and he should pretend to enjoy them even if he secretly disliked them. In truth, Frederick lacked the ability to handle his job effectively. As the First Elector of the

Empire he had important responsibilities, and he had also inherited the leadership of the Union of Protestant Princes, which involved difficult negotiations between Lutherans and Calvinists. But he was weak and easily overwhelmed.

For the moment, however, calm prevailed, and soon Elizabeth found herself expecting another child. The couple's second son, Charles Louis, was born on 22 December 1617, followed almost exactly a year later, on 26 December 1618, by their first daughter, Elizabeth. But by this time, the simmering tension evident in Germany for some time had developed into a full-blown crisis which threatened to tear the Empire apart. 'The world is in a slumber,' Sir Walter Raleigh had written prophetically a few years earlier, 'and this long calm will shortly break into some terrible tempest.'[10]

Triumph and Disaster

Germany in the early seventeenth century was divided and subdivided into a multiplicity of principalities, duchies, bishoprics, and other statelets, all of them quarrelsome and intractable. To the east of the Upper Palatinate lay the Kingdom of Bohemia, an independent state that did not form part of the Holy Roman Empire but whose King was one of the four lay members of the electoral college which chose every new occupant of the imperial throne. In theory, the office of Holy Roman Emperor was elective, as was that of King of Bohemia, but in practice both had by now become hereditary in the Catholic Habsburg family. However, since the Reformation, many German states had become either Lutheran or Calvinist, and in Bohemia the religious balance was particularly fraught. Ever since the revolt of Jan Hus, burned as a heretic in 1415, the country had been an explosive centre of dissent, but by the early seventeenth century the Protestants were in a majority.

At the time of Elizabeth's marriage to the Prince Palatine, the current holder of the offices of Holy Roman Emperor and King of Bohemia and Hungary was a mild, elderly, and tolerant gentleman named Matthias. Matthias had no son, and it had been agreed among the Habsburgs that after his death the succession should go to his nephew, the fiercely anti-Protestant Archduke Ferdinand of Styria. In the hope of securing a peaceful succession, the Emperor decided to abdicate as King of Bohemia and Hungary and hand over the succession to his heir during his lifetime. Formal elections were held, and in July 1617 Ferdinand was crowned in Prague as the new King of Bohemia.

In other German states Ferdinand had already made harsh attacks on Protestants, and following his coronation in Prague he began to impose the same measures in Bohemia, in violation, so the Protestants maintained, of the so-called 'Letter of Majesty' granted to them by the Emperor Rudolf II in 1612, which accorded them complete liberty of conscience. The upshot was the dramatic incident known to history as the Defenestration of Prague. On 16 May 1618, the leading Bohemian Protestants, led by Count Matthias Thurn, proceeded to the Hradčany Palace to confront the new Emperor and his advisors. The Emperor, eager not to inflame tensions, had retired to Vienna, but his two principal advisors, Jaroslav Bořita and Vilem Slavata, found themselves cornered in the palace and unceremoniously thrown out of a high window into the moat below. A secretary, Fabritius, who was brave enough to attempt to remonstrate followed his unfortunate masters out of the window too. They fell nearly 60 feet, but luckily for them all three landed on a dungheap and walked away unscathed.

After this dramatic start to their rebellion, the Bohemians formally deposed Ferdinand and established a provisional government in preparation for the election of a new King. They began the process of raising an army, which in the following months inflicted a series of defeats on imperial forces. The situation was delicate, with the Spanish seriously alarmed at the possibility that Frederick, the Elector Palatine, newly allied by marriage to the King of Great Britain, might be elected as King of Bohemia. King James, by temperament a man of peace, worried about the danger of war. With tensions rising in Germany, he could see the peril of foreign powers being dragged into a conflict. Quite apart from anything else, he was in the process of trying to negotiate a Spanish match for his son, and the Bohemian adventure threatened to ruin this plan. He decided to send an ambassador to try and negotiate a way out of the impasse.

James I's chosen ambassador was James Hay, Lord Doncaster. A genial man with a reputation for extravagance, Doncaster was one of James's more agreeable favourites. Elizabeth had a soft spot for him, nicknaming him 'Camel's face' because of his protuberant nose. He was famous for his lavish embassies and 'double suppers', in which guests would be treated to a sumptuous display of dishes which would suddenly be whisked away before the guests had a chance to start eating, to be replaced by other, even more sumptuous dishes. His embassy to Germany consisted of some thirty coach-loads of assorted peers and gentlemen. From Heidelberg he sent home enthusiastic reports of his host and hostess.

> His Highness is, much beyond his years, religious, wise, active and valiant. [And as for Elizabeth,] I can say no more than that she is that same devout, good, sweet Princess your majesty's daughter should be, and she was ever; obliging all hearts that come near her by her courtesy, and so dearly loving and beloved of the Prince her husband, that it is a joy to all that behold them.[1]

After urging Frederick not to accept the crown of Bohemia if it was offered to him, Doncaster passed on to Munich and then to Salzburg, where he met the Emperor.

The Bohemians had now begun to debate whom to elect as their new king. Who more suitable than the young Elector whose territories bordered Bohemia, who was leader of the Union of Protestant Princes, and who was bound by marriage to the powerful King of Great Britain? For the Bohemians the choice seemed eminently sensible. At this point the Emperor Matthias died, and on 28 August the Archduke Ferdinand, titular King of Bohemia, was elected in his place. The Bohemians now found themselves in revolt against the Holy Roman Emperor himself.

By the end of August 1618 the provisional government of Bohemia had formally elected Frederick as their new king, at the same time sending a deputation to invite his acceptance. In Heidelberg, the invitation prompted a flurry of diplomatic activity to sound out the opinion of interested parties. Frederick's Chancellor, Prince Christian of Anhalt, the scheming mastermind behind Palatinate politics, argued strongly for what he saw as a triumph for Protestantism and a defeat for the forces of the Antichrist. Frederick's Dutch uncles, Princes Maurice and Frederick Henry of Orange, both saw an opportunity to advance the Protestant cause. But fourteen out of eighteen of Frederick's councillors were opposed, and the Dowager Electress Louisa Juliana urged her son to decline the offer, predicting only trouble ahead if he accepted.

Elizabeth, for her part, wrote urgently to England for advice. The Archbishop of Canterbury, George Abbot, urged acceptance, as did the Marquess of Buckingham. Elizabeth certainly liked the idea of being a queen, perhaps still resenting her mother's jibes of 'Goody Palsgrave', but she did not seek to influence her husband's decision. On hearing of Frederick's election, she replied that she would leave the decision to him. Habsburg propagandists—with little justification—invariably blamed Frederick's fateful decision on Elizabeth's ambition, disseminating cartoons showing her as a lioness importuning her mate to forage for food for her cubs. Meanwhile, Frederick had made his decision. The Bohemian envoys were pressing, and he felt unable to wait for a reply from England. He could not, he decided, refuse the divine call conveyed by the votes of the Bohemian estates. On 28 September, he signed a paper agreeing to meet Bohemian deputies on the border. If the conditions were satisfactory, he would proceed on to Prague to be crowned King.

Preparations for the journey were quickly made. Although in an advanced state of pregnancy, Elizabeth insisted on accompanying her husband. Frederick Henry, aged six, was to travel with his parents, but the two younger children, Charles Louis and Elizabeth, were to remain behind with their grandmother. On the morning of 7 October 1619, the expedition set out from Heidelberg in a large, lumbering procession of some 153 baggage wagons, containing everything from boxes of toys for Frederick Henry to Elizabeth's favourite monkey, Jack, who travelled in the company of Elizabeth's English ladies-in-waiting, cloaked and hooded against the cold. It was an emotional moment. Elizabeth was cheerily convinced, with her usual optimism, that all would be well. One member of her retinue published an impassioned account of the departure from Heidelberg.

> And no heart would have been ravished but to have seen the sweet demeanour of that great lady, at her departure, with tears trickling down her cheeks, so mild, courteous and affable [...]. What good man would not adventure his life, and run even in the face of death such a lady going before, and marching in the front?[2]

At Amberg, the capital of the Upper Palatinate, Frederick was met by an envoy of the Emperor Ferdinand, who made a last attempt to change his mind. But it was too late for second thoughts, and the procession moved on to the town of Waldsassen on the Bohemian border. Here, on 24 October, Frederick was met by representatives of the provisional government of Bohemia. He accepted the terms offered, and was proclaimed King Frederick of Bohemia.

Next day the new King and Queen crossed the frontier into their kingdom, and on 31 October, to cheering crowds, they made a triumphal entry into their new capital. The magnificent skyline of Prague, then as now, was dominated by the spire of St Vitus's Cathedral, surrounded by the spires and towers of churches, palaces, and monasteries ranged along the hilltop overlooking the River Vltava. The King and Queen were conducted to their residence in the medieval apartments of the Hradčany Palace, and the next day they walked to the Great Gallery to admire the magnificent collection of paintings, sculpture, clocks, and curiosities of all kinds assembled by the late Emperor Rudolf. A few days later, on 4 November, Frederick was crowned King in a splendid ceremony in St Vitus's Cathedral, and three days later it was Elizabeth's turn to be crowned Queen.

Upon receiving word of the developments in Prague, James I's reaction was one of dismay. Clearly the Emperor would never accept Frederick as King of Bohemia, and it was quite obvious to him that his nephew's escapade could only lead to war and ruin. James himself would be urged to throw his weight behind the Protestant cause and contribute troops and money, with the probability that England would be forced into a war against the Habsburg powers. And anyway, as a staunch believer in the Divine Right of Kings, he had a strong distaste for the rebels who had had the temerity to remove their own king and elect his son-in-law instead.

James's subjects, however, thought differently. In England, there were scenes of jubilation when news arrived of Elizabeth's coronation as Queen of Bohemia. Bonfires were lit, church bells were rung, and prayers were said in churches up and down the land. The people's beloved Lady Elizabeth was now a queen—a queen, moreover, who would be at the forefront of the great battle for the Protestant cause. She would be taking over the mantle of the great Queen Elizabeth as the champion of Protestant Europe. Soldiers flocked to offer themselves as volunteers, contributions poured in, and there were vociferous demonstrations of support for the defence of Bohemia.

> With what great and general love Britain burned towards Frederic and Queen Elizabeth I can scarcely describe. There was not a soldier, officer, or knight that did not beg to be allowed to go to the help of Bohemia. As the exchequer was empty and did not suffice for domestic expense, men and women even brought money, with most willing minds, to sustain the war.[3]

James was in a quandary. Though he was strongly opposed to his son-in-law's adventurism, he was very aware that his subjects thought differently. James was not the most popular of kings, and he could see the dangers if he failed to support his daughter. So when the Palatine envoy, Baron Christopher Dohna, arrived in London to solicit his advice, he prevaricated, saying that he would have to satisfy himself as to the validity of the Bohemian election, and that he had already sent an embassy under Viscount Doncaster to discuss the problem with the Emperor. Meanwhile, James forbade his subjects, in the face of popular outrage, from lighting bonfires or ringing bells, or from praying for Frederick as King of Bohemia.

Nevertheless, James was at least prepared to authorise Dohna to levy a body of volunteers, at his own cost, to defend the Palatinate. Dohna began by making a public appeal for funds, 'on behalf of the King my master, and of his Queen, the only daughter of the King your sovereign, the most glorious mother and fruitful nursery of the royal plants.'[4] Dohna was not disappointed; money quickly began to pour in, and he set about trying to raise troops. He began by recruiting the veteran soldier Sir Horace Vere, the ablest military officer of the period, as commander. James had only permitted the levying of one regiment, but volunteers flocked to join and in the end it consisted of 2,200 men.

The Jesuits had predicted that Frederick would only remain King for a winter; he would surely disappear with the snows, they said. So it was to prove, and forever after Frederick and Elizabeth would become known as the Winter King and Queen. But the reign of the new King and Queen of Bohemia started promisingly enough, even if both Frederick and Elizabeth managed to upset the burghers of Prague in different ways. Elizabeth could be tactless, as on the occasion when she failed to appreciate the significance of a traditional gift of confectionary on her name day, and allowed her courtiers to laugh at the triviality of the present. But she did her best to make up for such tactlessness, making sure to thank another delegation profusely when they arrived with the present of an ebony and ivory cradle for her forthcoming child. It was the religious sensibilities of the Bohemians that Frederick managed to upset. Prague was a venerable city of great beauty and ancient traditions. The Protestants now in power were tolerant Lutherans, while Frederick was a rigid Calvinist who regarded the many relics of the city's Catholic past as hateful monuments to superstition. Among his first acts was to order the removal of offending pictures and statues from the cathedral, and of the ancient statues which from time immemorial had guarded the Charles Bridge. It was not long before the citizens made their displeasure known, and Frederick quickly ordered their reinstatement.

The coronation was followed by an uneasy period of calm. A few weeks later, on 17 December 1619, Elizabeth gave birth to her fourth child; he was named Rupert, after a member of the Palatine family who had been elected as both Emperor and King of Bohemia in 1400. To the outrage of most of his subjects, James forbade public rejoicings over the birth. 'He is a strange father,' wrote the courtier and prolific letter-writer John Chamberlain, 'who will neither fight for his children nor pray for them.'[5]

In the spring of 1620, the first rumblings of trouble appeared. In April the Emperor called on Frederick to resign his crown or face being put under the ban of the empire. Frederick refused, even though he knew full well that his refusal would almost certainly mean war. Over the next few months he toured his new kingdom in an attempt to rally his supporters, and he appealed to the other Protestant Princes of the Empire for support. His appeals fell on deaf ears. Members of the Protestant Union were wary of defying the Emperor, while James refused to commit himself to giving any military help. Even in Bohemia, as the prospect of war approached, the response was lukewarm.

James decided to send the diplomat and courtier Sir Henry Wotton to negotiate with the Emperor. Wotton was an able and cultured man whose chances of promotion to the post of Secretary had been ruined a few years earlier when he offended the King by his injudicious epigram that an ambassador was 'an honest man sent to lie abroad for the good of his country.' Wotton's attitude to the woman he called his 'royal mistress' was one of chivalrous devotion. On a summer's day in 1620 in Greenwich Park, before setting out on his mission, he composed the charming 'Sonnet of the Queen of Bohemia':

> You meaner beauties of the night,
> That poorly satisfy our eyes,
> More by your number than your light;
> You common people of the skies,
> What are you when the moon shall rise?
>
> You curious chanter of the wood,
> That warble forth dame Nature's lays,
> Thinking your passions understood
> By your weak accents, what's your praise,
> When Philomel his voice shall raise?
>
> You violets that first appear,
> By your pure purple mantle known,
> Like the proud virgins of the year,
> As if the spring were all your own;
> What are you, when the rose is blown?
>
> So when my mistress shall be seen,
> In form and beauty of her mind;
> By virtue first, then choice, a queen,
> Tell me, if she were not designed
> Th'eclipse and glory of her kind?

Among Elizabeth's champions perhaps the most useful, and certainly among the most faithful, was the diplomat Sir Thomas Roe, who exerted himself strenuously year after year to support her cause. In his youth, Roe had been a groom of the bedchamber to Queen Elizabeth. He had sent Princess Elizabeth a parrot from the Orinoco as a wedding present, and he was one of those who had accompanied her on her journey to Heidelberg in 1613. When news first arrived of Frederick's election as King of Bohemia, Roe had just returned from India after three years as ambassador to the Mughal court. He sent Elizabeth a pamphlet he had written justifying the Bohemians' actions. Elizabeth replied as follows:

Honest Thom Roe

I see your journey hath not altered you in your true professing of your love to me. I understand by the Baron of Dhona and Williams how diligentlie you labour in furthering anie thing that is for the good of our Bohemian affairs. If ever I have means and occasion to shew you my thankfullness, assure yourself I will. For I have ever wished well to Thom Roe, and will do so as long as I live….

Your most assured friend

Elizabeth

PS. I pray commend my love to your good wife. Your old friend Jack, my monkey, is in verie good health and commandes all my woemen pages with his teeth.

Prague June 19th[6]

It is a charming letter, typical of the cheery informality of address that makes Elizabeth so entertaining a correspondent. Roe's reply, for its part, was typically orotund in style: 'I am ready to serve your majesty to death, to poverty, and if you shall ever please to command, I will be converted to dust and ashes at your Majesties feete.'[7]

Prospects for a peaceful resolution to the crisis looked increasingly remote, and the bleak outlook was sorely evident to Elizabeth's newly arrived secretary, Sir Francis Nethersole. Formerly public orator at Cambridge University and then secretary to Lord Doncaster, Nethersole now filled the dual role of Elizabeth's secretary and James's agent to the German princes. In the years to come he was to suffer much tribulation through his dogged support of his mistress. His dispatches from Prague in the summer of 1620 gave a bleak assessment of the situation. The optimists in Prague deluded themselves that they were in no danger, Nethersole reported, but the wiser councillors all saw quite clearly that the differences between the Emperor and the King of Bohemia were so irreconcilable that 'in the end one of them must, of necessity, be ejected out of the Empire.'[8]

Already the Emperor's armies were on the march. Instead of moving on Prague, he decided to begin by striking at the Lower Palatinate with the 25,000-strong

Spanish army in the Netherlands, commanded by the famous general Ambrogio Spinola. On 28 August, Spinola crossed the border and advanced towards Heidelberg, and the Dowager Electress Louisa Juliana fled precipitately with her grandchildren to the Duke of Würtemberg. By late September most of the Lower Palatinate was lost, and Elizabeth wrote in desperation to her brother, Prince Charles, urging him to intercede with their father.

> Dear brother, be most earnest with him, for to speak freely to you, his slackness to assist us doth make the Princes of the Union slack too, who do nothing with their army; the King hath ever said he would not suffer the Palatinate to be taken; it was never in hazard but now.[9]

Nethersole urged that Elizabeth should leave Prague for her own safety, but she was 'irremovably resolved, out of her rare and admirable love to the King her husband,' to remain, 'lest her removing for her own safety might be the occasion of much danger by discouraging the hearts of this people.'[10] The people of Prague certainly did not wish their King and Queen to abandon them. Frederick joined his army in the field in Bohemia, after sending his eldest son, Frederick Henry, to safety in Berlin. In October another imperial army under the command of the formidable strategist Count Johann von Tilly crossed the borders of Bohemia. Frederick, too, urged Elizabeth to leave Prague:

> God grant that it may not be necessary [...] but it is best to prepare for the worst. Tell me, don't you think it might be better for you to withdraw in good order, while you can, rather than wait until the enemy comes too close, in which case your departure would rather resemble a flight? I would not urge you to leave against your will [...] I merely give my opinion. You are so bad at making up your mind.[11]

In early November Tilly started to advance on Prague, but the Bohemians under Anhalt moved speedily to defend the city, where the thunder of cannon could be heard by day and night.

Given that Prague was being defended by a Bohemian army of about 28,000, there shouldn't have been too much to worry about, even though the imperialist army was within 8 miles of the city. The Bohemians took up a position on the Weißenberg, or White Mountain, to the west of Prague, and Frederick returned to his wife to reassure her, 'with a countenance of glee', that there was no danger. But the following morning, Sunday 8 November, Tilly's army advanced further. Frederick was absent from the battlefield; not anticipating action, he had returned to the city to dine with his wife and the English ambassadors. In a few confused minutes the Bohemian Army was completely routed, despite the fierce fighting of the Calvinist Moravians. The Battle of the White Mountain was short but conclusive, more a skirmish than a battle. The defeated soldiers streamed back into Prague in headlong flight, many drowning in the Vltava in their panic.

In the palace, all was confusion. The royal coach was hurriedly summoned and the King and Queen, now heavily pregnant with her fifth child, headed a precipitate flight across the river. In the chaos of departure much was left behind, including the royal crown, Frederick's ceremonial garter, and many of his private papers. Prince Rupert, initially forgotten in the rush to leave, narrowly avoided the same fate. Fortunately, Frederick's chamberlain found him in an empty room while making a final check of the palace, and threw him unceremoniously into the royal coach as it was about to leave. The royal party crossed hurriedly over the Charles Bridge into the Old Town, where they stopped to regroup and consider how to proceed. Frederick sent for the two English ambassadors, Conway and Weston, who found him in conference in a private house 'accompanied with his blessed, undaunted lady, and all the chiefs of his army and council.'

The next day they left Prague, starting out north-eastwards through the heavy snow and trailing an army of camp-followers in their wake. There were about 300 coaches and wagons in total. Count Thurn offered to defend the bridge with a regiment of Moravian infantry for a day to secure their retreat, assuring Elizabeth that he would defend the bridge or die in the attempt. Sir Richard Weston's next dispatch told the story of the flight from Prague:

> That day's journey was long, of six great leagues, to a town called Limberge; by the way were many rumours and vain alarums. Truly the King bore himself through all the passages of this disaster with more clearness of judgment, constancy, and assurance, than any of the chiefs of his army, and indeed as well as could be looked for in such an unexpected change, and, a man may say, total disorder. But his incomparable lady, who truly saw the state she was in, did not let herself fall below the dignity of a queen, and kept the freedom of her countenance and discourse, with such an unchangeable temper, as at once did raise in all capable men this one thought—that her mind could not be brought under fortune.[12]

The huge, unwieldy convoy was threatened by troops of Cossack horsemen hovering in the vicinity, while some of the baggage waggons were pillaged by attendants. Not far from Prague, Elizabeth's carriage became irretrievably stuck in the snow, and for some distance she was forced to ride pillion behind an English captain, Ralph Hopton, who was later to fight for the Royalists in the Civil War. Later the same day, Maximilian of Bavaria, head of the junior branch of the Wittelsbachs, took possession of Prague in the name of the Emperor.

Pausing at Breslau in Silesia, Frederick appealed to the Protestant Union in an attempt to rally forces for a counter-attack. But no help came. Elizabeth pressed on northwards, attended by Baron Dohna and an escort of sixty horsemen. They headed towards Brandenburg, whose ruler, the Elector George William, was

Frederick's cousin. George William was unwilling to offend the Emperor by giving sanctuary to the couple who had so rashly defied the imperial will, but he could hardly refuse Elizabeth permission to stop temporarily in his territories to prepare for her confinement. Accordingly, she broke her journey at the grim castle of Cüstrin, to the north of Frankfurt-on-the-Oder, and there, on 6 January 1621, her fifth child was born. She decided to name him Maurice after Frederick's martial uncle the Prince of Orange, 'because he will have to be a fighter.'

As soon as she was fit to travel again, Elizabeth was obliged to resume her journey. Where, however, were she and her family to go? No invitation arrived from James, who carefully avoided offering refuge to his daughter. Her presence would strengthen the hand of his opponents, and the Spanish, whom he did not wish to provoke, also strongly opposed her presence in England. It was an unexpected rebuff, but Elizabeth let it be known that she had no desire to return to her homeland. She was highly relieved when an invitation came in April from Prince Maurice of Orange, offering the fugitive family asylum in the Hague.

3

The Queen of Hearts

The Hague, then as now a bustling centre of government swarming with foreigners, had begun life in the thirteenth century as a hunting lodge of the Counts of Holland, hence its official name, s'Gravenhague, or 'the Count's enclosure'. By the early seventeenth century, it had become the seat of government of the United Provinces, the seven northernmost provinces of what had previously been the Spanish Netherlands. Back in 1568, William Prince of Orange and Count of Nassau, known to history as William the Silent, had led an insurrection against Spanish rule. After his assassination in 1584, his son Prince Maurice of Orange continued the insurgency against Spain, with the help of a 6,000-strong English Army which Queen Elizabeth sent under the command of the Earl of Leicester.

The Princes of Orange resided in the Binnenhof, the rambling old castle in the centre of the Hague, its mellow brickwork reflected in the waters of the Hofvijver, the old castle moat. Officially, the Princes of Orange held the somewhat ambiguous position of Stadtholder (literally, governor) of the United Provinces, but in practice their authority came from their command of the Army and the prestige of their leadership of the Dutch revolt. In the rather convoluted constitution of the United Provinces, sovereignty rested with an oligarchy of Dutch burghers, the States General, who met in the Great Hall of the Binnenhof, which, according to English visitors, was 'not much inferior to ours at Westminster'.[1]

The Hague was a cosmopolitan town. Strictly speaking it was not a town at all but a village—'the largest village in Christendom'—since it did not have the privileges of a town. But its role as seat of government and residence of the Princes of Orange made it a most unusual village, its streets full of soldiers, refugees, deputies, and ambassadorial retinues. In an age when pomp and ceremony were calculated to impress, ambassadors were habitually driven in carriages drawn by six horses, preceded by trumpeters and attended by gentlemen in livery. In the 1590s, the English Ambassador in the Hague had seventy-nine men in livery, as well as six trumpeters and eight pages. Aside from the diplomatic contingent, the Hague was full of foreign soldiers, many from England and Scotland, in the service of the States Army. There were many religious and political refugees too, 'seen daily by the inhabitants of the Hague pacing the avenues with the restless strides of hunger, and misery, and hope.'[2]

Prince Maurice's invitation to the fugitive couple was a calculated one. He hoped that Elizabeth's presence in his country would be a means of securing English help in the war with Spain, which was about to resume on the expiry of the Nine Years' Truce. There were other considerations too. Traditionally the United Provinces had regarded the Palatinate as an important ally in the war against the Catholic enemy, due to its strategic location and the importance of its ruler as the head of the Union of Protestant Princes.

The offer of asylum having been accepted with grateful thanks, the Estates of Holland sent an escort of nineteen troops on horse to Bielefeld to accompany the King and Queen of Bohemia to the Hague. The party made its way through North Germany, accompanied as far as the borders of the Empire by Duke John Ernest of Saxe-Weimar with forty of his horsemen, and then down the Rhine to the safety of the United Provinces. In contrast to the dangerous and hectic flight from Prague, their journey through the United Provinces turned into something of a triumphal progress. From Delft the whole way was lined with cheering crowds, and their arrival in the Hague on 5 April, weary and travel-stained, took on the air of a celebration, with all the ambassadors turning out in their state coaches.

To begin with, Frederick and Elizabeth were offered an apartment in the Binnenhof. But since no one had a clear idea of how long they might be staying, the States General agreed to make another house available for them. Fortunately there was one which fitted the bill perfectly. The chosen mansion—or rather, two adjacent mansions which could be amalgamated into one—was situated just a short walk from the Binnenhof, along a short street known as the Kneuterdijk (originally the jousting field). The new home of the Palatine family stood at the far end, at its junction with a wide, tree-lined avenue, the Lange Voorhout. The larger house, the Wassenaer Hof, was set back from the road behind a walled courtyard, while its smaller neighbour, the Naaldwijk Hof, fronted the street next door to the Kloster Kirke, the church where many of the Palatine children would be christened. Both houses had recently been sequestered and so were conveniently empty. Their owner, Johan van Oldenbarnevelt, Grand Pensionary of the United Provinces, had lived in the Naaldwijk Hof, while the Wassenaer Hof had been occupied by his son-in-law, Cornelius van der Myle. Following a political disagreement with Prince Maurice, Oldenbarnevelt had been executed and van der Myle banished. His wife Maria, who still lived in the house, fortunately had no hesitation in agreeing to move up to the attic when asked.

A rambling, picturesque brick mansion of crow-stepped gables, dormer windows, and steep-pitched roofs, the Wassenaer Hof was adorned with richly ornamented chimneys and two small towers, together with a portico decorated with richly carved wooden armorial bearings. The States General decided that their royal guests should be housed in appropriate style, and three apartments in the mansion were splendidly redecorated and filled with fine paintings and furniture. An oak-panelled outer hall, hung with Flemish tapestries and fine oil paintings, contained a stone fireplace with a heavily carved overmantel. This room opened into the principal reception room, its walls hung with fashionable gilded leather, and beyond was the audience chamber, also lined with gilded leather and silk panels.[3]

On 4 April 1621, Frederick and Elizabeth moved into what they fervently hoped would be a temporary home. With them came their eldest son, Frederick Henry, who had arrived in the Netherlands before his parents, and Rupert. The other children were still scattered around northern Germany, Charles Louis and Elizabeth in the care of their grandmother Louisa Juliana in Brandenburg, and three-month-old Maurice in Berlin. Most of the 2,000 or so retainers and camp-followers who had fled from Bohemia with their King and Queen were found lodgings in the Hague, and the able-bodied men were offered places in the States Army. But the Wassenaer Hof still had to accommodate a large entourage. All in all, the royal household consisted of about 200 people and 50 horses. There were also assorted pet dogs and monkeys which Elizabeth had managed to bring with her, together with such clothes, plate, and jewels as had been saved in the panic of their sudden flight. Elizabeth's favourite monkey, Jack, had somehow survived all the tumult of the last year, and sat by her writing desk 'as knavish as ever he was' in Heidelberg or the Hradčany Palace. Her favourite puppy, Apollon, 'the most beautiful greyhound in Europe', had also travelled with her.[4]

On 13 April, a deputation from the States General paid a ceremonial visit to the King and Queen of Bohemia in their new home, and for the next three days Frederick and Elizabeth kept open house. It was Elizabeth's courage that struck people, her spirited determination in the face of disaster.

> His majesty's most royal daughter is, to use her godmother's [Elizabeth I's] impress, *semper eadem* [always the same], full of Princely courage, and therefore as well for that as her other admirable and royally shining virtues justly honoured, even by the enemies of her cause.[5]

On 27 April, Frederick had an audience with the States General. He thanked them for their kindness, and in return they agreed to pay 10,000 guilders a month towards the expenses of the family.

Frederick, weighed down with guilt at the loss of his patrimony and frustration at his enforced inactivity, never overcame his aversion to the Hague. Elizabeth, on the other hand, found plenty of sympathy and diversion in the large English community in the town. The Palatine family were regular attenders at the nearby English church, and Elizabeth became a close friend of the English ambassador Sir Dudley Carleton, whose wife helped her rebuild her depleted menagerie until it contained over thirty dogs and monkeys. Carleton was the object of Elizabeth's teasing, 'but her mirth,' he wrote, 'is mixed with as much sorrow and anger as the cheerfulness and sweetness of her disposition can permit.' He urged that she should be granted a monthly allowance of £1,000, and that her debts of £3,000 be paid off. According to Maurice of Nassau,

> The Queen of Bohemia [...] is accounted the most charming Princess of Europe, and called by some the Queen of Hearts. But she is far more than that—she is a true and faithful wife, and that too, of a husband who is in every respect her inferior.[6]

Certainly poor Frederick, melancholic and often irritable, always suffered from comparison with his wife. Her new nickname reflected the cult-like status she had acquired throughout Protestant Europe. William Trumball, the English agent in Flanders, wrote that

> For her Majesty I will spend the last drop of my blood; and if my eldest son should refuse to do the like, he should never enjoy one pennyworth of my poor estate.[7]

In the Spanish Netherlands and parts of Germany, by contrast, she had been dubbed 'the Helen of Germany', a woman who through her ambition to wear a crown had plunged the Empire into war. Of course it was not true, as Elizabeth was at pains to point out to visitors; she was careful to leave on prominent display in her withdrawing room a letter from the Archbishop of Canterbury dated two years earlier, which strongly advised her husband's acceptance of the crown of Bohemia.

What, however, was to be done now? All hopes rested on King James, and three weeks after Elizabeth's arrival in the Hague she dispatched Nethersole to England with a request that James give permission for them to retain the services of the Army of the Union of Protestant Princes. If Frederick were allowed to take command of this, she argued, he would be able to reconquer the Palatinate. Nethersole was in such haste to deliver his mistress's message that he crossed the Channel 'in a fisher boat, no other daring hazard such a storm.' James's answer, when it came, was a bitter disappointment. He would not agree to the proposal, but—one can imagine Elizabeth rolling her eyes with exasperation—he would be sending an ambassador extraordinaire, Lord Digby, to Vienna to negotiate the restoration of the Palatinate. Until then, his daughter and son-in-law had to be patient.

Thus began a stream of diplomatic activity, which invariably failed dismally. But in practice James had little alternative. War was an expensive business. Parliament might have been full of sympathy for the Palatine cause, but they still wouldn't grant subsidies without attaching to them demands for the redress of grievances—demands which James refused to grant. The only alternative was diplomacy, but diplomacy led nowhere, and in both England and Scotland there was a sense of outrage that the King did nothing to support his daughter. Not only was he damaging the cause of Protestantism by his failure to act, he was bringing shame on his dynasty too.

James's attitude provoked ribaldry among Catholic pamphleteers. He was pictured with a sword that would not leave its scabbard, and with an empty purse and empty pockets hanging out at his sides. As for his unfortunate daughter, Viennese cartoonists drew her as an Irish beggar, with her hair hanging about her ears and her child at her back, while her father carried the cradle behind her. The Jesuits staged a play in which a messenger arrived with the news that the Elector Palatine was shortly to acquire a huge army: the King of Denmark was to send 100,000, the Dutch 100,000, and the King of Great Britain 100,000. When asked, 100,000 of what, he replied that the King of Denmark would send him 100,000 red herrings, the Dutch 100,000 cheeses, and James 100,000 ambassadors.

Elizabeth's letters to her father grew increasingly desperate.

> Your majesty will understand by the King's letters how the Palatinate is in danger of being utterly lost if your majesty give us not some aid. I am sorry we are obliged to trouble your majesty so much with our affairs, but their urgency is so great that we cannot do otherwise.[8]

The news from Bohemia was grim. In June a group of twenty-seven leading patriots were executed in a particularly grisly way in the Old Town Square in Prague, the ringleaders' tongues ripped out and their severed heads grimly mounted on the towers of the Charles Bridge. Their estates were confiscated and the crown of Bohemia declared hereditary in the Habsburg family. The mood in the Wassenaer Hof was sombre, and Frederick began to relapse into his old melancholia, made worse by his forced inactivity. In August, to the intense annoyance of his father-in-law and the great anxiety of his wife, he decided to join the States Army as a volunteer.

The military picture was universally gloomy. In the absence of any lead from James, a variety of Protestant paladins had rallied to the cause of the deposed King and Queen. They included Ernst, Count Mansfeld, an ambitious soldier of fortune whom Frederick had appointed as his commander in Bohemia. A resourceful but not altogether trustworthy character, Mansfeld had published an *Apologie* in which he presented himself as a chivalrous knight defending the honour of the Queen of Bohemia. His 12,000-strong army, augmented by troops from the disbanded forces of the Protestant Princes, was engaged in defending the passes between Bohemia and the Upper Palatinate. Mansfeld's troops were notorious for their brutal and undisciplined behaviour, habitually doing as much damage to the surrounding countryside as any hostile army. And Mansfeld's loyalty was always questionable. Formerly in the service of the imperial Army, he had decided to change sides and fight for Frederick. As the imperial diplomats in Vienna spun out negotiations with Lord Digby, Mansfeld retreated to the Lower Palatinate. There he joined forces with General Vere in October, relieved the siege of Frankenthal, and proceeded to Heidelberg, which was anxiously awaiting a siege by the army of Count Tilly.

The other paladin who rallied in support of the Palatinate cause was, on the whole, a more attractive character. Duke Christian of Brunswick, or 'the mad Halberstädter', was a wild adventurer with a romantic streak. Officially, he was the administrator of the bishopric of Halberstadt—not that he possessed any particular qualification for this office. Instead, he far preferred war. The cause of the Queen of Bohemia gave an aura of chivalry to his hatred of the Habsburgs. In true knight-errant fashion, he wore a glove of Elizabeth's in his helmet, swearing that he would return it to her in Heidelberg once it had been recaptured, and he had the words 'Für Gott und für sie'—'for God and for her'—woven into his banners. Christian was prone to grand gestures. He blasted the city of Münster with his cannon after its citizens refused to give up some personal property belonging to the King and Queen of Bohemia, which had been pillaged in Prague.[9] In the autumn of 1621, he raised a 10,000-strong army to support the Palatine cause. He had few financial resources of his own, but successfully raised enormous sums from the bishoprics of Münster and Paderborn with the help of dramatic letters, deliberately burnt at the four corners, which he issued to every village he passed.

The Palatinate was in a desperate state. General Vere's tiny army had no hope of defending it against Spinola's vastly superior forces, even without James's insistence that they should act strictly on the defensive. James objected strongly to Frederick's taking up arms, protesting that it was likely to complicate negotiations in Vienna. He ordered his son-in-law to return to the Hague, and in October Frederick did so with a bad grace, complaining bitterly that he wished he had married the daughter of a beggar rather than the daughter of the King of Great Britain. At James's insistence, he reluctantly signed an instrument renouncing the throne of Bohemia and craving pardon from the Emperor for his rash conduct.

In England popular tracts began to appear promoting the cause of the exiled Queen. The *vox populi* waxed indignant at James's inaction:

> Sir, God hath made her your daughter, and our Princess, and adorned her with so many virtues, as she rather deserves to be empress of the whole world, than a lady of a small province; she inheriteth the name and virtues, the majesty and generosity, of our immortal Queen Elizabeth, and is a Princess of such excellent hopes and exquisite perfections, that I cannot speak of her without praise [...] and yet will your Majesty neglect her and will you not draw your sword in her just quarrel whose fame and virtue hath drawn most hearts to adore, all to admire her.[10]

James summoned Parliament in January 1622, and declared his intention of sending an expeditionary force to assist Mansfeld in the Palatinate. But although the House of Commons was every bit as keen to relieve the Palatinate, it insisted in discussing James's foreign policy, and an exasperated King promptly dissolved Parliament. In the end, the planned expeditionary force consisted of just a few extra troops for Vere, paid for with money raised in Scotland.

Feelings in both England and Scotland were running high, and those found to have spoken disrespectfully of the King and Queen of Bohemia were given harsh treatment. In April 1621, a Catholic Shropshire barrister, Edward Floyd, was reported to have remarked scornfully: 'I have heard that Goodman Palsgrave and Goodwife Palsgrave have taken their heels; and as I have heard Goodwife Palsgrave is a prisoner.' He had as much right to be King of Wales, said Floyd, as Frederick had to be King of Bohemia.[11] For these unwise comments, Floyd was called before the bar of the House of Commons and accused of having 'uttered openly false, malicious, and disrespectful speeches' about the King and Queen of Bohemia. As punishment Parliament ruled that he should be degraded from the estate of a gentleman, branded, fined £5,000, and sent to Newgate for life—by any standards a severe sentence. Another offender had his ears nailed to the pillory, while a third was condemned to life imprisonment after narrowly escaping being torn to pieces by a mob.

In London, the gentlemen of the Inns of Court shared in the widespread sympathy for Elizabeth. At Christmas 1621, it was reported that

> The Lieutenant of the Middle Temple played a game this Christmastide whereat his Majesty was highly displeased. He made choice of some thirty of the civellest and best-fashioned gentlemen of that house to sup with him, and being at supper, took a cup of wine in one hand and held his sword drawn in the other, and so began a health 'to the distressed Lady Elizabeth', and having drunk, kissed his sword and laying his hand upon it, took an oath to live and die in her service.[12]

How many of these gentleman fulfilled their vows history does not relate, but some may well have joined Vere's regiment in the Palatinate. Many more would no doubt have gone if James had agreed to send more troops. In February 1622, Frederick, to his great relief, obtained permission from James to go to fight in the Palatinate. With the newly arrived forces of Christian of Brunswick and Mansfeld, together with Mansfeld's ally the Margrave of Baden Durlach and the English and Scottish troops of General Vere, the Palatine forces were now comfortably superior in numbers to the imperialist armies. However, they were disastrously hampered by divisions between the commanders and, not least, by James's scruples. Still, with luck Frederick's presence would enable the different factions to make peace. In late March he set off for Paris, disguised as a young German merchant, and then made his way to the Palatinate.

On 7 April 1622, Elizabeth's sixth child, a daughter, was born. Eight days later she was christened Louise Hollandine; her godparents included the States of Holland and Elizabeth's new champion, Christian of Brunswick. Christian, busy fighting in the Palatinate, sent a christening present in the shape of a hefty ransom he had just received from a wealthy prisoner of war. Word arrived of Frederick's safe arrival in the Palatinate; on the day of his daughter's christening he slept in Heidelberg Castle for the first time for many years. The season began well when Mansfeld defeated Tilly at Wiesloch in late April. But in June Christian suffered a serious defeat at Höchst, escaping with most of his army but losing all his baggage. In the dejected aftermath of the battle, he wrote an emotional letter to his heroine (who, by the way, he had never actually met) begging her forgiveness.

Madame, my dearest and most beloved queen [...] I entreat you, most humbly, not to be angry with your faithful slave for this disaster, nor take away the affection which your majesty has hitherto shown to one who loves you above all in this world [...]. Courage will never fail me to die in your majesty's service, for I esteem your favour a hundred times dearer than life; and be assured that I will try with all my power not only to reassemble my troops but also moreover to raise as many more that I may be in better condition to serve faithfully your majesty, whom I love outre le possible, assuring you that as long as God gives me life I shall serve you faithfully and expend all I have in the world for you.

Your most humble, most constant, most faithful, most affectionate and most obedient slave who loves you and will love you, infinitely and incessantly to death. Christian.[13]

He was as good as his word and promptly set about rallying his troops, while Mansfeld mounted a raid into neighbouring Hesse–Darmstadt. But just as the fortunes of war seemed to be turning, James sent a messenger in the shape of Lord Chichester with an urgent demand that fighting cease. He had only authorised Vere's troops to fight defensively, he wrote, and furthermore he was in the midst of delicate negotiations with the Spanish; the Palatinate, he insisted, was on the point of being restored by treaty. Chichester promised on James's behalf that if by some mischance the treaty were to fail the King would provide Frederick with an army of 10,000 men the following year.

In July Frederick relented and disbanded his army. He dismissed Mansfeld and Christian and retired to Sedan, and the army was promptly rehired by Frederick Henry, who had by this time succeeded his brother as Prince of Orange. Mansfeld and Christian marched off towards the United Provinces, which they managed to reach after a sharp engagement with the Spanish Army of the Palatinate at Fleurus at the end of August. Christian displayed his usual reckless courage, leading four unsuccessful cavalry charges before he finally broke through with the fifth. The victory came at a huge price; in the battle he lost not just the majority of his infantry, but also his left arm. He retired to Breda, where, in an extraordinary show of bravery, he had the arm amputated above the elbow in an operation which was performed to a fanfare of trumpets. He commemorated the occasion by issuing a medal with the inscription *Altera restat* ('I've still got the other one'), and sent word to Elizabeth that he was 'already devising how to make an iron arm for his bridle hand.'[14]

This was a tense period for Elizabeth. Each letter seemed to increase her melancholy, such that, wrote Carleton, the days without letters were the easiest. News from the Palatinate became grimmer and grimmer. Tilly had renewed his siege of Heidelberg, with extreme violence and cruelty, and on 11 September 1622 he finally broke the city defences. The castle was badly damaged and the famous library broken up, the majority of it sent to the Vatican.

In mid–October, Frederick returned to the Hague. Diplomacy had clearly failed, and in September, in what seemed a final blow to Frederick's hopes, the Emperor transferred the Palatine electorate from Frederick to his cousin Maximilian, Duke of Bavaria. Perhaps now James would finally give his daughter and son-in-law the help they so desperately needed. There was great excitement in England. Prince Charles, on bended knee, begged his father to take pity on his poor distressed daughter and to permit him to raise an army of loyal subjects.

In November, Sir Horace Vere, who had been holding out at Mannheim, surrendered after a long and bitter struggle. To Frederick and Elizabeth the news was shattering. Sir Dudley Carleton wrote that

> Of all the ill news which have come unto him, like Job's messengers, I have observed none since his first arrival in these parts, to drive him into so much distemper and passion as this, for which the sorrow of Her Highness's heart (who was present at the reading of the letters) was seen in her watery eyes and silence. God send them both patience.[15]

Feelings in England were running as high as ever, and at Christmas the gentlemen of the Middle Temple repeated their ceremony, drinking the health of the distressed lady Elizabeth and swearing to live and die in her service.[16]

Only Frankenthal, Elizabeth's dower town, now remained uncaptured. But this last stronghold, defended valiantly by Sir John Burrough, was surrendered without a fight at James's insistence, with the inevitably empty promise that it would be restored within eighteen months if a general peace had not been signed. Privately Elizabeth was scathing about her father's ineffectual negotiations. He 'hath hitherto done us more harm than good,' she wrote; he was being 'cozened and abused, but will not see it till it be too late.' Finally, after much prevaricating and after Christian had been badly defeated at Stadtlohn in August 1623, Frederick bowed to James's demand and signed an armistice with the Emperor, which omitted any mention of the Palatinate.

If Frederick's response was to lapse into depression, Elizabeth was made of sterner stuff, and ambitious plans were made at the Wassenaer Hof for an anti-Habsburg alliance. 'Though I have cause enough to be sad,' she wrote to Sir Thomas Roe, 'yet am I still of my wild humour to be as merry as I can in spite of fortune.'[17]

It was increasingly obvious that there would be no imminent return to the Palatinate. In the summer of 1623 pressure of space in the Wassenaer Hof lessened after Frederick obtained from Prince Maurice the gift of a house in Leiden, not far from the Hague, where their children could be brought up. 'Their highnesses are in part compelled to this course,' wrote Carleton, 'by reason of the greatness of their family, which exceeds the proportion of the small house they have here.'[18] Originally a convent, the house at Leiden, pleasantly situated beside a canal flowing past the university, had been converted into a residence for the Prince of Orange. It was known as the Prinsenhof. In the summer of 1623, the first group of royal children arrived: Frederick Henry, aged nine, Rupert, aged four, and Louise, aged fifteen months. The following year they were joined by Charles Louis, Elizabeth's second son and her favourite child, who had been staying with his aunt in Brandenburg, and a few years later by Elizabeth and Maurice, who had been left dispersed around the courts of Germany during the flight from Prague. New children appeared every year or two and were duly dispatched to Leiden as soon as was convenient. Sophie, Elizabeth's youngest daughter, wrote in her memoirs:

> No sooner was I strong enough to be moved, than the Queen my mother sent me to Leyden [...] where her Majesty had her whole family brought up apart from herself, preferring the sight of her monkeys and dogs to that of her children.[19]

Certainly Elizabeth was fond of monkeys and dogs, but Sophie was hardly being fair; there was just not enough room for a large brood of children in the cramped confines of the Wassenaer Hof.

At Leiden the children were put into the charge of Frederick's former governess, the elderly Madame de Ples, who was assisted by her two severe daughters. It was a strict Calvinist upbringing based on the routine of the Heidelberg court and characterised by extreme formality. To Sophie's annoyance, the children underwent a stringent regime of lessons punctuated by rigorous ceremonial. They rose every morning at seven, and received religious instruction based on the Heidelberg Confession until breakfast at 8.30. Thereafter followed a regular succession of teacher after teacher, 'except when, to my comfort, kind Providence sent them a cold in the head.' An hour with the dancing master was followed by dinner at eleven.

> This meal always took place with great ceremony at a long table. On entering the dining room I found all my brothers drawn up in front, with all their governors and gentlemen posted behind in the same order side by side.

Before sitting down, Sophie was obliged to make nine curtsies: a very deep one to her brothers and a smaller one to their attendants, one in reply to the governess, another on handing her gloves to an attendant, and

> [...] again on placing myself opposite my brothers, again when the gentleman brought me a large basin in which to wash my hands, again after grace was said, and for the eighth and last time on seating myself at table.[20]

Sophie was a quick learner. Her teachers believed that she would turn into a prodigy, but her only object was to finish her studies as quickly as possible. Still, the Palatine children all received a first-class education at Leiden; they learnt French, German, English, Dutch, Latin, Greek, theology, history, mathematics, and law. At the age of nine or ten the children were removed from the Prinsenhof, the boys sent abroad to travel and the girls brought to live in the Hague.

The Gentleman Volunteer

As the exiled King and Queen of Bohemia were fast losing hope of a swift return to the Palatinate, and as their children were hard at work at their studies at Leiden, the fifteen-year-old William Craven was beginning his own studies at Trinity College, Oxford.

Although Craven's family was of humble origins, he was heir to a spectacular fortune. His father, Sir William Craven, had been a highly successful London merchant who had held the office of Lord Mayor of London in 1610–11. Born to poor parents in the West Yorkshire village of Appletreewick, at the age of thirteen or fourteen William Craven senior had been sent down to London by the common carrier and bound as apprentice to a merchant tailor. After seven years he was admitted to the Merchant Taylors' Company. He made a fortune initially in the wholesaling of cloth, but later became a moneylender on an enormous scale, advancing substantial loans to James I, whose money problems were always acute, and to various members of the aristocracy. In 1597, at the relatively advanced age of fifty-two, he married Elizabeth Whitmore, the seventeen-year-old daughter of an influential merchant and city alderman, and quickly fathered two daughters, Elizabeth and Mary.

In 1603, William Craven was granted one of James I's extravagant shower of knighthoods marking his accession to the English throne. Four years later, the family moved to a substantial house on the south side of Leadenhall Street, on the site now occupied by the Lloyds insurance building. It was a splendid and lavishly decorated sixty-two-room mansion, recently built on the site of the former Zouche's Inn, complete with blue and white marble paving, carved hall screen, and banqueting house in the garden—a suitably grand residence in which to hold receptions during Craven's term as Lord Mayor. After a splendid Lord Mayor's Show (by this time the processions had come to include pageants, trumpeters, and standard bearers) he had hosted a lavish dinner at the Guildhall, at which Prince Christian of Anhalt was guest of honour. The year after they moved to Leadenhall Street, their eldest son, William, was born. With great exactitude Sir William Craven made a careful note, on a back page of one of his voluminous ledgers, of the time as well as the date of birth of each of his children. It tells us that William was born at one o'clock in the afternoon of Friday 17 June 1608.[1] Nine days later, on 26 June, he was baptised in the nearby church of St Andrew's Undershaft, just across the street from his house. Two years later came another son, John, followed in 1616 by a third, Thomas.

William Craven grew up in his father's mansion in Leadenhall Street. Probably, like many children of the wealthy at this period, he received lessons from a private tutor. In 1618, when he was ten years old, his father died. Sir William had been a powerful and influential city father, and his funeral at St Andrew's Undershaft was attended by around 500 mourners. After leaving numerous legacies, including money to found a grammar school in Burnsall near Appletreewick, he left his widow, Elizabeth, a gigantic fortune, estimated at some £125,000.[2] Widows, as well as daughters, of City magnates were in this period among the most desirable catches in the country, since by the Custom of London widows were entitled to one-third of their husband's personal estate if there were children, and half if there were none. As a result, they were much courted by noblemen anxious to improve their finances. 'No sooner is the wealthy merchant dead, his wife left in fair possession,' wrote the playwright John Marston, 'then thither flock a rout of crazed fortunes, whose cracked states gape to be solder'd up by the rich mass of the deceased's labours.'[3]

Elizabeth Craven was evidently a tough nut to crack. A few months after her husband's death, she received an offer of marriage from Edmund Sheffield, third Baron Sheffield and later first Earl of Mulgrave. His first wife had died a few months previously, leaving him with nine daughters, and the sixty-three-year-old Sheffield asked the then Marquis of Buckingham to help him 'in beeinge a suitor to the greate riche widow of Sir William Craven.'[4] Whether pressure was applied to Elizabeth Craven is not recorded, but if so she successfully rebuffed the approach. She seems to have avoided any penalties too, unlike Sir Sebastian Harvey, Lord Mayor of London in 1619. King James went to great lengths to bully Harvey into marrying his daughter to one of Buckingham's brothers. Harvey resisted threats and blandishments, but the following year was fined £2,000 in the Star Chamber on a trumped-up charge to make him pay for his obstinacy. Poor Sheffield, having failed in his attempt to secure a rich widow, instead married a relatively penniless sixteen-year-old girl, who provided him with a further five children to add to his financial tribulations.[5]

As well as having the strength to resist pressure to remarry, Elizabeth Craven was a formidable businesswoman in her own right. As a widow she engaged in moneylending on a scale on a par with her husband's, with thousands of pounds coming in and going out each week. Sir William Craven's will had stipulated that the bulk of his fortune was to be invested in land for the benefit of his three sons, and so in 1620 she began a massive series of land purchases. Much of the land was bought jointly with her father, Sir William Whitmore, a former Lord Mayor of London who served as High Sheriff of Shropshire in 1620, and her nephew, Sir Edmund Sawyer, one of the auditors of the Exchequer.

A large proportion of the land Elizabeth Craven bought was in Berkshire. In 1620 she purchased the manors of Hamstead Marshall, Uffington, and Compton from Francis Jjones, who had bought them only a few years earlier from the heirs of Sir Thomas Parry. At Hamstead Marshall Parry had constructed a substantial manor house, to which Elizabeth Craven began to make alterations. Also in Berkshire she bought Benham Valence Manor, and in Shropshire she purchased a large estate centred around Stokesay Castle (for which she paid £4,000, although it was worth £7,000). She also acquired land in Somerset and Herefordshire, and in 1622 she spent £36,000 on purchasing the estate of Combe Abbey in Warwickshire from the capable patroness of the arts Lucy, Countess of Bedford. The countess's father, Lord Harrington, had been the guardian of the young Princess Elizabeth, who had spent much of her childhood there. Unfortunately Harrington had spent huge sums on making his house a worthy home for the Princess and on keeping her in appropriate style. He had died heavily in debt, and in consequence Lady Bedford was forced to sell Combe Abbey. In 1624 Elizabeth Craven settled the estate on her three sons.

As for Craven House, Sir William Craven's house in Leadenhall Street, his widow leased it to the East India Company, who promptly demolished it to build their own grand offices. Instead she purchased Drury House, a substantial mansion situated where Wych Street (now the Aldwych) turns into Drury Lane. It was a part of London popular with the nobility and gentry, with large town houses springing up apace. Drury House itself had been built by Sir William Drury K.G. (died 1579), but its most notable recent inhabitant was John Donne, a friend of the Drurys who had lived in one of the small houses in the courtyard for some years until moving to the deanery of St Paul's in 1621, probably the same year Elizabeth Craven bought the mansion.[6]

In 1622 there was talk of Elizabeth Craven's eldest daughter, the twenty-three-year-old Elizabeth, marrying Lord Mandeville's eldest son, bringing with her a dowry of £25,000. But the match did not take place, and instead Mandeville was pressured by the Marquis of Buckingham into marrying a comparatively penniless relative of his, one Susan Hill; 'indeed he [Mandeville] had need of some amends having forsaken a match of £25,000 certain with the lady Craven's daughter that was designed and reserved for him.'[7] Instead, the fortunate man who carried off the heiress was Sir Percy Herbert, eldest son of William Herbert, first Baron Powis and owner of the ancient stronghold of Powis Castle in the Welsh Marches.

Sir Percy had been named after his maternal grandfather Henry Percy, eighth Earl of Northumberland. He was currently the MP for Shaftesbury, and on his marriage he was granted, in quick succession, first a knighthood and then a baronetcy. The Herberts of Powis Castle came from a recusant branch of the Herbert family. By and large, Catholics in seventeenth-century England married other Catholics, and so Sir Percy's match was fairly unusual. It may well have been a love match, and perhaps if Elizabeth's godly father had been alive it would never have been permitted. The marriage was a happy one, but Elizabeth's decision some years later to convert to her husband's faith was to cause great distress to her brother, while Sir Percy's father never reconciled himself to the match. The chief causes of his happiness, Sir Percy wrote to his wife many years later, were, first, that her fortune had made up his estate and, second, that his conversation had rendered her a Catholic. But, as if God had always intended a moderation of their felicities, his father's crossness had always interrupted their contentment, and God had only bestowed two children on them.[8]

On 11 July 1623, a year after his elder sister's marriage, the fifteen-year-old William Craven matriculated as a gentleman commoner at Trinity College, Oxford. There would have been about 100 commoners in residence at Trinity College, studying, for the most part, Latin and Greek. The president of the college was Ralph Kettell, who, if John Aubrey is to be believed, was a figure of both awe and ridicule to generations of undergraduates, who would mimic the way he dragged his foot and copy his high-pitched singing voice. 'His gowne and surplice and hood being on,' wrote Aubrey, 'he had a terrible gigantique aspect with his sharp gray eies.'[9] Those with long hair, much disapproved of by Kettell, would live in fear of the president whipping out a pair of scissors as he passed them in the dining hall and slicing off any offending locks. He made numerous improvements to Trinity and built up its financial resources, ensuring that former undergraduates gave generously to college funds. Craven did not disappoint him, donating £100 in 1630 for Kettell's newly extended library. Later, after the Restoration, Craven also gave generously towards the furnishings of the new chapel planned by Dr Ralph Bathurst, Kettell's successor.

Among Craven's fellow undergraduates at Oxford was John Donne the younger, the dissolute son of the famous poet, 'a man of eccentric and scandalous character but of considerable talent.' Donne, who was at Christ Church, was just a few months younger than Craven, and they remained life-long friends. Donne remembered Craven as 'a little, learned, active man of extraordinary energy', a description certainly borne out by Craven's later career.[10] His small stature was often remarked upon, especially by those who disliked him. Though he did not spend long at Oxford, and though his grasp of Latin was evidently shaky, over the course of his life he was the dedicatee of a number of literary, religious, and military works, and he was friendly with writers such as Ben Jonson. Of his extraordinary energy there is no doubt.

In October, a few months after Craven's arrival at Oxford, there were scenes of jubilation in the city when news arrived of Prince Charles's safe return from Spain. The church bells rang all day and all the next; every college celebrated with speeches and bonfires, and the lucky undergraduates were even treated to an extra course for supper. Further celebrations, sermons, and a public oration on the third day were rounded off by bonfires, fireworks, drums, and celebratory gunfire until after midnight. Similar demonstrations of public joy were repeated everywhere, with street parties and bonfires.[11] There was more jubilation the following March, when it became known that negotiations over the Spanish marriage had broken down. The talk now was of war with Spain as the only means of regaining the Palatinate. Parliament voted for war, and James promised to pay Count Mansfeld a subsidy of £20,000 a month.

In April 1624 Mansfeld crossed over to London to offer his services to lead an army for the reconquest of the Palatinate. He was greeted warmly by Prince Charles and the Duke of Buckingham, and given lodgings in St James's Palace. In emotional scenes Charles and Mansfeld rode side by side through the streets of the capital, with bystanders crying 'Long live Mansfeld! God bless you, m'lord', and pressing to kiss the hem of his mantle. A few months later, recruitment for the new army began. Mansfeld was to have an army of 8,000 English and 4,000 Scots, divided into six regiments, but the authorities had to resort to pressing. 'God speed them whatsover they do or wheresoever they go,' wrote Chamberlain, 'but it is beyond my experience or reading to have such a body of English committed and commanded by a stranger.'[12]

But Mansfeld's was not the only English Army being raised in 1624, and it was not one that a gentleman would have even considered joining. His armies were notorious for their brutality and ill-discipline, and the men who enlisted or were pressed into them were by and large the dregs of society. However, that same summer the drums began to beat in London to levy troops for fighting in the Netherlands. There were to be 7,000 men, divided into four regiments under the command respectively of the Earls of Oxford, Southampton, and Essex, and Lord Willoughby. Prince Maurice of Orange had made an urgent request for reinforcements to relieve the city of Breda, which was being threatened by a Spanish army under Spinola, and so the cry went out for 'gentlemen and other voluntaries that will serve the States General'.[13]

Ever since the Earl of Leicester's expedition back in Queen Elizabeth's day, a season or two of campaigning in the Netherlands had been a standard rite of passage for a young gentleman—a means of gaining honour and reputation, and a useful credential for social advancement. So it was that William Craven left Oxford after just one year and joined one of the four new regiments marching to the relief of Breda. As *Chambers Book of Days* charmingly put it in 1869,

> At that period wealth alone, without the addition of a long pedigree, had not the position which it now enjoys; though military renown was considered sufficient cover for any deficiency of birth. Probably for this reason, William Craven, the wealthy grandson of a Yorkshire peasant, at an early age took service in the army of Henry, Prince of Orange, and acquitted himself with honour and distinction.[14]

Prince Frederick Henry of Orange, like Gustavus Adolphus a few years later, welcomed gentlemen volunteers into his army, believing that their example stiffened the courage of men of humbler birth who were more likely to be motivated by money and plunder rather than honour.[15] For many volunteers, service in the ranks was little more than a way of burnishing their social credentials, but in the absence of any real military academies, others regarded it as a form of apprenticeship in arms. Their duties would typically include mounting the guard and leading advance parties to scout enemy lines. They would usually serve in special companies, commanded by the colonel of the regiment, which acted almost as small military academies, with the cadets receiving instruction not just in military exercises but also in mathematics, fencing, and dancing.[16]

For the most part, a military campaign would last from spring until late autumn, when the army would go into winter quarters. We know nothing about the actions in which the young William Craven was involved, but in the autumn of 1624, at the end of the season's campaigning, he seems to have returned to England. In August his mother had died, at the age of forty-four. She must have been ill for some time, because among the Craven Papers is a licence dating from 1622 allowing her to eat flesh, presumably to give her some extra strength. Towards the end of August 1624, Elizabeth Craven was buried, like her husband, at St Andrew's Undershaft in the City of London. She was given 'but a reasonable funeral, for perhaps the richest widow that ever died, of a London lady.'[17]

All three of Elizabeth's sons were now orphans and therefore wards of court, a state of affairs fraught with danger. In the early seventeenth century it was still not uncommon for wealthy wards to see their fortunes vanish as their estates were plundered by unscrupulous administrators. The Earl of Shaftesbury was one such unfortunate who saw a large part of his fortune disappear while still a ward of court. In other cases, the wards found themselves purchased by peers who married them off to their own children. In the case of the Cravens, however, the family seems to have extracted an assurance that the wardships would not be abused. Shortly before Elizabeth Craven's death, the acting Treasurer to the Exchequer, Sir Richard Weston, wrote to the Secretary of State, Sir Edward Conway, urging that 'care should be taken that the King is not abused about the wardship of young Craven.' Conway in turn wrote to the Chancellor of the Exchequer, instructing him to 'take care that the King receives no prejudice in the disposition of the ward fallen to him by the death of the Lady Craven.'[18] Certainly the interlinked city dynasties of the Cravens and Whitmores, with their financial clout, had the power to exert considerable influence. After Lady Craven's death the Craven moneylending operations continued uninterrupted; in the first three months of 1625 the family agents lent out the astonishing sum of £23,644 and received back £21,789.[19]

Elizabeth Craven left the bulk of her fortune to her eldest son, but his two brothers, John and Thomas, inherited extensive property in Northamptonshire, Sussex, Berkshire, and Middlesex. Chamberlain reported, rightly or wrongly, that she had left £8,000 to William and £5,000 to John.[20] William Craven's movements during these years are difficult to follow. After returning to England following his mother's death he seems to have remained in the country for much of 1625, among other things supervising building operations at Hamstead Marshall. For roughly a year after October 1624, there are numerous entries in the account book such as, '£10 paid to William Craven in gold the same day he went to Hamstead', and '£43 to William Craven in gold, being sent to him at Hamstead.'[21]

It seems that during these years the earlier mansion built at Hamstead Marshall by Sir Thomas Parry was substantially remodelled. Certainly there was a large amount of construction work going on, with the accounts including numerous payments for bricklaying and wainscotting. Judging by the much later engraving by Kip and Knyff, the building that arose was a substantial mansion of traditional design around three sides of a courtyard, its central section, featuring a series of two-storied bays with large mullioned and transomed windows, probably retained from the earlier mansion.

William Craven probably returned to the United Provinces in the spring of 1626. He may well have served in the regiment of Sir Edward Harwood, one of the seven English and three Scottish regiments in the States Army. The young man had a great respect for Harwood; when Harwood was killed a few years later, Craven is said to have cast himself on his bed, crying out that he had lost his father, 'such was his love and opinion of him'.[22] History does not relate the actions in which the young volunteer was involved, but by all accounts he showed great promise. 'In addition to the most determined bravery,' wrote Edmund Lodge, Craven 'is said to have displayed all those qualities of mind that are esteemed in the character of a commander.' It must have been during this period that he first made the acquaintance of the King and Queen of Bohemia, whose doors were always open to any English or Scottish gentlemen in the United Provinces. Elizabeth, for her part, must have felt kindly disposed to the young owner of Combe Abbey.

For the royal exiles, prospects of an imminent return to the Palatinate had steadily diminished. The fortunes of war ebbed and flowed, but mainly they ebbed. John Howell wrote in 1635,

> It seems there is some angry star that hath hung over this business of the Palatinate from the beginning of these German wars to this very day [...]. You may remember how poorly Prague was lost; the Bishop of Halverstadt and Count Mansfeld shuffled up and down a good while and did great matters, but all came to nothing at last.[23]

Hopes were raised for a time by Charles's accession to the throne. But Charles, though sympathetic, lacked the money to help. In Germany things seemed to go from bad to worse. In 1626, Count Mansfeld was defeated by the rising imperialist commander Albrecht von Wallenstein, and later that year Christian of Brunswick died of fever. In his will he left the Queen of Bohemia a brooch with his mother's name, Elizabeth, on it, while to the end of her days she wore a bracelet engraved with his initials.

At the end of that season's campaigning, William Craven returned to England. The following spring, on 4 March 1627, he was knighted by Charles I at Newmarket. Eight days later, after paying £7,000 into the Exchequer, he was created Baron Craven of Hamstead Marshall, with a special remainder to his brothers John and Thomas. The motto he adopted was very characteristic: *Virtus in Actione Consistit*. Rumour had it that a condition of his peerage was that he should marry Elizabeth Ashburnham, one of Henrietta Maria's maids of honour and a kinswoman, inevitably, of the Duke of Buckingham.[24] Many of those offered peerages would find themselves being pressured to marry a member of the enormous Villiers clan. 'Whilst that duke [Buckingham] lived,' wrote Gervase Holles, 'scarce any man acquired any honour, but such as were either his kindred or had the fortune (or misfortune) to marry with his kindred or mistresses.'[25] Buckingham was a much resented man among the nobility, not least because of his sales of peerages. The following year he was stabbed to death, and immediately the sales of peerages ground to a halt.

It was also rumoured, however, that Craven was not willing to marry Elizabeth Ashburnham, but that, in a further twist, Lord Coventry, the Lord Keeper of the Privy Seal, had succeeded in arranging a double marriage with the Craven family. His son Thomas was to marry the twenty-five-year-old Mary Craven, while his daughter Elizabeth would marry her younger brother, the newly ennobled Baron Craven. Joseph Mead, the recipient of this titbit of gossip, noted that the marriage between Thomas Coventry and Mary Craven was

> [...] consummate with £27,000, and they say £3,000 more litigious, to make it up to £30,000, if my lord keeper can do himself right. But that it should be a cross match, and Baron Craven marry the keeper's daughter, I hear no confirmation, and suppose it to be a mistake, or a mere conjecture.[26]

It might have been no more than idle conjecture, but the rumour certainly throws a fascinating light on the ruthlessly mercenary nature of the contemporary marriage market; no wonder Pepys, writing many years later, described Lord Coventry as a 'cunning, crafty man'.[27] The minor matter of the wishes of the couple seldom came into the picture where marriage was concerned, although attitudes on the subject were beginning to change. Whether Mary Craven was happy to have her future bargained away in this way we have no idea, but the experience may have left a distinctly bitter taste in her brother's mouth. His first foray into literary patronage, not long afterwards, was to fund John Ford's play *The Broken Heart*, published in 1633 but probably written some years earlier. It is an unhappy tale of forced marriages which end in tragedy, while the only marriage that prospers is one based on love and entered into freely.[28] Oddly enough Elizabeth Ashburnham, spurned by Craven, was one of the few who did make a love match. In a romance at court a few years later, she fell in love with Sir Frederick Cornwallis, one of the King's equerries. Frederick's formidable mother was vehemently opposed to the match on the grounds that Elizabeth possessed neither rank nor fortune, but the King and Queen were warmly supportive, doing their best to reconcile her to the match.[29]

As for Craven, he was more interested in gaining glory on the battlefield than being caught in the soft entanglements of matrimony; he was, after all, still only nineteen. He succeeded, anyway, in acquiring his barony without having to marry as part of the bargain, but, as we saw, he was obliged to pay a cool £7,000 for his title. In almost all cases, the recipients of honours paid their money over to the hated Duke of Buckingham, by now the grand dispenser of royal patronage—but Craven, almost uniquely, circumvented the Duke by paying the sum directly into the Exchequer. Perhaps it was the only way to avoid having to marry Elizabeth Ashburnham. Since he was not yet of age, he was also obliged to pay a hefty wardship fine of £8,000, an exorbitant rate which no doubt reflected his status as a nouveau riche with no influence at court.[30] At the same time, he was appointed to the Council of War, possibly as a kind of fig leaf to conceal the fact that he had bought his title—'some excuse unto the world why his Majesty should receive him in this honour,' as John Holles, anxious to conceal the fact that he was paying for an earldom, wrote in 1624.[31]

In April 1627, Mary Craven duly married Thomas Coventry at St Andrew's Undershaft, and the Lord Keeper got his £30,000.[32] Five years later she died in childbirth, and her grieving husband erected an elaborate monument in her memory in the Coventry family Valhalla in the Church of St Mary Magdalene at Croome D'Abitot, the inscription noting her kinship to 'the illustrious Lord Craven'.

A month or two later, the newly ennobled Baron Craven returned to the Netherlands, where he re-joined the States Army. While not on campaign he found time to accompany Frederick, King of Bohemia, on hunting expeditions, and in August the two of them spent time in the countryside around Amerongen, in the Province of Utrecht on the lower Rhine. It was a country of water meadows, woodland, and heather—fine country for hunting, though boggy in places. On one occasion Frederick found his horse sinking into the boggy ground, but fortunately Craven was at hand to help him onto dry land. 'Without him,' Frederick wrote to his wife, 'I would have had great difficulty getting out.' Frederick's horse was no longer fit to ride, and instead Craven lent the King one of his own mounts, a fine grey horse with which Frederick was very pleased. He found the young man a pleasant travelling companion; Craven's company whiled away the time, he wrote, which would otherwise have hung heavily.[33] Frederick's melancholia had not gone away.

By now Craven was a regular guest at the small court of the King and Queen of Bohemia, which included men and women of English, German, and Bohemian nationality. Its general tone, in contrast to the sober and austere court of the Prince of Orange, was one of careless gaiety. The presence of the Winter King and Queen had transformed the Hague into a rich cultural capital, a fertile environment for all kinds of courtly activities; tournaments, tilting, art, plays, masques, ballets, and other performances. But inevitably, the passage of time and the repeated setbacks the exiles had suffered diminished their prestige. Their finances were in increasingly dire straits, their debts to the long-suffering tradesmen of the Hague ever-increasing. On 1 January 1628, their unpaid household debts included £16 to the egg-wife, £554 to the chandler, £400 to the butcher, £464 to the poulterer, and £1,000 for the stables. It did not help that the allowance from England arrived on an irregular basis, since Charles was not exactly flush with money himself. In July 1626 he had promised the exiles £10,000, but the money had not materialised.

Frederick had come to loathe what he called the *canaille* of the Hague, and he and Elizabeth increasingly preferred to spend their summers in Rhenen, close to Amerongen on the lower Rhine. To begin with they stayed in lodgings in the town, but Frederick conceived a project of building a hunting lodge on the site of a disused Augustinian nunnery adjoining the twelfth-century church of St Cunera. It might have seemed rash for a desperately impoverished couple to embark on an ambitious building project, but Frederick decided that he would finance it by drawing on the interest of the sum he had received as payment for the town of Lixheim, which he had sold to the Duke of Lorraine in 1623 for 130,000 rixdollars. Half of this sum had been seized by the Emperor, but the other half was earning good interest in the Bank of Holland. Soon work on demolishing the old nunnery began and the 'Palazzo Renense', as the couple jokingly called their new hunting lodge, began to take shape, and from then on they would habitually spend the summer there. They would usually bring their children with them, and Rupert, at least, shared his parents' love of hunting. A story was related of him that once, when out hunting at Rhenen as a boy, his favourite dog disappeared underground in pursuit of a fox. When it did not reappear Rupert squeezed down the hole after it and eventually got hold of its hind legs, but was unable to wriggle back out of the hole. By this time Rupert's companion was getting worried, so he crawled far enough down the hole to reach Rupert's legs, but was also unable to get back out. Eventually the companion's legs were discovered and after much effort he was pulled out, followed by the Prince, still hanging onto the dog, which in turn was firmly gripping the fox.

'Cartropes shall not detain me longer in this place'

Lord Craven was to become a frequent visitor to Rhenen, but now, with a peerage and a few years as a gentleman volunteer under his belt, he decided to embark on that essential component of a young gentleman's education—foreign travel. Since the early sixteenth century, tours of France and Italy had become increasingly fashionable. For much of the 1620s there had been something of a hiatus because of war with France and Spain, but by 1628 the difficulties had begun to ease. Following Buckingham's assassination in September of that year, peace treaties were concluded with both France and Spain. With France now open again and the plague having abated somewhat in Italy, increasing numbers of young Englishmen began to embark on excursions on the continent.

In September 1627, Craven wrote to Lord Conway explaining that 'curiosity drawes mee to see Italy.' He had already obtained a licence from the King to travel through France and Italy, but for the sake of convenience he wished to get permission to pass through Spanish territory in northern Italy.[1] He remained in the Netherlands until the following spring, and then spent the rest of the year in France and Lorraine.[2] What was he doing? The French historian Jaques Boulenger maintained that Craven was involved in secret communications between the Duchesse de Chevreuse, that beautiful but mischievous intriguer at the French court, and Anne of Austria, wife of Louis XIII and sister of the Spanish King.[3] According to Boulenger, Craven, together with Anne of Austria's servant La Porte and other faithful gentlemen such as La Rochefoucauld, helped to carry secret letters between the two women. Madame de Chevreuse had recently been banished to her estate at Dampierre, near Paris, after the discovery of a plot she had hatched against the French state, motivated by her intense hatred of Richelieu. Instead she was busy fomenting another plot, this time involving secret communications with the English court. Evidence for Craven's involvement in such matters seems remarkable by its absence, but it is tempting to think that, beguiled like so many by the beauty of the Duchesse de Chevreuse, he might have been drawn into her intrigues. Alas, we can only speculate.

In early December 1628, the Earl of Carlisle (none other than the former Viscount Doncaster, the Queen of Bohemia's old friend 'Camel's face') wrote to

Craven asking him to go out to Italy to accompany his fifteen-year-old son James, Viscount Doncaster, who was touring Italy in the company of a tutor. Carlisle had included his son in the entourage of his lavish 100-strong embassy, which had been making its stately way around the capitals of Europe. It turned out to be a largely fruitless mission, and following Buckingham's assassination in September Carlisle returned post-haste to London, leaving his son to complete his travels.

Craven agreed to Carlisle's request, though by this time his enthusiasm for travelling to Italy had undergone a distinct cooling; evidently he was enjoying himself in France. He would happily wait upon Lord Doncaster as soon as he was able to travel, he replied. But he wished it were in any place other than Italy, where there was nothing to satisfy his curiosity. If he had not troubled Carlisle to beg a warrant from the King to go to Rome, he would not be prepared to linger out the winter in 'so woeful a dull country, where there is no more conversation than among the dead'.[4]

A few weeks later Craven set out for Italy, armed with a licence from the King to travel for two years 'in the countries of any Princes or states whatsoever', along with Doncaster and five or more servants. No doubt he took with him copious quantities of luggage, servants, and horses. A glance at the items which Craven's youngest brother Thomas took with him on his own European tour a few years later throws an intriguing light on just what a wealthy young gentleman of the period typically carried with him on his travels. Thomas Craven's tour was cut tragically short when he died suddenly of the plague in Paris in February 1636, at the age of nineteen, and he was buried in the Protestant cemetery of the temple of Charenton, just outside Paris. He died intestate, but after much delay his possessions were eventually returned to his family in England. The resulting inventory and valuation includes the following:

One suite of cloth and cloake lined with sky-coloured plush: £8
One blackcloth suite with cloake lined with plush and a black satin doublett: £10
One other suite and cloake of black satin embroidered worth: £25
One cloth suite and cloake laced with silk lace and lined with flower satin: £15
A tent of thick cords and other furniture to it: £8
A tent bedstead, two trunks to it with a blue canvas canopy: £6
A large covering of craiecloth [cerecloth?] guarded with stripes: 50s.
One buffecoat [a leather coat worn under armour]: £6
A set of arms: £15
Six pairs of pistols: £12
A sword with silver hilt and silver spurs: £12
Two diamond rings: £40
Two silver candlesticks with sockets, two spoons and two porringers: £10 9s 4d
Four pairs of sheets: £4

Nine pewter bottles, a dozen dishes, a dozen trenchers, a basin and ewer, two beakers, a salt, two candlesticks and six spoons, all of pewter and latten: 50s
Some books: 10s[5]

The inclusion of a sword, arms, spurs, and buffcoat in Thomas's luggage suggests that he too had intended to spend a period as a volunteer, probably on campaign with the Prince of Orange. The pistols would perhaps have been more for self-defence, though six pairs seem rather excessive. Perhaps he was collecting them. The total value of his possessions repatriated from France, including all the fine clothes, jewellery, arms, and assorted domestic items, came to more than £180 (roughly £18,000 today), and it is a fair assumption that his eldest brother, a young nobleman and heir to a much larger fortune, would have been even more stylishly kitted out, especially once he had agreed to accompany Lord Carlisle's son and heir. Prior to setting out for Italy, Craven spent a large sum of money on suitable apparel, and on returning to the United Provinces after his Italian interlude he ordered two saddles, one of scarlet and one of green velvet.[6]

After travelling south through France and northern Italy, in the middle of January 1629 Craven caught up with Doncaster and his suite in Florence. Doncaster was accompanied by his tutor, James Traill, an able Scot from Fife, and John Spelman, son of the antiquary Sir Henry Spelman. Their tour had got off to an unlucky start when Doncaster caught smallpox in Turin, and they had remained in the city for over a month while Sir Isaac Wake, the English ambassador, kept a benevolent eye on them. By mid–December Doncaster had recovered, and the party set out northwards by coach for Geneva. After a few days there they retraced their steps through Piedmont and passed through the Spanish territories of northern Italy, and on to Florence.

Then as now, travel abroad involved jumping through an irksome series of bureaucratic hoops, and Doncaster's party needed separate passes for each duchy. In Tuscany they were stopped because of difficulties with their paperwork, but fortunately Lord Dudley managed to sort out a pass for them. From there the party made a brief excursion eastwards towards the Adriatic coast, only to be stopped at Cervia because of a suspected outbreak of plague. They returned to Florence, then after a few weeks continued southwards, stopping at Siena, and in mid–February they reached Rome. Traill sent encouraging reports home about Doncaster's progress in learning Italian.

Because of the sensitive nature of his father's diplomacy, Doncaster had been enjoined to be discreet about his identity. In Rome, nobody but the Venetian and Savoyard ambassadors knew who he was—nobody, that is, apart from George Conn, a Scottish Catholic who was well known to Carlisle as part of his efficient private intelligence network. '[T]his signior George,' wrote William Prynne, 'was a very fair youth of some fifteene yeares of age and of a fair disposition, having also access to his holiness.'[7] In Rome, Conn habitually gave a warm welcome on the

Pope's behalf to any English, Scottish, or Irish visitors, bringing them delicacies, treating them to lavish meals, and conducting them round the seven pilgrimage churches of Rome. Even Protestant tourists received this lavish welcome, meant no doubt to seduce heretics back into the true faith. A few years later Conn was to become the papal agent in London, where he was remarkably successful in converting ladies in the Queen's circle.

Doncaster, Craven, and their suite seem to have resisted any blandishments. They spent a few weeks in Rome, enjoying Conn's hospitality and 'wandering and wondering,' according to Traill, 'among the ruins of ancient magnificence and the monuments of newer greatness.'[8] On a lighter note, they found time to enjoy the carnival as well. Once they had had their fill of sightseeing in Rome they had planned to travel south to Naples, but in the event it proved impossible to get passes, so instead they retraced their steps northwards to Florence. They were aware that disturbances in Savoy, still a battleground between pro-French and pro-Spanish factions, might well hold up their return journey, and so it proved. Unable to get passes to proceed north, they decided to return instead to Rome for a few weeks more before heading north again to Florence and then to Venice, that inevitable magnet for travellers to Italy.

Back in Florence, Traill did his best to fulfil a request from Carlisle's secretary, William Boswell. Boswell was among the first Englishmen to be aware of Galileo and his discoveries, and he begged Traill and Spelman to do their utmost to acquire any books of his they could find. Recently released from prison by the Inquisition, Galileo was currently living some 30 miles outside Florence. Because of the distance Traill felt unable to deliver Boswell's letter in person, but he sent it on, promising Boswell he would forward any books he managed to procure. Spelman had more luck, succeeding in acquiring two of the famous astronomer's works.

Craven's main preoccupation, by contrast, was to leave Italy as soon as possible. 'Cartropes shall not detain me longer in this place,' he wrote emphatically to Boswell in early May, 'unless the sun were more temperate or the people less dogmatic.'[9] At the same time Doncaster wrote to his father to say that his Italian was progressing nicely, but that Craven was obliged to return to England and, not wishing to stay on in Italy by himself, he planned to return too. They spent a few more weeks in Venice and Milan, until word finally came from Sir Isaac Wake that it was safe to proceed. Leaving their trunks at Leghorn to be transported back to England by sea, they made their way northwards, over the Alps, and through France.[10] Only now did it become apparent why Craven and Doncaster had been so impatient to leave Italy. Instead of returning to England, they and Spelman made their way via Antwerp to the United Provinces, where Frederick Henry, Prince of Orange had just launched a new military campaign. Compared to this the attractions of wandering among the ruins of ancient greatness evidently didn't hold much appeal.

The new campaign, the first for many years, had been financed by the recent capture of the Spanish treasure fleet, a windfall which had transformed the financial position of the United Provinces. As a result the States Army had the wherewithal to mount an ambitious campaign, and after some discussion the objective chosen was the fortress of 's-Hertogenbosch, or Bois-le-Duc, the most important stronghold in the Netherlands still in Habsburg hands. Large numbers of English volunteers came to take part in the siege of 's-Hertogenbosch, including many who would go on to become commanders in the Civil War. Four English regiments were recruited to join the siege, commanded respectively by General Vere, Viscount Wimbledon, Sir Charles Morgan, and Sir Edward Harwood. Craven and Doncaster, along with thirty-seven other gentlemen volunteers, joined Wimbledon's regiment.[11]

Also among the volunteers was the forlorn and unhappy figure of the King of Bohemia, feeling the need for displacement activity after the tragic death of his eldest son, Prince Frederick Henry, a few months earlier. A lively and intelligent youth of fifteen, the Prince had planned to join the States Army as a volunteer in the spring. But on 2 January he had gone with his father to view the Dutch fleet which had just returned from the West Indies, laden with valuable prizes captured from the Spanish. Enormous crowds had come to view the fleet, and at Haarlem father and son embarked in an overladen boat, which then collided with a larger vessel and sank. Frederick managed to clamber out of the freezing water onto a passing boat, but his son was not so lucky. Frederick spent most of the night in a frantic search, but the next morning the Prince's body was found, frozen to the mast of the upturned boat.

It was a few months after this that Craven, Doncaster, and Spelman made for Rhenen, where the Queen of Bohemia was spending the summer in order to be close to her husband and to oversee construction work on the new Palatine hunting lodge. Inspecting the building work with Frederick and Elizabeth, the visitors noticed that the building materials were being stored in the former abbey, a profanity which shocked the pious Spelman. His father, Sir Henry Spelman, recorded the exchange that followed.

> It chanced that the truly noble Lord Craven, returning out of Italy (where my Son was very happily fallen into his Company) he went to this place [Rhenen] to visit the Prince, whom they called the King of Bohemia. My son seeing what the King was about, and how he had profaned the church by making it a Store-house, said to my Lord Craven, That he fear'd it might be ominous to the King; my Lord answer'd, I will tell him what you say; and, turning to the King, said, This gentleman fears this that your Majesty doth will not be prosperous to you; the King answered, That was but a Conceit, and so passed it over. But mark what followed upon it. Frederick's eldest son drowned shortly afterwards [in fact, as we have seen, he had drowned a few months earlier], and Frederick himself was shortly to die of the plague. [...] God's judgements are his Secrets, I only tell Concurrences.[12]

Craven, for his part, seems to have been more interested in flirting with Elizabeth's maids of honour, one of whom, Mademoiselle de Nassau, gave another, Jane Rupa, a fine pair of gloves to present to him. As a result, wrote Frederick afterwards, Mademoiselle de Nassau was more in Craven's good graces than Rupa. Little is known of Mademoiselle de Nassau, but Jane Rupa, a long-standing member of Elizabeth's entourage, was the daughter of a Bohemian patriot, Baron Wenceslas Rupa, who had fled with the King and Queen in the debacle of 1620. Elizabeth became very fond of the attractive sylph-like girl, whom she nicknamed 'Queen Mab' after the supposed queen of the fairies.

From Rhenen Craven and Doncaster proceeded on to the Prince of Orange's camp outside 's-Hertogenbosch, where Frederick greeted him warmly. 'I find Craven the same as ever,' he wrote to Elizabeth; 'he is a good lad and always has a fund of stories to tell.'[13] The city of 's-Hertogenbosch, surrounded as it was by marshy ground unsuitable for digging trenches, had long been regarded as practically impregnable. But the States Army had a wealth of expertise in siege warfare, 'learnt by many years' experience in the school of pickaxe and spade.'[14] Frederick Henry's ingenious scheme was to divert the two streams funnelling into the marshes, the Aa and the Dommel, by digging a double dyke 30 miles long to completely enclose the city. After this the marshes were drained by means of horse-powered mills. Trenches of circumvallation were dug, bristling with ravellins, redoubts, and traverses strong enough to withstand any attack by the 30,000-strong army of Count de Berge, which was in the vicinity. De Berge kept the besiegers awake for three months by constant alarms, then withdrew in an attempt to draw the States Army away from the siege.

In August the attackers at last began to push forward their lines, their zig-zagging trenches steadily approaching the walls. Craven, with boundless energy, flitted between the different English regiments as they mounted the watch. Henry Hexham, an English soldier who wrote a history of the siege, wrote on 18 August that

> My Lord of Craven, whose worth and bounty to my Lord of Wimbleton's company was known to us, this night and the day following watched with my Lord of Oxford. The next night with my Lord Cecil's company, and the third night with General Morgan's regiment.[15]

Early on 11 September a mine was exploded, creating a large breach in the walls, and three days later the city's governor surrendered. A large group assembled to watch the triumphant spectacle as the defeated Spanish garrison marched out of one gate while the Prince of Orange's victorious troops marched in at another, and a few days later the Prince threw a grand fête in celebration. The siege had lasted five months, and casualties among the attackers had been high. Sir Edward Vere himself had been mortally wounded by a musket shot.

The fall of 's-Hertogenbosch was widely celebrated as a triumph for the Protestant cause. In England, Alexander Gill the younger, Usher of St Paul's School and future friend and teacher of John Milton, published a poem in Latin entitled 'Sylva Ducis' (the Latin version of 's-Hertogenbosch). It lauded the bravery of the commanders, 'fierce Vere' and 'fierce Cecil', as well as 'handsome Craven, who frightened the terrified enemy with youthful arms'. Gill, as it happens, was under suspicion after an evening spent drinking in the buttery at Trinity College, Oxford the previous year, in the company of Craven's younger brother John, then a commoner at Trinity, and William Pickering, who was probably John Craven's private tutor. Also present was the theologian William Chillingworth, a newly elected fellow of the college. It was just after the Duke of Buckingham's murder at the hands of John Felton, and Gill called for a health to Felton, declaring that the duke was in hell with King James, who 'was fitter to stand in a Cheapside shop with an apron before him and cry "What do you lack" than to govern a kingdom.' This seditious remark was reported to Archbishop Laud by Chillingworth, his godson, and Gill was dragged from his classroom and committed to the gatehouse.[16]

Following the siege of 's-Hertogenbosch, Craven fell dangerously ill and remained in the United Provinces for a few more months.[17] In England there was speculation as to his whereabouts, and rumours too of a possible marriage in the offing. In November, George Aglionby, the newly appointed tutor to the Cavendish family, wrote a gossipy letter to his friend Thomas Hobbes, his predecessor as tutor.

> My Lady Anne [Cavendish] [...] is (you know) fair and ripe, and tis pitty she is so long a forbidden fruit. I am sure she would be willing to be gathered by my Lord Craven, but because I hear nothing of him having been in England this month, I fear his hands are already full.[18]

Ripe, fair, and willing to be gathered by Craven she may have been, but Craven refused to gather her, probably because he was still more intent on winning glory on the battlefield, and a few years later she married Robert Rich, eldest son of the Earl of Warwick. Craven did not stay in the Netherlands for much longer, however, and the following month, December 1629, he returned to England. By this time the pictures and other goods which he had purchased in Italy had arrived home.[19]

The previous June he had turned twenty-one, and to mark the first Christmas after his coming of age he spent £3,000 on freeing poor debtors from London prisons. 'The Lord Craven hath kept the noblest Christmas of any here,' wrote Lord Manchester's steward early the following year, 'and hath rescued poor prisoners out of gaols that lay for debt, some 20 shillings, some 30 shillings, 40, 50, 60, out of all prisons in town, to the total of £3,000 value.'[20] It was rather as if a tap had been turned on, which was to run freely for the rest of Craven's life, except for the years of comparative penury after his estates were sequestered by the Commonwealth.

Craven now decided to resume his voyages abroad, and he obtained leave to travel in France and Italy for a further two years. But first he returned to the Hague, where he donated a fine gilt communion cup and cover to the English Church.[21] Later that year he set off for France and Italy, staying for a while in Paris and paying another visit to Rome. We only know about the latter visit because while in Rome he received a letter from John Donne, his friend from Oxford and son of the Dean of St Paul's. Donne enclosed a verse which shows, if nothing else, that his poetry was not up to the standard of his father:

A verse written to Lord Craven

My Lord, now you're at Rome and there behold
Things which are wonders when in England told.[22]

Later in 1630 he returned to England, where he donated £100 to the new library at Trinity College. As far as we know, his generosity had not yet begun to extend to the King and Queen of Bohemia—except for the gift of a horse in 1627—although as soon as the opportunity arose his munificence was to show no bounds. But in 1630 the Palatine family was still in the direst state of poverty, and hopes of restitution were lower than ever. King Charles had begun conducting negotiations for a peace treaty with Spain, negotiations which the King and Queen of Bohemia regarded with suspicion, fearing—with every justification—that their interests would be overlooked. Charles I assured his sister that their restitution would be a *sine qua non* of the talks, but when the final version of the treaty was agreed, it made no mention of the Palatinate beyond a general promise that the King of Spain would put in a good word for the King and Queen of Bohemia at the electoral diet about to be held in Ratisbon.

In April 1630, Charles sent Sir Henry Vane to the Hague to break the unwelcome news that he was preparing to sign a treaty with Spain. Vane decided that the most tactful way of conveying his message would be to hand over Charles's letter to his sister and let the couple peruse its contents in private. Shortly afterwards, Frederick arrived at Vane's lodgings and burst into a fit of hysterical sobbing, declaring that he had been forsaken by all the world. Vane did his best to persuade Frederick that the draft treaty represented the best that could be secured. 'That evening,' wrote Vane, 'I waited upon the queen, whom I found a little distracted between the love of a husband and a brother.' Next morning, Frederick told Vane that he had only £200 left in the world, and did not know where to turn for more. Vane reported to Charles,

The first word he said unto me was that he was reduced to that want and necessity by the non-payment of the queen's pension, as that, if I had not brought money with me to supply their present wants, he was resolved to put away all his servants, himself to live obscurely with a couple of men, and to send the queen by the next passage to England, to throw herself at your Majesty's feet, for that he was not able to put bread in her mouth.[23]

Vane hurriedly arranged to extend credit to them to stave off the day of reckoning. The Winter Queen, however, was not one to dwell on her misfortunes. In June we find her writing to the Earl of Carlisle in characteristic style from the newly completed Palazzo Renense:

> Thou ugly, filthy camel's face,
> You chide me once for not writing to you; now I have my revenge, and more justly chide you, for not having heard from you so long as I fear you have forgot to write. I have charged this fat fellow [Sir Henry Vane, who carried the latter back to England] to tell you all this, and that I cannot forget your villany. He can inform [you] how all things are here, and what they say to the peace with Spain; and though I confess I am not much rejoiced at it, yet I am so confident of my dear brother's love, and the promise he hath made me, not to forsake our cause, that it troubles me the less. I must desire your sweet face to continue your help to us, in this business which concerns me so near; and in spite of you, I am ever constantly
>
>> Your most affectionate friend
>> Elizabeth[24]

Elizabeth remained at Rhenen for the summer, hunting with Frederick, before returning to the Hague at the last possible moment for the birth of her twelfth child. The baby, a girl, arrived in mid–October. The parents were hard pressed even to find a suitable name for her, given that most plausible options and godparents had already been used up. Their solution was to write a selection of girls' names on slips of paper and draw lots; the name that came up was Sophie.

The following year the situation was to change utterly, and Craven would throw everything he could into an attempt to regain the Palatinate, risking his life in the process.

In which our hero's bravery impresses the Great Gustavus

'Superior to the vulgar ambition, which can rest satisfied with rank and power, Lord Craven aspired to fame, and the first, if not the only object of his pursuit, was glory.' So wrote Elizabeth Benger in 1825. 'The enterprise of Gustavus presented an irresistible attraction to the gallant spirits of the age.'[1]

The enterprise of Gustavus Adolphus, the warrior King of Sweden, came just when the imperialists appeared to have triumphed everywhere. So confident of his final victory was the Emperor that in 1629 he issued an Edict of Restitution which reversed the rights that the Protestant states of the Empire had won in the previous century. He began to root out any remaining Protestant institutions in his territories and to expel anyone who obstinately refused to convert to Catholicism. He also dismissed Wallenstein, the resourceful general who had been responsible for his victories but had incurred many enemies along the way. In the absence of its commander, Wallenstein's army rapidly melted away.

It was at this point that the course of the war changed dramatically with the sudden intervention of Gustavus Adolphus. In a short space of time, this extraordinary man won a series of stunning victories which left him the master of a large swathe of Germany. Gustavus was a commander of genius. He owed his success in large part to military innovations such as smaller and lighter weapons which enabled his troops to deploy and fight more quickly, and he pioneered the use of cavalry as a sort of battering ram to scatter the enemy by shock action. He also arranged for his army to buy provisions from the local people instead of plundering the countryside, as was the usual practice in war.

After landing in Pomerania in June 1630 with just 4,000 troops, Gustavus Adolphus rapidly amassed a large army, including a sizeable contingent of battle-hardened Scots previously employed by the Prince of Orange. The Scottish contingent, in fact, made up a significant proportion of the Swedish Army, Gustavus admiring their fighting spirit. After consolidating his position in Mecklenburg and Pomerania and signing a treaty with France that would ensure plentiful French gold for his army, in March 1631 Gustavus went on the offensive. He began by capturing Frankfurt-on-the-Oder, and then marched quickly through Brandenburg. Despite his speed, however, he failed to prevent Count Tilly from capturing Magdeburg in early May after a lengthy siege, then burning the city to the ground and massacring the entire population of 42,000. Even by the brutal standards of the German wars, this was an atrocity which sent a wave of shocked revulsion through Europe. After joining forces with the Elector of Saxony, Gustavus crushed Tilly's army at Breitenfeld, near Leipzig, in September.

To the Palatine family, watching the unfolding of this dramatic campaign with astonishment, it seemed that after long years of waiting they would soon be restored to their patrimony. In London, there was much discussion about the practicalities of sending an army to help Gustavus. Not that there hadn't already been English contributions to the Swedish war effort, but, as with all English interventions in the German wars, they had been badly planned, under-financed, and dogged by misfortune. Charles had already agreed to pay for a 6,000-strong army raised by the Marquess of Hamilton. The plan was that Charles would finance the recruitment and launch of Hamilton's army, while Gustavus would take over responsibility once it had landed in Germany. In the event the expedition was more or less a total disaster, earning Hamilton the soubriquet of 'Captain Luckless'. The recruitment of sufficient troops proved difficult, but by the summer of 1631 Hamilton had succeeded in raising 5,000 English and 1,000 Scots troops. Although the whole purpose of the exercise had been to assist in the recovery of the Palatinate, there were disastrous differences with Gustavus over exactly where Hamilton's army was to land. In July, after much wrangling, the troops landed in Pomerania on the Baltic coast, and then spent a few less than glorious months guarding the fortresses on the Oder and attempting to besiege Magdeburg, before abandoning the siege in early January 1632. Soon the army was hit by plague, famine, and sickness, and by mid–October only 2,500 of the original 6,000 men were left.

By and large, English volunteers who wished to spend a season on campaign still joined the States Army. In the summer of 1631, while Gustavus was marching triumphantly through the heart of Germany, Lord Craven, now back in France, was engaged in collecting a company of volunteers for a new campaign in the United Provinces. In the middle of June it was reported that he had sent a servant across to Dover in search of a ship 'to waft his Lord to Holland', and towards the end of the month the *Bonaventure* sailed to Calais to collect Craven and his volunteers and transport them to Brill in the United Provinces.[2]

Two months later, in early September, they took part in the Battle of the Slaak, a notable Dutch maritime victory near the island of Tholen. A large Spanish army, transported on a fleet of barges, had attempted to land in Zeeland with the intention of laying siege to the strategic town of Bergen-op-Zoom. But the Spanish were ill-acquainted with the tortuous navigation among the islands of Zeeland, and on 5 September their attempt to capture Tholen was defeated when part of their fleet ran aground in the shallows. For the Prince of Orange, this was an opportunity not to be missed. He despatched a fleet of about thirty vessels, with a mixture of English, Scots, French, and Dutch troops, in an attempt to cut off the stranded ships and barges and prevent any other troops from landing. French troops led the vanguard while the Earl of Oxford, with Craven's company, brought up the rear.

The battle went on all night but, finally, Craven reported, 'they like frightful hares taken in a nest rendered themselves into their chasers' hands.' The entire Spanish fleet was captured and some 5,000 men taken prisoner,[3] and it was reported that Craven was expected to receive a commission in recognition of his services.[4] After the battle Craven stayed in Bergen-op-Zoom for a few weeks more. He planned to join the victorious Swedish Army in Germany, at least for a few months, after which he thought of returning to Paris.

Following his victory at Breitenfeld, Gustavus had marched westwards across Germany in a triumphal drive, capturing Würzburg in mid–October and then proceeding on down the River Main. In mid–November he captured Frankfurt and began to advance towards Heidelberg, but with winter setting in he decided to turn back. A few days before Christmas he captured Mainz, and there he decided to stop for the winter and establish his court, the new and undisputed leader of Protestant Europe. To Gustavus's court in Mainz came representatives of the Protestant states of Germany and the ambassadors of England and France.

The Swedish King appeared to be on the point of reconquering the Palatinate, and towards the end of September Charles I had sent Sir Henry Vane to begin negotiations on English assistance towards its reconquest. For Gustavus, restitution of the Palatinate was largely a bargaining chip to obtain worthwhile English support for his army. He offered to re-establish the Elector Palatine in Heidelberg on condition that Charles agreed to supply him with 20,000 foot soldiers and 5,000 cavalry, as well as £6,000 a month towards their maintenance. This, of course, was the sticking point. Charles had no money to spare, and he was unwilling to recall Parliament to raise funds. It was said that he was already in debt to the tune of £2 million, and that there was only £4,000 in the Exchequer. Matters were not helped by the fact that relations between Gustavus and Vane soured quickly. The months went by without any agreement, and Elizabeth resorted to appealing directly to her brother. If anything were to be achieved, she urged, it would have to be by force of arms, not by endless, fruitless negotiations; 'if you now do nothing but treat,' she wrote, 'I beseech you to give me leave to say, that the world will wonder at it.'[5]

Over in London, discussion continued over possible assistance for Gustavus. The States Army was prepared to supply 12,000 men for a new Palatine Army if Charles I would agree to pay for their upkeep.[6] So at least went one rumour, while others reported that a combined force of 24,000 men was to be raised from England, Scotland, and the United Provinces.

In early November, Sir Edmund Moundeford, a Norfolk politician with Puritan sympathies, reported that 'our brave city soldier the noble Lord Craven' had been on the point of going to join the Swedish Army when he received a summons to come to England to recruit volunteers to join the King of Bohemia's rumoured 24,000-strong army.[7] This huge force remained in the realms of fantasy, but when

Craven arrived in London at the end of November, he asked for permission to raise a regiment of 3,000 men at his own expense, and he undertook to pay for coats of arms and victuals for the troops until they arrived in Germany. It was even rumoured that he had already bought arms for 2,000 men.[8]

It was a remarkably generous offer, but one about which the King's ministers were unenthusiastic, according to the well-informed Venetian ambassador Giovanni Soranzo.

> Many announced that he [Craven] is to serve for the Palatinate. Here the ministers do not allow anything whatever to come out about it, indeed they say that this thoughtless young man, being very rich, wishes to make this honourable coup for the King of Sweden.[9]

Nevertheless, Soranzo continued, it was thought that the King would grant him the levy.

Brave city soldier or thoughtless young man with too much money, in the event Craven didn't get his permission. The King argued that he could not make any decision until he had heard the result of Vane's negotiations with Gustavus.[10] In any case, Craven could hardly have expected to recruit 3,000 men at the drop of a hat. It had taken the Marquess of Hamilton the best part of a year to recruit his regiment, and in the end he had been reduced to scouring London for vagrants to make up the numbers. Even so, if Craven had only made his request either a little earlier or a little later, he might have had more luck; a few months earlier, Lord Reay had obtained permission to levy troops for the same purpose, although in the event they consisted of just 500 or so reinforcements for Hamilton, and a little later, in April 1632, Colonel Fleetwood also received permission to raise troops for the Swedish service.

Having failed in his attempt to raise a regiment, Craven returned to the United Provinces shortly afterwards with what Soranzo termed 'a few adventurers' (or 'some competent officers', according to his successor).[11] They included men such as Lieutenant-Colonel Talbot, a relative of the Earl of Shrewsbury, and Sir Francis Fane, a kinsman of the Earl of Westmoreland. Others volunteers, including Robert Marsham, may have joined Craven for a spot of fighting after travelling out in Vane's ambassadorial entourage. In total Craven's volunteers probably numbered about forty. From London they made their way to the Hague in order to accompany Frederick on his journey to the King of Sweden's camp.[12]

In November 1631, Frederick had sent a message of congratulation to Gustavus, offering to join his army as a volunteer, and in reply the Swedish King had sent a warm invitation to Frederick to come to his court in Mainz. It was not an entirely disinterested invitation; Gustavus was eager to secure Frederick's presence as a means of increasing his own legitimacy with the Protestant German princes. He suggested to Frederick that to help with the reconquest of the Palatinate he should first raise an army for himself, to be paid for by Charles I. When Frederick replied that he had no army nor any prospect of raising one, Gustavus was unimpressed.

What, a brother of the King of Great Britain and protected by the States, and must he come to me in his doublet and hose? Let him come, however, and I will do my best to restore him to his patrimony.[13]

Still, with Craven's volunteers Frederick would at least have a respectable escort for his journey to Mainz.

Elizabeth's thirteenth child, a boy, was born on 2 January 1632. He was a handsome but sickly child. Frederick had wanted to christen him after their eldest son, Frederick Henry, drowned three years earlier, but Elizabeth was keen that the child should be named after the family's new champion, Gustavus Adolphus, who agreed to stand as godfather. The second godfather was Lord Craven. It was a remarkable honour for the young man, given that all the other Palatine godparents had been either relatives, royalty, or else official bodies such as the States of Holland, who agreed to stand as a third sponsor to young Prince Gustavus Adolphus. Craven, by contrast, was an unknown youth whose friendship with the King and Queen of Bohemia only dated back a few years. Not only that, but he came, as Elizabeth might have put it, of ignoble lineage. She had a keen awareness of status and was always quick to complain when a messenger turned out to be a mere merchant's son. But Craven had already shown the depth of his commitment to the Palatine cause with his offer to raise and equip a whole regiment. It is easy to imagine him in long discussions with Frederick and Elizabeth, dreaming of glory on the battlefield in a noble cause.

The christening of Prince Gustavus Adolphus took place on 13 January. Like all the Palatine christenings in the Hague, the ceremony took place at the Kloster Kirche, a few doors down from the Wassenaer Hof, with the Swedish King represented by a proxy. As a christening present Craven gave a silver gift worth £1,500, together with the assurance of a lifetime pension of £200 a year, and the city of Amsterdam also made the gift of an annuity.

On the eve of his departure, the Estates General granted Frederick a ceremonial audience. They contributed 50,000 francs towards his military expenses, and the Prince of Orange gave him an additional 20,000 francs for his personal use. Frederick settled his affairs, making an inventory of his possessions, and withdrew funds from the Bank of Holland in Amsterdam in expectation of his imminent return to the Palatinate. His luggage—coffers containing his clothes, a portfolio of maps, a pewter camp service, a small writing desk, and portraits of his wife and mother—was loaded onto the coaches. On 16 January, a few days after his son's christening, Frederick left the Hague in a procession of forty coaches, accompanied by Craven at the head of his English volunteers and the Prince of Orange with a troop of 2,500 horsemen.

Frederick's hopes were high. The restitution for which he had waited so impatiently seemed in sight at last. His first stop was a farewell visit to his children at Leiden, where he found time to attend a public examination of the university students, in which Charles Louis and Rupert both excelled themselves. From

Leiden the party proceeded on to Rhenen, where they spent the night in the Palatine hunting lodge. The Prince of Orange accompanied Frederick as far as Wesel, just over the border in the Duchy of Cleves, and then turned back, leaving his troop of horsemen to escort Frederick through enemy territory. In atrocious weather they proceeded through the devastated wasteland which was Germany after twelve years of warfare, famine, and disease.

The roads in the Rhineland were in an appalling condition, and at more than one ford Frederick's carriage seat was flooded. At Kreutzen, near Dortmund, Craven came close to drowning when his own carriage overturned. In the nearby village of Mengede, Frederick decided to spend the night in a house whose owner was absent, but the servants had to be threatened with pistols before the party could gain entry.[14] The following day they continued on into Hesse-Cassel, where the Dutch troops left Frederick to return to the Hague, leaving the Landgrave of Hesse-Cassel to provide a guard for the last part of the increasingly sodden journey. Frederick and his entourage arrived on horseback in Hanau, where they had to wait for two days to allow the coaches and baggage, stuck in the mud further back, to catch up. Encouragingly for Frederick, he was greeted with scenes of jubilation; the people of Hanau came out in the pouring rain to shout '*Vive le Roi de Bohême!*' Finally, on 10 February, the party caught up with the Swedish Army at Frankfurt-am-Main, and Frederick entered the city with an escort of seventy horses. He had expected to meet the Swedish King there, but Gustavus had absented himself to avoid the palaver of a formal reception, and the following day Frederick travelled to Höchst to see him, accompanied by Craven and twenty gentlemen. Gustavus greeted Frederick with scrupulous respect, addressing him repeatedly as '*mon frère*' and upbraiding the Landgrave of Hesse-Darmstadt for failing to address him as King of Bohemia.

A few days later, the Swedish Army advanced into the Lower Palatinate to more enthusiastic displays of welcome. The devastation was heart-breaking. The famine in the Rhine Valley that winter was so severe that peasants from miles around had come to work on the fortifications of Mainz in return for scraps of bread.

In the Lower Palatinate, only three fortresses—Kreutznach, Frankenthal, and Heidelberg—remained in Spanish hands, and Gustavus began by laying siege to the closest, Kreutznach, which was defended by a garrison of 600 Spanish troops. On 18 February he despatched 300 Scots soldiers under Lieutenant-Colonel George Douglas to begin the siege, accompanied by Craven's volunteers. It helped that the local people welcomed the besiegers with enthusiasm, working hard to improve the roads and supplying them with information about the defences. The winter was cold, and digging trenches in the frozen ground was arduous and slow work. But the next morning the attackers stormed one of the gates and the town was easily captured, the Swedes strictly observing their policy of humane treatment of the inhabitants. The garrison withdrew into the castle, the Kauzenburg, whose situation made it one of the strongest in Germany.

Gustavus viewed the fortifications carefully. On the lower side, the castle walls rose one above another in a pattern that could be easily defended. They were, he said, 'the devil's works'. One crescent-shaped bastion in particular he dubbed 'the devil's head'. He decided to make his approach on the other side and deployed Douglas's Scots near the walls. Walking up to view the castle at close quarters, he had a near escape when a stone thrown from the walls fell just short of him, and a man standing next to him was shot dead. Then he climbed to the top of a nearby hill to assess the fortifications, lying flat on his stomach, and returned to the camp, saying with blithe confidence, 'Now I will be master of yonder castle by five o'clock tomorrow evening.'[15]

Most assaults took a familiar course, with the attackers attempting to bring forward scaling ladders to the foot of the walls, after filling up the ditch as far as possible with turf and faggots. The initial assault, the forlorn hope, was always dangerous. The term 'forlorn hope' comes from the Dutch for 'lost heap' or 'lost troop'. It was, as its name suggests, always a risky enterprise, in which the chances of being killed or wounded were considerable, but with luck any survivors would manage to seize a foothold which could then be reinforced in the next assault. The forlorn hope would typically be made up of volunteers led by a junior officer eager to prove his valour, and despite its extreme danger there was usually stiff competition for the command.

The next morning Gustavus sprang a mine, which opened a narrow but steep breach in the walls, full of loose rocks. He ordered a general storm under the command of General Winckle, with English and French volunteers forming the forlorn hope, the English commanded by Craven and the French by Colonel Boulin, Quartermaster-General of the Swedish Army. Craven led the first assault, with around forty volunteers, including Robert Marsham and Lieutenant-Colonel Talbot. They were met with a withering hail of partisans (a type of spear), halberds, stones, and firebrands from the defenders, and, after suffering many casualties, they were forced to retreat back down the steep slope. Gustavus, looking on impatiently from its foot, ordered them to move their scaling ladders to another section of the breach.

The attack recommenced, and Gustavus noted Craven's reckless bravery with approval. He gave him a jovial clap on the back, saying with a chuckle, 'Young man, I see you're happy to give your younger brother a good chance of succeeding to your estates.' The second assault was also beaten back, but Craven led on a third. After two hours of fierce fighting one of the defenders shouted out the words 'quarter' and 'surrender', to the dismay of others who wished to fight on. Craven, in the thick of it, heard the words and with an admirable presence of mind shook one of the enemy captains by the hand, and it was all over.[16] The town's capitulation was quickly signed by Craven and Boulin. The casualties had been high; Captain Douglas and Lieutenant-Colonel Talbot had both been killed, the latter shot while standing just next to Craven. None of the English officers had escaped without injury; the wounded volunteers included Lieutenant-Colonel

Henry Winde and Sir Francis Fane, shot in the hip, as well as Craven himself, wounded in the thigh by a pike. It is said that Gustavus knighted Craven as he lay wounded on the ground. Certainly, the young man's bravery at Kreutznach attracted widespread admiration.

News of the capture of Kreutznach soon arrived in England from various quarters. There was as yet no official confirmation, but Vicenzo Gussoni, the new Venetian ambassador in London, reported that Craven's relatives had sent word of the fall of the town to the King.[17]

The terms of the surrender were that the garrison should, within three hours, march out of the town under Swedish escort, without their colours but taking their arms with them. The citizens of Kreutznach rejoiced at the relatively painless nature of the siege, and threw open their doors to their liberators. Afterwards a review of the whole army took place, during which Frederick congratulated the English brigade, thanking them for their services to date and wishing them equal success in the future.

Only two towns now remained unconquered in the Palatinate: Frankenthal and Heidelberg itself, its castle now partially burnt by Spanish troops in the expectation of its imminent recapture. But in early March, Gustavus decided to leave the Palatinate and march eastwards to confront Count Tilly, who had just defeated Swedish troops under the command of Gustav Horn at Bamberg in Bavaria. The Swedish Army had been on the point of reconquering the whole of the Palatinate, but now, to the intense irritation of Frederick and the English volunteers, victory would have to wait. Gustavus waved aside any discussions of the terms of Frederick's restoration, and when Frederick asked him for permission to levy his own troops in the Palatinate to accompany the Swedish King 'with a better garb', Gustavus refused on the grounds that he was levying troops there himself. If Frederick really wished to see some action, then Gustavus would give him Oppenheim to fortify: when that was done, he could have further troops to besiege Heidelberg. And anyway, said Gustavus, he would be no man's servant for £40,000, which was the paltry sum he had been offered by Charles I. Frederick was insulted by this exchange, but afterwards, Craven wrote to Vane, he was 'treated with more courtesy and fair show of welcome than what he hath been heretofore, which I think is only to take away the ill relish of this sour pill.'[18]

Had Frederick been allowed to levy his own forces, Craven would doubtless have been given a high command in them, but it was not to be. Instead, Frederick took Vane's advice that he should remain with the Swedish King, although he complained bitterly to Elizabeth that he couldn't understand why Gustavus had wanted him to come. He might just as well have stayed in the Hague, he grumbled; 'the trade of a volunteer is tiresome enough.' Craven remained with Frederick, grumbling too about the conditions. In fact the Swedish Army was none too popular with the English volunteers, many declaring that it was the worst army they had ever been in. Quite apart from anything else the war-ravaged German countryside was a grim place. In the middle of March Craven wrote in a letter to Vane that:

> Sweet Holland is often thought on. For my owne part could I but once see the Kinge
> of Bohemia in a good way for to be reestablished in his owne possessions I would
> leave the Kinge of Swede to enjoy his victories, & [...] would content my selfe with
> the noble and honnest conversation which the good Ile of Brittaine affords.[19]

Gustavus insisted that he still had every intention of restoring Frederick to his patrimony, but in return Charles must send another 12,000 troops and pay a subsidy of £25,000 per month—a colossal sum, far more than the £10,000 a month which Charles was now offering. So for the moment things remained, with Frederick still an unwilling volunteer. It did not help that Gustavus Adolphus, hot-tempered and impetuous, took an instant dislike to Vane, the portly, pompous ambassador. His dislike was so intense that it was suspected that he was insisting on impossible conditions for the return of the Palatinate in the hope of driving Vane away. Elizabeth on the other hand liked Vane, even though his negotiations failed to do much to help her cause. The cheerful 'fat booby ambassador' was on close enough terms to be subjected to her good-natured banter. 'I must tell you,' she wrote in April 1632, 'that if you do not come home this way there will no mercy for you, but a perpetuall warr therefore looke to it.'

Gustavus insisted that Frederick guarantee freedom of worship for Lutherans in the Palatinate; that the conquered strongholds remain in Swedish hands for the duration of the war; and that Frederick also conclude a binding alliance with Sweden. The reconquered Palatinate would, in effect, be a fiefdom of the Swedish crown, leaving Frederick, as he complained bitterly, as no more than a marionette. He rejected the terms, declaring to Vane and the Marquess of Hamilton, with tears in his eyes, that he was horrified at the thought of being restored only to be in perpetual subjection to the King of Sweden. He would rather accept a small portion of his estates unfettered than be curbed with so dishonourable a condition. It appeared alarmingly as if Gustavus was merely spinning out negotiations and had no intention of signing any agreement at all. 'The treaty with the King of Sweden will be dragged out to infinity,' Frederick complained. 'He takes up the subject since he wants money but commits himself to nothing.'

On 5 March 1632, the Swedish Army began to move eastwards, the English volunteers now attached to the 800-strong green brigade of the doughty Scottish commander Sir John Hepburn. From Mainz they marched 30 miles on the first day to Aschaffenburg. By 10 March the whole 23,000-strong Army was assembled at Weinsheim, and from there it began to move into Bavaria. In Nuremberg the two Kings dined in public with the burghers, after which Gustavus toured the town on foot. From Nuremberg the Swedish Army headed south towards the Danube and towards Count Tilly. But 'the subtle fox', as Craven called him, was proving elusive.[20] He had destroyed all the bridges on this stretch of the Danube except for one at the strategically important town of Donauwörth, defended by a 2,500-strong garrison. Because the town was surrounded by high ground it was vulnerable, but Tilly had begun to build formidable fortifications to improve the town's defences.

On 5 April, after a brisk march which took his enemies by surprise, Gustavus arrived at Donauwörth, and by the following morning his troops had created a large battery on a hillside commanding the town. After easily capturing the outer defences on the north-eastern side, he despatched a trumpeter to summon the governor to capitulate. The answer came that Gustavus should know better than anyone else the duty of the defenders, who had nothing to rely on except honour and the point of a sword, and so the governor would pay no tribute except gunpowder. 'Upon this,' wrote Harte, 'both parties performed their respective business with great earnestness.'

The siege was a brief affair, due partly to the initiative of Hepburn, who pointed out to the Swedish King the strategic importance of the narrow angle of land formed by the confluence of the Wernitz with the Danube. Capturing that position would give them command of the Danube Bridge. Realising the soundness of this advice, Gustavus ordered Hepburn to march his brigade 5 miles up the Wernitz to the bridge at Hasfort, and then back down on the other bank to the confluence with the Danube, from where they could effectively command the bridge. They marched in silence, arriving a little after midnight at the appointed place, and Hepburn deployed them among the garden walls, hedges and ditches flanking the bridge.[21] The besiegers now surrounded the town on all sides. Craven reported to Vane,

> After a warm disputing for a whole day and night and the loss of some on each side, the town of Donaver [sic] was rendered up to his majestie. We may thank both his expedition in his journey which passed upon his enemies unawares, and the good service Colonel Hebron [sic] did him, otherwise the town would not so soon have been in his possession.[22]

After most of the garrison had made their escape, Gustavus entered the town at the head of his men, sword in hand. But he was beaten to it by Hepburn's Scots, who were first inside, accompanied by some of the English volunteers, including Lord Craven, Robert Marsham, Nicholas Slanning, and Mr Russell. Donauwörth had fallen in just forty-eight hours.

In his regimental chronicle Monro, *His Expedition with the Worthy Scots Regiment*, Robert Monro praised Craven for 'his prowess and Heroicke spirit at the intaking of Donavert.' In fact, Craven was the only English volunteer whom Munro deemed worth a mention.

> Where he [Craven] did merit so much, that I having reason to have said more, could say no lesse. His worth being knowne, his affection to the cause, and his respects to his Majesty of Bohemia whom he followed, merits a well-deserving

reward from his Majesties Royal Issue.[23]

Like most of the Scots in the Swedish Army, Monro was equally motivated by affection for the cause; that is to say, by devotion to the Queen of Bohemia, and so by extension to the Palatine cause. 'They all fought for her as much as for the cause,' wrote Walter Harte, who maintained, no doubt with a touch of exaggeration, that half the Swedish Army was in love with her.[24]

Following the capture of Donauwörth, the English volunteers hoped that Gustavus would permit Frederick to return to the Palatinate. Gustavus had reportedly agreed to appoint a place as a rendezvous for Frederick, 'which,' wrote Craven, 'when I see I will believe but not one minute before.'[25] Having crossed the Danube, Gustavus intended to march directly to Munich, but it soon became apparent that crossing the River Lech would be a difficult undertaking, because Tilly's 25,000-strong army was encamped on the opposite bank. Before they left Donauwörth, the Swedes collected as many planks and bulwarks as they could muster to construct a bridge. Two weeks later, in one of the Swedish King's most brilliant feats of arms, they crossed the Lech under fire and forced Tilly to retreat. The Swedes advanced to Augsburg and then to Munich, where Frederick had the satisfaction of dining with Gustavus in the palace of his cousin, Maximilian of Bavaria. But Frederick was feeling increasingly frustrated. 'Time drags terribly for me here,' he wrote from Nuremberg in early August, 'for nothing is happening.' He begged that Gustavus should at least restore to him the portion of the Palatinate which had been reconquered, but still the Swedish King prevaricated.

Craven had no more desire than Frederick to remain with the Swedish Army, and at the end of May he left Augsburg and made his way back to the United Provinces, leaving Frederick still grumbling over his shoddy treatment. Craven took with him a letter from Frederick to his wife. Craven, wrote Frederick,

> has behaved highly commendably in this campaign and has shown great courage and affection to me; he would certainly have proved this beyond any doubt if the King of Sweden had thought fit to allow me to raise an army. Nevertheless I am extremely indebted to him and would dearly like to be able to show him the esteem in which I hold him and that he left here as content with me as I am with him. I pray you to assure him of this and how I appreciated the affection he showed me.[26]

Back in the United Provinces Craven delivered Frederick's letter to Elizabeth in the Hague, and then plunged straight back into action. A few weeks earlier the States Army had begun besieging the strategic town of Maastricht, and in early July Craven made his way to the Prince of Orange's camp, where he joined Lord Vere's regiment. Also in the camp was his younger brother John, who had decided to take time out from the Inns of Court for a season's campaigning in the Netherlands. In the middle of June Colonel Harwood had begun to dig his circumvallation trenches, in the face of regular sorties by the garrison. The trenches steadily advanced towards the walls in two zigzag lines, until in early August a breach was made in the walls. A first assault was driven back, and the defenders succeeded in exploding a mine under the English approaches. The garrison made a determined sortie, and there was fierce fighting by push of pike around the advance party of the English attackers. Their commander was killed, but Craven and Philip Skippon, who was to become a parliamentary commander during the Civil War, led a counter-attack and succeeded in driving the defenders back towards the walls.[27]

Back in Bavaria Gustavus had decided to confront Wallenstein, who had been recalled by the Emperor and had speedily reconquered much of Bohemia. When the Swedish Army moved off eastwards in October, Frederick obtained Gustavus's agreement to leave him and tour the liberated parts of the Palatinate. He found the scenes of devastation heartbreaking. At Oppenheim half the town had been burnt, and the house where he and Elizabeth had stayed on their journey to Heidelberg was a tragic ruin. Frederick diverted himself in hunting, but the tragedy of the situation weighed on him. Aged only thirty-six, he had become so worn down with care that his own brother had difficulty in recognising him.[29] He did not remain in the Palatinate for long. With Spanish troops still in the vicinity he did not feel altogether safe, and he accepted an offer to stay in the castle at Mainz, which at least had some creature comforts.

News arrived of Gustavus. Wallenstein had captured Leipzig, and Gustavus was angling to confront him. 'God grant,' wrote Frederick, 'that his accustomed success awaits him.' But this time the Swedish King's luck did not hold. On 6 November 1632, the two armies finally met at Lützen. The Swedes were victorious, but at disastrous cost. In the evening, after Wallenstein had sounded the retreat, the body of Gustavus was discovered dead on the field of battle. It was a disastrous blow for the Protestant cause. The Swedish King's death removed the last of the great military commanders who could have swung the tide of war.

A few days after Lützen, Frederick, still wandering disconsolately through the ruined Palatinate, visited the town of Bacharach, a short distance down the Rhine from Mainz. It was a foolhardy visit because plague had been reported in the town, and it soon became apparent that Frederick had himself succumbed. It appeared to be only a mild infection, but news of Gustavus's death seems to have overwhelmed him as he was struggling to recover. On 19 November, Frederick died at Mainz. The two figureheads of the Protestant cause in Germany had died within two weeks of each other, Frederick, with tragic irony, just as he was on the point of regaining the major part of his patrimony.

The news of her husband's death came just as Elizabeth was beginning to indulge hopes of returning to the Palatinate. In his last letter, Frederick had told her that he would send for her as soon as Heidelberg had fallen, an event which was expected imminently, and she was full of anticipation. The task of breaking the dreadful news was given to Dr Rumph, doctor to the Palatine family and long-standing friend of both Frederick and Elizabeth. Rumph performed the difficult task with all the tact he could muster, but there was little he could do to soften the blow. The news left Elizabeth stunned. For three days she remained in her bed, without eating, drinking, or sleeping, and without uttering a word. Sir J. Meautys remarked,

> [...] what an afflicted and grieved lady the Queen of Bohemia is, for the death of the King [...]. Certainly no woman could take the death of a husband more to heart than this queen doth.[30]

Charles I put his court into mourning and sent Nethersole to the Hague bearing a letter of commiseration, in which he invited his sister to return to England. He even sent a formal embassy under the Earl of Arundel to accompany her to London. But she declined the offer:

> I must entreat you to pardon me, if I cannot at present obey your command and my own wishes; the custom in Germany being not to stir out of the house for some time, after such a misfortune.[31]

Perhaps more importantly, she had decided that her priority must be to fight for her sons' patrimony, and for the next few years, until her eldest son came of age, she proceeded to steer Palatine affairs with a single-minded tenacity of purpose.

It was just one year since Craven had thrown all his energy into the Palatine cause. He had fought bravely with the Swedish Army, only to see the reconquest postponed. The Swedes still remained in control of most of the Palatinate, but for the moment there was nothing more to be done. After a visit to the Hague in November to see the disconsolate Elizabeth, Craven returned to England to attend to his affairs back home.

Back in England

The most urgent matter now, at the end of 1632, was to secure funds to honour a provisional agreement regarding the Palatinate. The Swedish Chancellor, Axel Oxenstierna, who was now in charge of Swedish policy, had agreed to restore most of the Palatinate to its heir on the payment of 6,000 rixdollars for Swedish expenses, and on condition that the free exercise of Lutheranism be allowed. Half of this sum would be paid by the Administrator of the Palatinate, Frederick's younger brother the Duke of Simmern, but the remainder, plus further money for defence, would have to be furnished by Charles I. In total, a sum of £30,000 was required, and there was some urgency because French forces were poised to take over the strongholds of the Palatinate on the departure of the Swedes.

Elizabeth, already annoyed by her brother's tardiness in providing funds, suggested to him that the sum could be raised through a voluntary contribution, and she proposed that a letter inviting contributions for the relief of the Palatinate be circulated. Charles agreed in principle, though he refused to allow any mention in the letter of the calling of a Parliament, and the faithful Nethersole travelled over to London again for negotiations. He succeeded in obtaining from the King a declaration concerning the proposed appeal, and accordingly drafted a letter to be issued in the King's name and circulated to the magistrates in every county. The letters went out and contributions began to come in. They trickled in, however, with frustrating slowness, and so Nethersole came up with an alternative plan: he would raise a loan of £30,000 from London merchants, to be repaid out of contributions raised by an appeal in the sole name of the Queen of Bohemia. Charles was unimpressed, denouncing the scheme as rash and extravagant, but Nethersole went ahead anyway. On 30 May he showed the King's declaration to Lord Craven, who was in Greenwich to wait on the Queen before departing for Edinburgh to see the King. Craven agreed with alacrity to act as guarantor, and on the strength of this Nethersole negotiated a loan of £31,000 from two London merchants, Sir William Curteen and Samuel Aldersey.

Craven meanwhile decided to discuss Nethersole's proposed scheme with Lord Goring, who shared the King's opinion that it was dubious and impractical. The result was that Craven too began to have second thoughts. Goring then made the whole scheme public, adding disobliging comments about Nethersole into the bargain. This stung Nethersole into writing an emotional letter to Goring, accusing him of failing in his duty to the King and his love of the Queen of Bohemia by revealing the scheme prematurely. Goring, put out by this imputed stain on his reputation, made the letter public and asked that the matter be referred to the board of the Council of State. The whole affair caused much laughter at Nethersole's expense. Goring wrote to the Secretary of State, Francis Windebank, enclosing one of Nethersole's over-emotional letters and asking for a meeting the following morning; the afternoons, he added nonchalantly, always belonged to his mistresses.[1]

At the council Nethersole behaved with an unfortunate tactlessness. First of all he refused to kneel, causing great offence, and then, after judgment was given against him and in favour of Goring, he wrote intemperate letters pinning the blame for the loss of the Palatinate on the King. There was some justice in the accusation, of course, but it was tactless of Nethersole to point it out. Charles was outraged and ordered Nethersole's arrest. He was freed after a few months, but only after the King had extracted a promise from his sister that she would never employ Nethersole in her service again. To replace him Elizabeth sent over her secretary Sir John Dineley, formerly tutor to the Palatine children at the Prinsenhof. Any further attempts to raise money for the relief of the Palatinate were abandoned when Charles I accepted the advice of the lord treasurer, Lord Portland, who opposed English involvement in the German wars. The inevitable result was that on the departure of the Swedish Army the Palatine fortresses were, as expected, taken over by the French. So ended yet another failed attempt to regain the Palatinate. Never again, in the twists and turns of the succeeding years, would success come so close. It was particularly frustrating because Craven easily had the wherewithal to supply the £30,000 required by Oxenstierna, and in the years to come he was to spend far greater sums on more failed attempts at reconquest.

For Craven there was nothing to do now except to wait and hope that a new opportunity would present itself. For the next few years he remained in England, managing his estates and supervising building projects, attending court now and again, taking on assorted administrative duties, and becoming something of a literary patron, while keeping a weather eye on affairs in Germany and the United Provinces. On 24 November 1633 he took part in the christening of the King's second child, James, Duke of York, in the Chapel Royal at Whitehall, helping to bear the canopy carried over the baby as the party proceeded to the chapel. He attended court on a few other occasions; the following March he accompanied the Swedish ambassador extraordinary, Henry Oxenstierne, in his coach for the journey from Greenwich to Whitehall Palace. The Swedish Chancellor's son had been sent to London in an effort to find out if there was any chance of English assistance in the restoration of the Palatinate and to seek Charles's support for the Protestant League of Heilbronn.

When in London Craven lived at Drury House, situated where Wych Street (now the Aldwych) turns into Drury Lane. It was a substantial building on the east side of the street, its forecourt surrounded by ranges of smaller houses and stables, and behind the house lay a large garden. After his return to England in late 1632, Craven seems to have decided to rebuild the Elizabethan structure along more up-to-date lines. The new Drury House was a large three-storied brick mansion with casement windows, its upper floors decorated with pilasters. The building has traditionally been attributed to Sir Balthasar Gerbier, although it seems more probable that the designer was an anonymous local mason.

Out in the country Craven began to busy himself in building work and in the development of his estates. In 1633 he bought Caversham Park in Oxfordshire for £10,000, and over the next few years he spent another £20,000 on repairs and improvements to the house. The following year he obtained a licence to enclose 650 acres at Combe Abbey to create a park. His brother John had recently settled not far away at Winwick, over the border into Northamptonshire, and in December 1634 he married a near neighbour, Elizabeth Spencer, daughter of William Spencer, second Baron Spencer of Wormleighton, who lived at nearby Althorp.

In 1633 Lord Craven was appointed to the Council of Wales, which met at Ludlow Castle. His sister Elizabeth Herbert was living not far away at Powis Castle, and during these years he became a frequent visitor. Sir Percy Herbert was a Catholic and Elizabeth, much to her brother's distress, was considering converting to her husband's faith. Craven's visits were evidently characterised by fierce arguments over religion, but he seemed confident of his powers of persuasion. On a visit to Powis Castle in August 1633, he penned the following declaration:

Lord Craven declaration at Powys Castle

If I do not prove the possession of the doctrine now held in the Church of England from our Saviour's time until this present day I oblige myself never to dispute with my sister concerning matters of controversy in religion. The which I am confident to prove, and will do my endeavour herein.

W. Craven 29 August 1633.[2]

It rather sounds as though the Herberts were a touch exasperated by their guest's harping on about religion. Perhaps even then the topic was regarded as one best avoided at dinner parties. Alas, Craven was less persuasive than his brother-in-law, and soon afterwards, to his horror, Elizabeth decided to convert to Catholicism. Two years later he was still trying to persuade her that she had made a mistake.[3] He never succeeded, but he remained close to his sister and her family, while never ceasing to lament that she had been debauched from the faith in which she had been raised. It is a measure of the appeal of Catholicism in the higher echelons of society in these years that Craven's brother John was also flirting with conversion. At Trinity College, Oxford, John Craven had made the acquaintance of the Catholic convert William Chillingworth, who was a fellow there. Chillingworth set to work on him, but on learning about this danger to John's immortal soul, William sent a message to Chillingworth through a mutual friend, the noted Catholic convert Elizabeth Lady Falkland, forbidding Chillingworth from approaching his house. 'This communication,' wrote Lady Falkland's biographer, 'was received with much patience by Mr Chillingworth, who treated it as a calumny brought upon him by his zeal for God's cause.'[4]

Craven's entry in Collins's Peerage of England tells us,

> His Lordship in his younger days was one of the most accomplished gentlemen in Europe; an useful subject, charitable, abstemious as to himself, generous to others, familiar in his conversation, and universally beloved.[5]

Allowing for the usual oleaginous quality of such descriptions, at least part of this is entirely accurate. Of Craven's generosity and charitable instincts there is no doubt. Though many at court looked down on him because of his humble origins, he was certainly popular among Londoners, who celebrated his martial prowess in atrocious poetry.

> London's bright gem, his house's honour, and
> A great assistant of the Netherland
> Bounty and valour make thy name shine clear
> By Nassau graced, by Swedeland's King most dear
> Who, when on Crusnacke walls, he understood
> Thee wounded, came to knight thee in thy blood:
> To whom then folded in his arms he said
> Rise bravest spirit that thy city bred.[6]

Intriguing hints of Craven's activities during these years in England appear in 'The Progresse', a libellous poem of around 1634 full of tittle-tattle about the nobility and their mistresses. Sandwiched between bawdy verses about Lord Goring ('Lusty Ld. Goring cannot bee mist, For then should some want to be kist') and Lord Grandison ('Gandison [sic] too did there resort, But yet his Mistres was not at Court') are these verses about Lord Craven:

> Craven comes not to boast of bloud
> Whats ere defective his purse makes good,
> Who would not then his mistres be
> That is more Franck then two, or three.

> But some say he does this to spare
> For wives more costly than mistresses are,
> Besides if one please not his minde
> Hee finds another thats more kind.[7]

In other words, Craven makes up for his humble origins by the lavishness of his generosity, which has the added advantage of making him attractive to women. He has had two or three mistresses, including, perhaps, one called Francis—or perhaps she was French. And some say he prefers mistresses to wives because they are cheaper, and because if he gets bored with one he can easily change her for another.

There is certainly no doubt about Craven's generosity, even leaving aside his donations to the Palatine cause. He seems to have gone around, chequebook in hand as it were, doling out money with abandon. His record of generosity began when he celebrated his coming of age by paying the debts of hundreds of poor people in debtors' prisons. His years in England were marked by literary patronage and a donation to his college library. But in addition he seems to have been always open with his purse, regularly contributing funds for example to help support John Dury, the advocate of Protestant reunion. One contemporary wrote that Craven 'deserves to have his name written on pillars of brass' in recognition of his 'many great, noble and pious works.'[8]

In these few short years in England—he was to return to the continent in 1637—Craven embarked on a veritable flurry of literary patronage. Between 1634 and 1637 he was the dedicatee of a large number of classical, military, and religious works, with dedications ranging from the stodgy to the obsequious. There were plays—such as John Ford's *The Broken Heart* and Mary Fage's *Famous Roule*—and translations—such as Thomas Farnaby's translations of Virgil, Edward Grimeston's translation of *The History of Polybius the Megalopolitan*, and William Tyrwhitt's translation of *The Letters of Monsieur de Balzac*. There were dictionaries—Francis Holyoke's *Dictionarum etymologium latinum*—and military works—John Russell's *The two famous pitched battles of Lypsich and Lützen*. Robert Basset's dedication at the front of his *Curiosities or the Cabinet of Nature* (1637) gives an intriguing summary of Craven's career to date.

> One whose birth ranked him not in the extremes, by Education trayned up in the learned Qualities, by an innated desire of a melioration, a Travailer in forraine parts, at length by accident a Souldier, who at length, seeing that Bellum was but *Jactis Aleae* [the casting of dice], making a faire retreate, and resigning his Sword to Mars, retyred himselfe to the former unforgotten tranquillity of his pleasing and most recreative studies; amongst the rest, being desirous to breath himself of his last and lost laborious times, happened upon the ever-verdant and private walkes of Naturall Philosophie.[9]

It seems a touch improbable that Craven really became a soldier by accident, but at least for the moment he did indeed return to the 'former unforgotten tranquillity' of his life in England, where he indulged his literary interests. Among the writers whose acquaintance he cultivated was the poet Ben Jonson. We only know as much from an old joke— admittedly not a very good one—which relates how Craven once invited Jonson to dinner.

At the appointed time Ben trudged off in his usual poor clothes, patched all over, and knocked at his lordship's door. The astonished porter scratched his head, and before he conducted the stranger in sent to inform Lord Craven that a shabby clodhopper who called himself Ben Jonson desired to see him. His lordship flew to the door to welcome the poet, but started back in surprise when he saw such a figure. 'You Ben Jonson, indeed! Shouldn't care for your clothes, but your face— zounds! You couldn't say "Bo" to a goose.'

'Bo,' said Ben.

His lordship burst into a hearty laugh, and, satisfied by the joke of the personal identity of the famous guest, conducted him in.[10]

After leaving England in 1637, Craven's literary patronage continued, though on a smaller scale. In 1640 Sir Richard Baker, who died in a debtors' prison, dedicated a book of reflections on the psalms to Craven, thanking him for 'the remission of a great debt'.[11] After the sequestration of his estates in 1653, Craven no longer had the means to support needy writers. In 1657, admittedly, he was the dedicatee of a play by George Gerbier d'Ouvilly entitled *The False Favourite Disgraced, and the Reward of Loyalty*, but this dedication had more to do with loyalty than patronage; in 1637 Craven had made d'Ouvilly a captain in the newly formed Palatine Army.

But this is to look ahead. After successive failures, military and diplomatic, restitution of the Palatinate seemed as far off as ever, and prospects grew even darker in 1635 when the sixty-seven-year-old Maximilian, Duke of Bavaria married the Emperor's daughter Maria, aged twenty-seven. Under the terms of the Treaty of Prague, the Palatine electoral title was transferred to Maximilian. For the Queen of Bohemia, this represented something of a low point.

Charles Louis, the young Prince Palatine, was due to turn eighteen in December 1635, and Elizabeth decided that his first official foray into the outside world should be to travel to London to pay his respects to his uncle. Elizabeth hoped that a personal entreaty to Charles to give worthwhile support to the Palatine cause would have more chance of success than yet another letter of supplication. She wrote to Archbishop Laud and the Marquis of Hamilton informing them of her intention, but she carefully omitted to tell the English ambassador at the Hague, fearing that if she did so her plans might be thwarted.

She also wrote to Sir Harry Vane, begging him to give her son his best advice and to protect him from the disadvantages of inexperience. He was, she explained, very young and inept:

I fear damnablie how he will do with your ladies, for he is a verie ill courtier; therefore I pray, desire them not to laugh too much at him, but be mercifull to him.[12]

Charles Louis had grown into a careful, rather melancholy youth, but as Elizabeth's son he was ensured of an enthusiastic welcome in England. 'The coming of the Prince,' wrote the Venetian ambassador Anzolo Correr, 'will certainly be greeted by acclamations from the general [population], with whom he is very popular because of his mother.'[13] There was a general expectation that the Prince's arrival would finally galvanise Charles into giving help, but Elizabeth impressed upon her son that he should not annoy his uncle with 'impatient pressings'.

In early December 1635 Charles Louis sailed for England, taking with him an entourage of seventy. Prominent among them were Craven, Sir John Dineley, and Colonel Thomas Ferencz, 'a gentleman of great valour, judgment and appearance' who had been granted leave from the States Army so that he could accompany the Prince to London. There was a great sense of excitement in England, and frustration when Charles Louis' journey was delayed by contrary winds. His arrival at Dover was marked by an unfortunate mishap when, in a display of astonishingly inept gunnery, one of the cannons firing a salute managed to score a direct hit on the Prince's ship. Five of his entourage were killed, including two German gentlemen standing just a few paces away from him.[14] After this unpromising start Charles Louis came ashore, where he was greeted by the Earl of Arundel and conducted ceremoniously up to London. He was welcomed warmly by the King and Queen, and given lodgings in Whitehall Palace.

The King's warmth towards his nephew seemed to augur well. Correr reported that

His Majesty, indeed, neglects nothing that is likely to give pleasure to his nephew. He always wants him near, makes him dine with him nearly every morning, visits him frequently in his own rooms and treats him with a familiarity and affection that cannot be exaggerated.[15]

It seemed to indicate that Charles might at last make some sort of provision for his nephew, and there was even talk of him being given a fleet.

Charles Louis wrote enthusiastically to his mother about the court, though he complained about 'perpetual hunting and changing of lodgings'. He was invited to Theobalds, 'one of the most charming places belonging to the crown near London and especially enjoyable for every kind of hunting.' It was unfortunate that, not long after their arrival, several members of the Prince's entourage, Craven among them, fell ill with 'a most pestilential fever' which was feared to be the plague. The doctors were doubtful; it may have been just a case of the measles. Yet plague was certainly rife all over Europe during those months; only a few weeks later, in

February 1636, Craven's brother Thomas died of the plague in Paris. Lord Craven himself soon recovered, though another member of the Prince's suite, a son of Lord Saye, succumbed.[16]

At Whitehall the court was fully occupied with Christmas revelries.

> Comedies, festivities and balls are the order of the day here, and are indulged in every day at court for the Prince's sake, while all the greatest lords vie with each other in entertaining him.[17]

The Prince worked hard to mobilise support for his cause, going out of his way to cultivate the growing number of influential men, many of them with Puritan sympathies, who distrusted the King and disapproved of his policies. He took care, however, not to identify himself with any one faction, and a few days after Christmas he went to dine with the Archbishop of Canterbury at Lambeth Palace, accompanied by Craven and the Earl of Dover.[18]

All this hospitality took its toll on the Prince, and early in January he fell ill with a fever brought on, or so Correr suspected, by a surfeit of good living. He soon recovered, and set out with the King, accompanied by Craven and a few others, on a hunting expedition to Newmarket. Soon afterwards, however, he fell ill again. This time the cause was rumoured to be deep melancholy. It was becoming increasingly obvious to him that there was little immediate prospect of help from his uncle, and 'although they neglect nothing to keep the Prince diverted and happy,' reported Correr, 'he seems careworn and sad at seeing his affairs go on in the same old way.'[19] No promises of help were forthcoming, and he even began to talk about returning to the Hague. Ideas were floated—a fleet for the Prince, a grand alliance with France—but no decisions were ever made, 'and thus,' wrote Dineley to Roe, 'affairs are floating in the world as though all were in shipwreck without England.'[20]

Later in January 1636, Elizabeth decided to send her second son, Rupert, to join Charles Louis at his uncle's court. Since the departure of Charles Louis, the sixteen-year-old Rupert had been clamouring to be allowed to join his elder brother in England. Rupert had grown into an intriguing youth. Energetic and charming, tall and strong, but blunt of speech and with an uncontrollable temper, he was known by his brothers and sisters as Rupert le Diable. From an early age he had been fascinated by the art of war, and it was said that at the age of eight he already handled his arms like an experienced soldier. At the age of thirteen he had been on his first military campaign with the Prince of Orange, and had won much praise for his 'manly carriage'. He had a talent too for drawing and sketching, and was an accomplished linguist.

Late at night on 7 February, Rupert arrived at the garden steps at Whitehall Palace, to be greeted by the Earl of Arundel. Elizabeth had been nervous about her second son's reception in England, afraid that his manners might seem too rough for the sophisticated London courtiers. Charles treated his nephew warmly, but many at court, remembering that the Queen of Bohemia had plenty of other penniless sons growing up in the Hague, were less enthusiastic, 'because they fear,' reported Correr, 'that by degrees they will all come and will take root.'[21]

It was not long, however, before Rupert, with his spontaneous manner and graceful bearing, became popular at Whitehall. He in turn was enchanted by its lavishness, a marked contrast to his mother's impoverished, threadbare establishment, and he became deeply devoted to the King and Queen. In particular, Elizabeth heard worrying reports that her younger son was spending time in the company of Henrietta Maria and her Papist entourage. It was true; the Queen had adopted Rupert into her circle. Elizabeth appealed to Roe to persuade Rupert to return to the Netherlands so that he could begin learning the art of war in the camp of the Prince of Orange, 'as he spends his time and idly in England.' Sir Thomas thought it would be unfair to recall the young man quite yet. 'His spirit is too active to be wasted in the softness and entanglings of pleasure,' he wrote, '[but] there is nothing ill in his stay here.'[22] So despite his mother's misgivings Rupert remained in England, where Craven kept a watchful eye on him, assisting the young Prince with both money and advice.

Roe thought highly of Rupert:

[he was] full of spirit of action, full of observation and judgment. Certainly he will réussir un *grand homme*, for whatever he wills, he wills vehemently, so that to what he bends, he will be in it excellent. I am glad he stays here while he cannot be employed in a school of honour, for his Majesty takes great pleasure in his unrestfulness, for he is never idle, and in his sports serious, in his conversation retired, but sharp and witty when occasion provokes him.[23]

By this time, it had begun to seem that at last English help might be forthcoming for the recovery of the Palatinate. France and Spain were now at war, and in June 1636 the Spanish Army in Flanders invaded France. In England the anti-Spanish faction at court was urging the King to enter into an alliance with France and join the war against Spain. Discussions continued over a possible agreement, under the terms of which England would declare war on the Habsburgs while France would undertake to continue the war until the Palatinate had been restored. There was much discussion of raising an army, but more astute observers doubted whether talk would ever lead to action. The unavoidable fact was that there simply wasn't enough money in the royal coffers. 'The Spaniards are well aware of this,' wrote Correr, 'and set about to confuse the issue with their subtleties, so as to make it go on for ever.'[24] The carrot which the Spanish held out was the restitution of the Lower Palatinate. Talks meandered along exasperatingly, until in April Charles despatched the Earl of Arundel to the Emperor in Vienna, 'as they are tired of being put off with ambiguities.'

Though the Winter Queen's two sons came together on ceremonial occasions, they mostly went their separate ways. The King and Queen began to cast around for ways of helping Rupert and providing him with employment, or at least to provide him with an income. An early suggestion was that he should marry a wealthy heiress, a very practical suggestion for a poverty-stricken Palatine. The heiress in question was Marguerite de Rohan, daughter of the Huguenot Duc de Rohan. Elizabeth was in favour of the match, as it seems was Marguerite herself, but Rupert showed little enthusiasm. Negotiations continued for a while, but meanwhile Rupert's imagination was captured by what seemed a much more interesting possibility; he would head a merchant squadron whose aim would be to colonise the island of Madagascar, of which Rupert himself would become governor. Elizabeth was alarmed by this madcap idea, denouncing the scheme as 'neither feasible, safe, nor honourable'. If he was looking for military glory, there was plenty to be had in Europe. Rupert, however, was not easily dissuaded, despite the best efforts of Roe and Elizabeth's councillor Johann van Rusdorf. Anxious about where all this might lead, Elizabeth wrote to her brother asking him to send Rupert back to the Hague, where he could be much more usefully employed in the army of the Prince of Orange.

With the plague still rife in London, the court was perpetually on the move. At the beginning of May 1636, Charles Louis accompanied Henrietta Maria to a play at Blackfriars, but later in the month the court moved out to Hampton Court. The summer was hot, and in July the plague came uncomfortably close when members of the Prince's entourage, including John Dineley, Thomas Ferencz, and Sir Richard Cave, were given lodgings in rooms in Holborn which, it was discovered too late, were suspected of harbouring the plague. To avoid any danger to the Prince, Craven invited all those who might have been infected to spend a month in quarantine at Combe Abbey, 'according to the zeal,' wrote Ferencz, 'which he has for Your Majesty and for His Highness.'[25] The mention of Combe must have stirred up happy memories for Elizabeth, memories of a happy and carefree childhood long ago.

An unfortunate result of the quarantine was that for a month the Prince Elector was deprived of his key advisors. It worried Roe a little; 'but,' he reasoned, 'he is so discreet, warye, and free from precipitation, that he may be trusted alone, and in the progresse he will not have much use.'[26]

The progress to which Roe referred consisted of a ceremonial visit to Oxford by the court at the end of August. The highlight of the Princes' stay in England, the visit consisted of three days of orations, sermons, plays, sightseeing, and dinners. It was masterminded by Archbishop Laud, Chancellor of the University of Oxford, who bore much of the expense himself. Preparations were exhaustive, with instructions going round to the undergraduates that they were

> to appear nowhere abroad without their caps, and in apparel of such colour and fashion as the statute prescribed, and particularly they were not to wear long hair,

nor any boots, nor double stockings rolled down or hanging loose about their legs, as the manner of some slovens is, nor to wear their gowns hanging loosely, with their capes below their shoulders.[27]

The King and Queen arrived in Oxford on 29 July, the two Palatine Princes riding with them in the royal coach. Two miles outside the city the royal party was met by the Chancellor, accompanied by all the university dignitaries and 'students of qualitie'. After a ceremonial Latin address by the Public Orator, William Strode, the King, Queen, and Princes were each presented with gifts, carefully chosen by the Chancellor, of religious (or military, in Rupert's case) books, and costly pairs of gloves. Arriving in the city, the King and Queen were escorted to lodgings at Christ Church, while the court was spread among the various other colleges. Craven was given lodgings at Trinity, his old college, and there, at Laud's request, he too was presented with a pair of gloves, which cost £2 15 s.[28]

This was a period when gloves, often extraordinarily elaborate, were highly prized as gifts. The most expensive were intricately embroidered satin gauntlets, embellished with silver thread and decorated with pearls and heraldic devices. Often such gloves would be given by gallants to their favourite ladies, or else by ladies to their favourite gallants, who would habitually wear them in their hats or helmets. In 1629, Craven had been greatly pleased by the present of gloves from Mademoiselle de Nassau, maid of honour to the Queen of Bohemia, and a few years earlier Duke Christian of Brunswick had worn Elizabeth's glove in his helmet, vowing to return to her in Heidelberg. On other occasions, as with Craven's gift from Trinity College, gloves were more in the nature of ceremonial presents. In 1634, Lord Craven's steward Lewis Ziegler was presented with a pair of gloves by George Weckherlin, poet and private secretary to successive English Secretaries of State. Intriguingly, this gift seems to have related to Weckherlin's initiation into Rosicrucianism, that fascinating hermetic philosophy which flourished briefly in the Palatinate in the years before the Thirty Years War.[29]

The royal party at Christ Church was regaled with more ceremonial speeches, and in the evening they were entertained in Christ Church Hall with a play by Strode, which, according to Lord Carnarvon, a member of the royal party, was 'the worst that ever he saw but one that he saw at Cambridge.'[30] After this everyone enjoyed a sumptuous banquet, at which the cooks had contrived the cooked meats so that 'there was first the forms of archbishops, then bishops, doctors, etc. seen in order, wherein the King and courtiers took much content.' The following day the royal party was conducted to the House of Convocation, where the Princes were invested as Masters of Arts by Sir Nathaniel Brent, Warden of Merton College. As a compliment to Laud both were entered as members of St John's, the Archbishop's old college. There followed more Latin speeches and a tour of the colleges, after which the Princes returned to Christ Church. Before the court left Oxford, Craven and others of the Palatine entourage were also invested as Masters of Arts at the special request of the Prince Elector. Twelve years after he had left Oxford at the age of fifteen to join the States Army, Craven had at last achieved his MA.[31]

In September 1636, Arundel returned from his fruitless embassy in Vienna. He travelled back via the Palatinate, where he witnessed the grim devastation wrought by years of warfare—towns ruined, villages depopulated, and dead bodies lying in the roads, their mouths filled with grass which they had been driven to eat. Following this latest diplomatic failure, Charles Louis began to despair of ever getting help from his uncle, though discussions continued over the much-debated alliance with France and a possible joint army under the command of either Charles Louis or French officers. Others proposed that the Prince could take the field in alliance with one of the two non-aligned Protestant armies in Germany, those of the Landgrave of Hesse-Cassel and of Duke Bernard of Saxe-Weimar. As always, however, there was much conversation but little action.

Charles Louis was increasingly tiring of inactivity. Correr reported that

> he shows great impatience at remaining idle here, and his countenance really betrays the most acute sense of shame, as he never takes part without blushing at any conference where the present agitations of the world are discussed. His brother, on the other hand, finds all his delight in the amenities of the court, and in particular passes his time by amusing himself in the society of the ladies, without any preoccupations besides what his own youthful inclinations at present supply him.[32]

Clearly, despite Roe's prediction, Rupert had learnt to enjoy the court's 'softness and entanglings of pleasure'. However he had not given up on the Madagascar scheme, and early in 1637 talk resumed, Elizabeth as vehemently opposed as ever. 'As for Rupert's romance of Madagascar,' she wrote in April, 'it sounds like one of Don Quixote's conquests, where he promised his trusty squire to make him King of an island.'[33] Roe advised her to wait for events to take their course. Although nothing would ever come of the plan to colonise Madagascar, it was a dream which continued to exercise men's imaginations. Others looked beyond Madagascar to Mauritius, and at about the same time an equally abortive scheme to send ships and planters to that island was promoted by John Craven and his wife's uncle the 4th Earl of Southampton. John Craven spent many thousands of pounds on this enterprise, only to be beaten to it by the Dutch, who began to plant settlers on the island in 1639.[34] Lord Craven was recorded as being the owner of the *Pennington*, a small ship of 80 tons, in 1637, and given his later interest in colonisation, perhaps he too was involved in the abandoned Mauritius expedition.

The Prince Elector's luck was beginning to change. Pressure had been steadily mounting on the King to recall Parliament, commit himself to an alliance with France, and declare war on the Emperor. In February 1637, a tentative agreement was reached with the French that if Charles were to declare war on the Empire, and also to provision thirty ships and permit the French to levy 6,000 troops in England, France would undertake to continue the war until the restitution of the Palatinate. With luck the Dutch would also join the alliance, with Charles Louis as High Admiral of the combined fleets of France and Holland. This would conveniently mean that England might not have to declare war, something that Charles desperately wished to avoid.

As a means of recapturing the Palatinate, hundreds of miles from the sea, a fleet was not on the face of it particularly useful—about as useful in fact as a Swiss navy. In reality, though, the plan was that it would be used to mount an attack on the Spanish treasure fleet returning from the Americas. Charles Louis, anyway, was overjoyed that at last a decision had been made. The proposed fleet was to consist of twenty-two ships, including some from the Royal Navy, and the government began to seize suitable merchantmen arriving in the Thames. To raise money to outfit them Charles drafted a letter to be read out in all parishes, requesting voluntary contributions. Offers of money came in from the Providence Island group and a few London merchants, but among the first contributors, needless to say, was Lord Craven, who with characteristic munificence offered £30,000.[35]

Craven's contribution led to much comment, not all of it favourable. Many Italian princes would shirk at such prodigality, wrote Nathaniel Hobart to his friend Sir Ralph Verney in February 1637.

> Though I dare not rank him [Craven] with kings and princes yet, trust mee, his bounty may challenge a prime place amongst them. I daresay there are some Italian princes would shrink at soe great an undertaking [as financing a fleet], nay, and they should pawn their titles, and spoyle their subjects, they would not be able to furnish such a sum. Yet what is this but a small part or portion of those vast treasures left him by his father?

But who was Craven, Hobart asked with towering condescension. A mere *filius populi*! And what stock had he to begin with? Only a groat! There followed a long diatribe about the meanness of Craven's pedigree, his small stature, his gargantuan wealth, and his boundless liberality, which 'begets in his inferiors a disguised friendship, and in his equals, envy.' His vanity made him accessible to his inferiors; the meanness of his birth and physique made him contemptible to his equals.

Hobart's extreme venom certainly shows the extent of aristocratic disdain for new money, not to mention the sheer unpleasantness of many courtiers. The fact of a mere merchant's son having such stupendous wealth and, worse, having bought his peerage, appeared a violation of the natural order of society. The court could indeed be an awkward place, and Craven probably suffered similar treatment to the financier Lord Cranfield, denounced in the House of Lords as an 'insolent merchant'.

Verney's reply to Hobart was equally condescending:

We hear much of a great navy, but more of my little Lord Craven, whose bounty makes him the subject of every man's discourse. By many he is condemned of prodigality, but by most of folly.[36]

All these slighting references to Craven's stature incidentally raise the question of how tall he really was. A full-length portrait of him by Honthorst shows a man of average height, but its low viewpoint no doubt exaggerates its subject's stature. He was probably a few inches shorter than the average for the period (about 5 foot 6 inches), but certainly men such as Rupert or Gustavus, both well over 6 feet tall, would have towered over him.

With regard to the proposed fleet, accusations of prodigality and folly were understandable. Certainly many were doubtful about the sense of spending huge sums on such a quixotic enterprise. Elizabeth disapproved of the idea altogether, regarding it as an unwise distraction. Practical as ever, she wished to see her son in command of an army in Germany. 'He will hardly get the Palatinate at sea,' she commented tartly to her friend the Landgrave of Hesse-Cassel, 'but if the King woulde but give my sonne 6 thousand men' he would be able to use it as the nucleus of a strong army.

Just at the moment, however, a fleet seemed to be all that was on offer, and Craven spent the first few months of 1637 hanging around Whitehall hoping that it would materialise. During these months at court he found himself drawn into some of the romances, quarrels, and intrigues that inevitably flourish in such an environment. Charles I's court, like any other, brought together a disparate group of people. Some came to mix in fashionable society, others to beg a favour, make a complaint, or ingratiate themselves with the powerful. Some simply kicked their heels on the fringes of the most sophisticated court in Europe. There were troublesome gossips, too, like Madge Crofts, a former maid of honour to the Queen of Bohemia who had returned to England after falling out spectacularly with her mistress. At Whitehall she enjoyed spreading tittle-tattle about Elizabeth's poverty-stricken court, while complaining loudly to Craven that the Palatine Princes, who loathed her, were ignoring her.

However, the first of this series of disparate events into which Craven found himself drawn was a marriage; not his own, but that of Barbara Sidney, a cousin by marriage of John Craven and the widow of Thomas Smythe, Viscount Strangford. After a lightning romance Barbara Sidney had married Thomas Colepeper, colonel of one of the English regiments in Dutch service. Colepeper had arrived in England a few weeks earlier with the brother of the Landgrave of Hesse-Cassel, whom he had brought to court to kiss the King's hand, and Craven probably introduced his comrade-in-arms to his cousin. However the couple met, it was evidently something of a *coup de foudre*. 'It is said that on two days' acquaintance she contracted herself to him,' wrote Barbara's sister-in-law the Countess of Leicester, 'and after a few more was married and given by my Lord Craven.'[37] The Sidneys disapproved strongly of the match and not a single member of the family was present at the wedding, so as a friend of both parties Craven performed the office of giving the bride away. When Colepeper called on the Countess a few weeks later, she was distinctly unimpressed: 'What she finds in him I do not know but if he be not a very ass I am deceived.'[38] Poor Colepeper; his career was distinguished enough. After long service in the States Army through the 1630s, he managed to secure the post of Lieutenant of Dover Castle.

Preparations continued for the proposed Palatine fleet; initially, five royal ships and ten merchantmen were selected, and the King's subjects were given leave to volunteer for the force. Meanwhile, pro-Spanish ministers whispered into the King's ear that if he gave the new fleet to the Spanish instead, they would restore Charles Louis to the Palatinate and marry him off into the bargain to the daughter of the Duke of Florence.[39] Astute observers such as the Venetians doubted that the fleet would ever materialise. In February Correr wrote that:

> So far, the only sure signs are the readiness of the leading nobles to contribute large sums of money, and a strong desire on the part of the idle youth to follow the Palatine's fortunes.[40]

But Correr was only half right. The idle youth might well have been keen, but contributions from the leading nobles were remarkably slow in coming in. 'Apart from Lord Craven,' Correr corrected himself at the end of March, 'few are willing to devote their capital for this, so that he [Charles Louis] cannot hope to have the following that was rumoured.'[41] At the same time, hopes were fading that the French and the Dutch would join the fleet.

Attempts continued to tap all possible sources of money. The previous December, Ferencz had paid a visit to the French court to ask for repayment of an old debt to the Palatine house. The French ambassador in London thought he would never succeed, commenting that 'the government of France is carried out by young men who have no memory of ancient things, so it is a waste of labour.'[42] Still, work continued on assembling and fitting out the Palatine fleet. By early May 1637, fifteen ships were ready, but still without enough volunteers to man them. 'There is not much preparation or speech of hastening the Prince Elector to sea,' lamented Roe to Elizabeth in May.[43]

The Prince Elector was not the only person frustrated by lack of progress. Most foreign governments looked on with bemusement at Charles's failure to support his nephew, and diplomats such as the Spanish ambassador in London, Count Ognate, found the English court remarkably trying. In July Correr reported,

> [Ognate] spoke to me in a very contemptuous manner about this Court. He said there was no school in the world where one could learn how to negotiate with the English, and he admitted that he was not capable of understanding their

humours. He had proposed conditions here calculated to adjust the Palatine's affairs. They had either not listened or not understood them, and to his great astonishment held them in so little account that in the very middle of them they had concluded an agreement with the Most Christian [his Most Christian Majesty, i.e. the French King].[44]

Not that an agreement with the Spanish was ever a realistic prospect either. Elizabeth had long given up any hope of a peaceful settlement, convinced that the Palatinate would only ever be recovered by force. Roe agreed with her that if at all possible, Charles Louis should take command of an army in Germany: even if he did not succeed in reconquering the Palatinate, his mere presence at the head of an army should strengthen his hand in the forthcoming negotiations in Hamburg. 'All Princes,' Roe wrote, 'make best conditions with their swords in their hands.' In fact, the Swedish government had promised that if Charles I were to send an army, however small, they would undertake to return all the territory between the Rhine and the Weser to Charles Louis.

Poor Charles Louis was a good deal less keen on the idea of leading troops in battle. Pacific by nature, he had never, wrote Correr, 'been able to conceal his apprehension of exposing himself in an army [...] these opinions confirm the impression of his lack of courage.'[45] When a new Spanish proposal surfaced Charles Louis leapt at the idea, but as ever the diplomacy went round in circles.

Elizabeth now wrote to her brother requesting that Charles Louis should not take command of the Palatine fleet after all; instead, she wished him to go to Germany, where there appeared to be a good chance that he would be able to take command of the Hessian Army. The Landgrave of Hesse-Cassel was one of the strongest supporters of the Protestant cause, and following a recent Hessian victory over Croat troops, his forces were available to mount a new campaign. The indefatigable Roe began negotiations with the Landgrave, and agreement appeared to be within reach.

All that remained was to find an army. Charles I appealed for volunteers and opened a subscription list to raise money. He made a generous start by donating £10,000, Craven matching the King's contribution exactly. 'And now,' wrote Charles Louis, 'we shall see whose professions are real or not: my Lord Craven has already offered ten thousand for his share: if all were like him, the affair would soon be completed.'[46] All, however, were not like him and as Correr had predicted, few others were willing to risk their capital.

Charles offered £12,000 a year towards the army's maintenance, as well as the 6,000 troops that Elizabeth had hoped for (though in the event only 2,000 materialised). With luck however their ranks would be swelled by the might of the Hessian Army. As so often, everything depended on whether Charles I would pay the subsidy required, but there were grounds for hoping that this time the treasury might be able to find the money. Craven now threw himself into the business of recruiting troops for the new Palatine Army, and in the spring of 1637 he succeeded in raising around 3,000 men, divided into between fifteen and seventeen companies.[47]

Then in June, just as Craven was preparing to leave the country, he became embroiled in a quarrel between his brother John and the politician and occasional masque-writer Sir John Maynard. Maynard had been a client of the Duke of Buckingham, but since the latter's murder in 1628 his career had stalled. One Tuesday in mid–June John (or Jack, as he was familiarly known) Craven had come with his brother to Whitehall. While Lord Craven was attending court, his brother and Maynard were enjoying a game of bowls in the company of Sir Percy Herbert, Craven's brother-in-law, and Herbert's kinsman the Earl of Pembroke, the Lord Chamberlain. In the course of the game Maynard accused Craven of failing to pay a debt, a claim which Craven hotly denied. The argument soon led to fisticuffs and Sir Percy Herbert intervened, only to be roundly thrashed by Maynard. The quarrel was hastily patched up by the Earl of Pembroke, but a breach of the peace within His Majesty's palace was a serious offence. All those involved were banished from London, John Craven retiring to his in-laws the Spencers in Northamptonshire, and Sir Percy Herbert going to Chester. Their punishment was in fact remarkably lenient, in striking contrast to the treatment meted out at a later date to Colonel Thomas Colepeper, son of the couple whose marriage Craven had attended in 1637. In 1685, the younger Colepeper struck the Earl of Devonshire in public in the precincts of Whitehall Palace, an assault which was witnessed by John Evelyn. Colepeper was imprisoned in the Marshalsea and condemned to lose his hand, though fortunately he was pardoned before the sentence could be carried out.[48]

The banishment of John Craven and his fellow brawlers, however, wasn't the end of the matter. The dispute appears to have ended up in court, where it was settled before Lord Craven's departure for the continent by the judge Sir Henry Marten, Craven's Berkshire neighbour.[49] In what might have been a gesture of thanks for settling the matter so speedily, Craven offered £500 for the repairing or rebuilding of St Andrew's Church in Shrivenham, on Marten's Berkshire estate in the Vale of White Horse. Work seems to have soon ground to a halt in the increasingly troubled condition of England, and it was not until 1660 that the rebuilding of the church really got underway, when Sir Henry Martin gave £4,000 for the purpose.[50] This two-stage reconstruction produced a church which, even though it was mostly rebuilt in the age of Wren, is still largely perpendicular gothic in style. It is an unusual structure, with a single wide roof sailing over the entire width of the building, its nave arcade carried on curiously bulbous Doric columns.

In which our hero is captured in Germany then apprehended in Paris

At the end of June 1637 the Palatine brothers travelled down to Greenwich, where they embarked on the St George to return to the Hague. A contemporary wrote that

> [...] both the Brothers went away unwillingly, but Prince Rupert expressed it most; for being a hunting that Morning with the King, he wished that he might break his Neck, so that he might leave his Bones in England.[1]

The princes left with generous gifts; Charles Louis took with him a present of £3,000 from his uncle and a confirmation of his annual pension of £12,000, and in addition both had been showered with presents of jewels and horses. Accompanied as far as the coast by the Earl of Arundel, they were escorted back to the United Provinces by the entire English fleet.

Among the large retinue the princes took with them were assorted soldiers and gallants. Some of them could probably have been classed as Correr's 'idle youth', while others were more serious soldiers. In addition to Lord Craven, the Palatine force included the Earl of Northampton and Viscount Grandison (the father of Charles II's future mistress Barbara Villiers).[2] Other members of the princes' retinue, such as Sir Jacob Astley, planned to join Rupert at the forthcoming siege of Breda, while some, like Jeffrey Hudson, Henrietta Maria's 18-inch-tall dwarf, planned to observe the siege from the relative safety and comfort of the Prince of Orange's camp.

On arrival in the United Provinces both princes went straight to join the siege of Breda, taking with them their younger brother Maurice, as well as Lords Northampton and Grandison. Both Charles Louis and Rupert acquitted themselves well in the siege, and on 10 October, much to Rupert's disappointment, Breda finally surrendered. Charles Louis now set himself to the business of recruiting troops for the proposed Palatine campaign, and he and Craven paid a visit to the Swedish Army under Marshal Johan Baner in Westphalia.

Meanwhile, negotiations continued to secure the support of the Hessian Army for the Palatine cause. In October the Landgrave of Hesse-Cassel died, but it still seemed likely that Charles Louis would be able to assume command of the Hessian forces. Both the Landgravine and the army commanders seemed amenable, as long as a suitable financial settlement could be reached. In November the Venetian ambassador reported that Charles Louis had decided to accept the command, and it was hoped that the French and the Dutch would bolster the Hessian Army with troops and money.[3]

Gradually, however, any chance of an agreement slipped away. The French continued to stall, while Charles Louis showed a distinct unwillingness to take up the command, deciding to postpone his departure for Hesse until the spring. He continued to press for French support, but the reply as always was that French help would be forthcoming once England declared war on the Emperor. At this juncture news arrived that the Hessian Army had in fact decided to swear fealty to the Landgrave's nine-year-old son and to the able German soldier Melander.

In the absence of any agreement with Hesse, the Palatines came up with a new plan for assembling an army. Key to this was the purchase of Meppen, a small town lying on the River Ems in Westphalia, 10 miles east of the Dutch border. Meppen was to be Charles Louis's seat of operations, a *place d'armes* from which to assemble an army. Once they had done this, the plan was to march south through Hesse to recapture the Palatinate. The owner of Meppen was the widow of Baron Knyphausen, a German soldier formerly in the Swedish Army who had been presented with the town by the Swedes as a reward for his services. Knyphausen had died in 1636, and his widow agreed to sell Meppen to Charles Louis for £9,500. Though the cost was substantial, the town was expected to render a revenue of £10,450 a year, so the outlay should be recouped in little more than a year. To pay for the purchase Charles Louis drew out a large sum from money deposited with the States of Holland and Utrecht. Elizabeth supplied £4,500, as well as roughly £20,000 for levies and other expenses. Craven contributed £5,000, and in addition pledged his own services and his credit for money to aid in the levies. Craven's help was certainly substantial. According to the ever-observant Venetian secretary in England, Francesco Zonca, since leaving London with the Princes Craven had withdrawn some 400,000 crowns in cash, 'and he still has a revenue of over 40,000 a year left him here.'[4]

Patents were issued for enlisting troops, and munitions were prepared. From the Hague Charles Louis wrote to his uncle begging for the help so frequently promised, arguing that if Charles would only agree to supply him with levies, France and Holland were bound to match the English offer. This time Charles did not disappoint, promising his nephew money and munitions, preparing remittances for £20,000 and giving leave to his subjects to serve in the Palatine Army. It was reported that a number of the younger lords were preparing to join the Prince. Roe, zealous as ever, was appointed as ambassador to the conference shortly to be held at Hamburg. At last it seemed that success was in the air. 'Everything conspires,' wrote Zonca, with a clear understanding of the risks involved, 'to help that Prince [Charles Louis] to seek every means of avenging his wrongs or perishing nobly.'[5]

Charles Louis and Rupert took their leave of their mother at her summer palace at Rhenen, and from there they travelled eastwards into Westphalia with a small group of companions. In March Knyphausen's widow let a small group, including Charles Louis, Rupert, Craven, and the Earl of Northampton, into Meppen.[6] It is not clear how many men the Palatines brought with them, but there cannot have been many. They had secured their place d'armes, but as yet they didn't have many troops to garrison it. It was a risky strategy, and the imperialists were not slow in countering the new threat. At about the same time that Charles Louis and his companions entered Meppen, General Melchior von Hatzfeldt received instructions to raise an army of 4,500 men from Westphalia with the aim of capturing the town. He wasted no time, and a few weeks later, on 19 May, his new force appeared outside the walls of Meppen. The town should have been easy to defend, given that during the past few years its Swedish defenders had built strong new fortifications, but its garrison, still only of negligible proportions, was caught off guard. The town was taken by surprise and seized with ease. Some of the defenders were captured, as well as twenty cannon, and the rest of the Palatine Army was forced to scatter.

This debacle did not bode well for the rest of Charles Louis's campaign. It is not clear who was in command in Meppen or how many men were taken prisoner, but the small army was now considerably depleted, and the £9,500 laid out on purchasing the town—money the Palatines could ill afford—had been utterly wasted. Charles Louis tried to make light of the setback, remarking nonchalantly that 'a misty morning often makes a cheerfuller day.' What, however, were the Palatines to do now? Roe argued that they should attempt to retake Meppen, but instead they decided to retreat south with the 1,700 survivors to Cleves, on the Rhine near the Dutch frontier, where they would be protected by Dutch forces. With permission from the Prince of Orange Charles Louis arranged to assemble his army at Wesel, a short distance upstream.

Charles I had agreed to advance £20,000 for the levying of troops, and shortly after the loss of Meppen Elizabeth received an advance payment from Whitehall of £1,200, the remainder being held up for a time by contrary winds. In mid–June guns, munitions, and officers began to arrive from London, together with generous amounts of money, and Charles Louis set about recruiting his force from Hamburg and North Germany.[7] The force was largely made up of cavalry suited to rapid movement, as well as a regiment of guards and some artillery. The first of the three cavalry regiments formed was put under the command of Rupert; the second was given to Thomas Ferencz, who was appointed Marshal of the Camp; and the third to Colonel Loe. Each regiment numbered around 600 men. At the same time Craven built up a 1,200-strong regiment of foot guards, consisting mostly of Swedish troops armed with pike, musket, steel-cap, and corselet, as well as two troops (about 200 men) of dragoons (in effect mounted infantry), who were veterans from the siege of Breda.[8]

'I give you thanks for your good wishes for my convoy to Germany,' wrote Craven to his sister in late June. 'I can assure you I have need of them.'[9] The levies were steadily coming in. In July Charles Louis sent an English officer, Lieutenant-Colonel Huncks, to London for permission to levy a regiment of 500 men, a request which was readily granted. Huncks reported to Charles I, rather optimistically, that his nephew had managed to collect about 5,000 troops, 'and will soon enter the enemy's country with good plans and hopes of success.'[10] In the end the extra levies from England only consisted of 600 foot, and they did not set sail until the end of September.[11] Charles Louis meanwhile paid a visit to the Prince of Orange in the hope of extracting a promise of more troops.

Things looked up a little in the autumn when, thanks to Roe's tireless diplomacy, 1,000 Swedish troops arrived in Wesel under the command of James King, a Scottish veteran in command of the Swedish Army in Westphalia. A former major general in Gustavus's army, King had had to leave Scotland in 1619 after killing a man with whom his family was at feud. As the most experienced man in the Palatine Army, he was deputed to act as Charles Louis's military advisor. There was rivalry, however, between King and Ferencz, who had been a senior officer in the States Army, and Elizabeth feared that Ferencz would not agree to serve under King. Fortunately Ferencz agreed. A German general, Hans Christoff von Königsmark, also brought a 200-strong cavalry regiment, and Charles Louis managed to recruit 300 men discharged by the Catholics in Cologne. In all the Palatine Army numbered about 4,000, about two thirds horse (including dragoons) and one third foot.

The army was worryingly small, far smaller than had been hoped and growing ever smaller due to lack of money for its support. Charles Louis had been expecting a sizeable force under the Scottish veteran Sir John Ruthven, who had undertaken to bring eight troops of cavalry and 1,200 foot from Scotland, but no sooner had the troops been mustered than Charles I decided that he needed them for his own purposes, and they were soon pressed into service in the First Bishops' War. In the end Charles only provided a fraction of the troops he had promised. At the same time, negotiations with Hesse had failed to secure very much in the way of support, although it seemed likely that Melander, the new Hessian commander, would be willing to provide a limited number of troops. For the Palatines to go into the field with such a small force was risky indeed. Matters were not helped by Charles Louis's failure to make any agreement with the Protestant rulers through whose territories he was to pass, or to make arrangements with the Swedish garrisons along the way.

Even so, the expedition might have succeeded had King and Königsmark not both turned out to be veritable masters of ineptitude. King's advice, sensibly enough, was to circumvent the strong garrisons further up the Rhine by marching eastwards through Westphalia and Lippe, states held by rulers who were well disposed to the Palatine cause, and close too to the Swedish garrisons on the Weser, and then to proceed down the valley of the Weser into Hesse-Cassel. Here they would be joined by the reinforcements promised them by Melander, and would then make their way south towards the Palatinate.

After joining up with King's Swedish troops at Stadtlohn in early September, the Palatine Army headed north with the intention of retaking Meppen. It was too strongly held, however, so instead they proceeded eastwards towards the Weser, where they hoped to capture the small Hansa town of Lemgo, with a view to using it as a new seat of operations. With luck they would be able to collect further reinforcements there, including Craven's English troops, who were making their way up the Weser in about eight or nine ships.[12]

Soon after setting out the Palatine Army passed close to the town of Rheine, which was weakly held by imperialist forces, and here followed the first and, as it turned out, the only successful engagement of the campaign. Rupert's regiment advanced towards the town, accompanied by Charles Louis, Craven, and Sir Richard Crane. On arrival they found three troops of cavalry drawn up outside the walls, and Rupert moved forward to attack them with his three troops. There followed the first of the irresistible Swedish-style cavalry charges for which Rupert became famous. For the last few months he had been working hard to train his regiment, mostly consisting of experienced German veterans but supplemented by a number of enthusiastic English volunteers. They charged straight at the defenders, there was a huge crash as the two sides met, and the enemy retreated hastily into the town, Rupert's troops hot on their heels.

Proceeding towards the Weser, on 15 October the Palatines reached Lemgo and prepared to lay siege to the town. But the following day a reconnaissance party brought news that Hatzfeldt's army was approaching from the south-west. It was considerably larger than the Palatine Army, numbering about 5,800 men, including eight regiments of Austrian cavalry, 1,800 infantry, and a regiment of Irish dragoons led by Colonel Devereux, who had gained notoriety four years earlier as the murderer of Wallenstein, the imperialist commander.

In view of Hatzfeldt's unexpected appearance, the Palatines hurriedly abandoned their siege. It was decided that the best course of action would be to withdraw towards Minden, a Swedish-held town a few days' journey to the north down the valley of the Weser. The most direct route went north through Vlotho, keeping on the west side of the Weser. The disadvantage of this route was that the Palatine Army would pass uncomfortably close to Hatzfeldt's force, but King argued that this was better than the alternative, which would mean crossing the Weser. Charles Louis accepted King's advice, and so on the night of 16 October the baggage was sent off towards Minden, followed early the next morning by the cavalry, the infantry, and the guns. However, the Palatine Army, slowed down by baggage and guns, was easily outpaced by the faster imperial cavalry, and when they approached the Weser at Vlotho they found Hatzfeldt's army drawn up in front of them.

It was obvious that a battle was unavoidable. General King advised that the Army should take up a position on a low hill known as the Eiberg. Charles Louis agreed, and King went back to bring forward Craven's infantry and the remaining guns. King also took the opportunity to send away his own baggage, a suspiciously defeatist action which led many to accuse him of treachery in the recriminations which were thrown around after the debacle. As soon as King had gone, Königsmark persuaded Charles Louis that the cavalry would be in a better position if they took up a position not on the Eiberg, but in a narrow valley closer to the enemy. The advantage of this would be that the imperialists would be forced to attack on a confined front, one regiment at a time, thereby compensating for the disparity in numbers. Charles Louis agreed, and so Königsmark, as the senior commander present, drew up his cavalry and the three Palatine cavalry regiments in the narrow valley. Königsmark declined the honour—which would by tradition have been his—of commanding the leading regiment, courteously conceding that place instead to the Palatine cavalry. The Palatines deployed, with Loe's regiment in front, followed by Ferencz, and with Rupert's regiment in the third row. Königsmark himself took up the rear.

As soon as the Palatine troops were in position, Hatzfeld's cavalry attacked. They charged with such momentum that they broke right through the first two Palatine regiments, leaving Rupert in the front line. Without waiting for the enemy to reach them, Rupert's regiment charged forward at full tilt, Rupert himself flanked on either side by Lords Grandison and Northampton. The imperialist cavalry wavered and then turned, and Rupert pursued them down the valley, killing the imperialist commander Colonel Pietro Götz. But his charge had taken him far away from the rest of the Palatine force, and he sent a messenger to ask Königsmark to back him up. Inexplicably, however, Königsmark did nothing. When Rupert reached the end of the valley he found himself surrounded by a fresh enemy regiment.

At this point Craven pushed his way through the confusion to Rupert's assistance with his two troops of dragoons and the remnants of the other two Palatine regiments of Loe and Ferencz, both of whom had been captured. Together, Rupert and Craven again forced the enemy out of the valley into the open, with great slaughter. But at this point a new enemy regiment, led by Colonels Lippe and Westerhold, attacked Rupert's flank, no longer protected by the sides of the valley, forcing the Palatine forces back into the gorge. Gradually they broke up into a number of small groups, each surrounded by superior numbers of enemy cavalry. On the other side, Colonel Westerhold had been killed.

It was not long before Craven, Ferencz, Loe, and Crane were all captured, Craven severely wounded in the leg and hand. Rupert was still fighting on. In order to identify himself to his men he was wearing a white cockade in his helmet, which by chance happened to be similar to those worn by the Austrians, and the fortunate result was that he was not attacked. In the confusion he could easily have slipped away, but just then he saw one of Craven's ensigns holding Charles Louis' standard but surrounded by enemy troops. He rode to the rescue, thereby identifying himself as a member of the Palatine forces.

In a last effort to break free Rupert set his horse at a stone wall, but the animal was too tired to jump it and Rupert was cornered and captured. Impressed by his ferocious resistance, Colonel Lippe approached the Prince as he lay exhausted on the ground. Pushing up his helmet, Lippe asked who he was. 'A colonel,' Rupert replied evasively. 'By God, you're a young 'un,' Lippe exclaimed. But a soldier named Bansbach recognised Rupert, and he was promptly taken prisoner by Devereux. Rupert tried to strike a deal with Devereux to allow him to escape, but the appearance of Hatzfeldt put paid to this scheme.

Königsmark, seeing the way the battle was going, abandoned his allies and managed to extract the Swedish contingent more or less intact. Meanwhile King, observing the disaster from the Eiberg, also realised that all was lost. He and Charles Louis jumped into a coach and fled from the field towards Minden, on the other side of the Weser. Both narrowly avoided drowning when their coach overturned in the flooded river. Horses and driver were swept away and drowned, but Charles Louis survived thanks to an overhanging willow branch which he fortunately managed to grab. All his baggage was lost, including his insignia of the Order of the Garter. He arrived at Minden, on foot and soaked to the skin.

The battle had lasted just three hours and the Palatine Army had been completely destroyed, with 1,200 men captured. Hatzfeldt by contrast had suffered just seventy-nine casualties. Reports of the battle soon filtered back to the Hague. Though Elizabeth tried to make light of what she referred to as 'a somewhat rough engagement', it had clearly been a disaster. Rupert forever after blamed King for the defeat because of his failure to back up Rupert's successful cavalry charge; that had been the one moment when the Palatine Army had stood a chance of success. Rupert also blamed King for persuading Charles Louis to take the Vlotho route. Since King had also sent away his baggage the night before the battle, he was suspected of betraying the Palatine Army to the enemy for profit. The allegations were never proven, but in the aftermath of the battle King was stripped of his command, recalled to Sweden, and charged with treason. He in turn blamed the defeat on Rupert's rashness, and the bitterness between the two persisted for many years. Meanwhile, Craven's troops making their way up the Weser arrived too late. On arrival at their rendezvous, they found no one to report to.[13]

The disaster was a fatal setback for the Palatine cause. Despite huge efforts Charles Louis had only managed to assemble a pitifully small army, which had easily been crushed. Enormous sums had been expended for nothing. Many hoped, however, that the defeat would at last spur Charles I to give more resolute help to his nephew and finally to declare war on the Empire. Certainly the French hoped so. Elizabeth, naturally, never gave up hope. Always undaunted but always destined to be disappointed, her response to the tragic news was to urge her brother to send another 4,000 foot. Charles was sympathetic, but there was little chance now of further help from him.

Rupert, Ferencz, and Craven were taken to the nearby town of Warrendorp, where they stayed until Craven was fit to travel. He obtained a permit to send Sir Richard Crane with a message from Rupert to the Hague with news of the disaster, Rupert taking care to assure his mother that 'neither good nor ill usage should ever make him change his religion'. The three prisoners were taken to Bamberg and then separated.[14] Craven applied to be allowed to share Rupert's captivity, but his appeal was denied. Instead he was kept in comfortable confinement in the castle of the Prince-Bishop of Würtzburg, while Rupert, despite his mother's best efforts to arrange an escape, was marched away, with an escort of 600 cuirassiers and 600 musketeers, to the distant castle of Linz on the banks of the Danube. He was given permission to take with him three gentlemen of his household, an Englishman, an Irishman, and a Scot.

It was at this point that hopes suddenly rose again that the reconquest of the Palatinate might still be possible after all. These hopes centred on the army of Duke Bernard of Saxe-Weimar. Duke Bernard, the youngest of seven Saxe-Weimar brothers, was an experienced, ambitious but mercurial soldier of fortune who had fought for Gustavus Adolphus and had assumed command of the Swedish Army on the King's death at Lützen. Since 1635 his 17,000-strong army, known as the Bernardines, had been subsidised by France, but there were hopes that he could be encouraged to become more independent of the French and put his weight behind the Palatine cause. In April 1638 Elizabeth had written to thank Bernard for his bravery, and he had paid a visit to the Hague. The Queen of Bohemia kept his portrait alongside those of her other champions, and there was even talk of cementing an alliance with a marriage between Duke Bernard and Princess Elizabeth.

A few months later, Bernard's army began to besiege the strategic fortress of Breisach on the Rhine, just to the south of the Lower Palatinate. He did so largely at the instigation of his French paymasters. For Richelieu control of Breisach was an important prize; it would bring Alsace under the control of the French crown, in effect extending France's eastern frontier as far as the Rhine, as well as cutting Spanish lines of communication with Flanders. But the Palatines also watched Bernard's progress with excitement. The general expectation was that once he had captured Breisach, Bernard would proceed northwards to reconquer the Lower Palatinate, and to that end large numbers of English and Scots soldiers were planning to join the Bernardines for the forthcoming campaign.[15]

In December 1638, after a long and terrible siege, Breisach fell. The understanding had been that after capturing it Bernard would hand the town over to the French, but instead, annoyed at the high-handed approach of their envoys and aware of the great power that possession of Breisach gave him, he announced that he had decided to keep it for himself. For six months Richelieu's emissaries argued with him, then, quite suddenly, towards the end of July Bernard died. It seems probable that he died of the plague, though his death was certainly suspiciously convenient for the French. In his will he bequeathed his army to his four deputy commanders, with instructions that they should sell it to the highest bidder.

Bernard's death led to a frantic scramble for control of his forces and the town they were occupying. Given the importance Richelieu attached to Breisach, and given the deep pockets of the French state, it would clearly be hard for anyone else to win the contest, but there was no shortage of other candidates, including the Emperor and the Swedes. First off the mark, however, was Charles Louis. The Bernardines were for the most part fellow Germans and fellow Protestants, by and large supporters of his cause, and not very happy to be in the pay of the French. For all these reasons there were grounds for believing that they could be persuaded to accept the Prince Elector as their commander, but to achieve control would require speed and guile, not to mention a good deal of money. It was an audacious scheme, one which bore the hallmarks of the Queen of Bohemia rather than of her cautious, unwarlike elder son.

There were others too who wished to see the Prince Elector as commander of the Bernardines, as a counterweight to French influence. Chief among these was Sir Oliver Fleming, the English resident in Zurich and a man of virulently anti-French views. The previous spring Fleming had been in London attempting to negotiate an agreement between the English crown and Duke Bernard in favour of the Palatine family. Fleming, who was of Scottish birth, of Puritan sympathies, and related to Oliver Cromwell, was later appointed by Parliament as Charles I's master of ceremonies, a post he continued to hold under Cromwell.

What gave the Queen of Bohemia and her eldest son particular grounds for optimism was the good news which seemed to be emanating from England. In June Charles had patched up a peace with the Scots, and there was even talk of General Leslie bringing a regiment of his Scottish Covenanter troops to fight for the Palatine cause in Germany. When Bernard died the following month, therefore, there seemed good reason to hope that this time Charles would give his wholehearted support to the cause. So it was that at the beginning of August, within a few days of Bernard's death, Charles Louis sent agents to the directors of the Bernardines with a message asking if they would accept him as their commander. The reply was encouraging, but any agreement would be dependent on a hefty monthly subsidy from Charles I. This, of course, was likely to prove the sticking point given that the royal Exchequer, needless to say, was virtually empty.

As so often, the Palatines were faced with a desperate need for funds, and as so often it was Craven who provided the money. From his captivity in Würtzburg he had evidently heard of the audacious scheme under consideration. At the end of July he arranged to buy his freedom for the enormous sum of £20,000. Sir Henry Wotton wrote:

We hear my Lord Craven has made his composition under 20,000 1 [£]. As for Ferents, I believe his own head must ransom him, or his heels.[16]

In fact within two months Ferencz had also regained his freedom by one means or another; perhaps Craven paid a ransom for him too. Craven, in any case, made his way through Germany back to the Netherlands, still limping as a result of his injuries, and after stopping briefly at Rhinberck to see the Prince of Orange he arrived back at the Hague. A few days later, Charles Louis and Craven left hurriedly for England.

On arrival at Dover on 6 August, Charles Louis hastened north to see the King. He missed Charles in Berwick but finally caught up with him in Durham, and as they returned together to London the Prince Elector unfolded his plan. The reaction was guardedly positive; at least Charles agreed to put the matter to his Council of State. Of course, given the popularity of the Palatine cause he could hardly have dismissed the suggestion out of hand. Both his own and the Scottish Covenanter Army would far rather have been fighting side by side for the Elector Palatine, so it was frequently said, than fighting one another. Lengthy discussions began at Whitehall, the two main questions being: where would the money come from, and could the French be squared? Charles sent letters to the Bernardines and to the Swiss. Nevertheless, his lack of sympathy for the Palatine cause was made painfully obvious by his treatment of a group of Scottish officers who arrived at Newcastle from Germany that summer, on their way back from fighting for the Prince Elector at Vlotho the previous November. Cross-questioned on arrival, they said that they had come to volunteer for the King. Charles doubted their word, suspecting them of planning to join the Covenanter Army, and without more ado they were thrown into jail.

Charles's Council of State was well aware that the French had their own designs on the Bernardines. According to the Venetian ambassador, Giovanni Giustinian,

> They certainly fear that the Most Christian [his Most Christian Majesty, i.e. the French King] may spoil the success of their projects. The wisest realise the very serious difficulties in the way, multiplied by the lack of money, the only thing that can give these transactions life.[17]

Not that the French did not support the Palatine cause. On the contrary, they were perfectly willing to support the Palatines as part of an anti-imperial alliance, to which England would have to supply money and troops. There was no chance of this, and instead discussions meandered along as always, with much talk but little action. 'Meanwhile,' Giustinian reported,

> the Palatine is enjoying the pleasures of the court. His suite state that the air of the country suits him, and that he wants to prolong his stay as long as possible though it is not thought that his uncle will allow him.[18]

Later in September, distinctly encouraging letters arrived from the Bernardines. If Charles were to pay his nephew a monthly subsidy sufficient to maintain their troops with vigour, the army directors would have no objection to accepting him as their commander. Reports were diligently circulated that Charles Louis would soon depart to take up the command, though everyone thought, reported

Craven.

1. William, 1st Earl of Craven, Lieutenant-General from 1678, by Gerrit van Honthorst, 1640s. (*National Trust Images*)

Queen of Bohemia.

2. Elizabeth, Queen of Bohemia, by Gerrit van Honthorst, 1642.

3. Ashdown House, Berkshire. (*Author's collection*)

4. Ashdown House. (*Author's collection*)

5. Ashdown House, the hall. (*Nicola Cornick's collection*)

WILLIAM EARL OF CRAVEN.

From a Picture in Craven Buildings, Drury Lane. This Nobleman was Son of Sir W.ᵐ Craven Lord Mayor of London, gained great reputation as a Soldier under Henry Prince of Orange, & Gustavus Adolphus King of Sweden, & took the strong fortress of Creutznack in Germany by storm, which is one of the most extraordinary actions recorded in the history of the Great Gustavus who Knighted him as he lay wounded before the said fortress.

Pub.ᵈ April 1 1794 by J. Smith N.ᵒ 81 O' Mean Buildings.

6. Fresco of William, 1st Earl of Craven, formerly in Craven Buildings, Drury Lane.

7. Princess Elizabeth by Robert Peake the Elder, 1603.

8. Princess Elizabeth by Isaac Oliver, 1610.

9. Frederick V, King of Bohemia in Roman dress, by Gerrit van Honthorst.

10. Peter Ernst II, Count Mansfeld.

11. Christian the Younger, Duke of Brunswick by Willem Jacobsz Delff, after Michiel Jansz.

12. Stokesay Castle, Shropshire.

13. Stokesay Castle gatehouse.

14. Gustavus Adolphus, King of Sweden, attributed to Jacob Hoefnagel, 1624.

15. Charles Louis, Elector Palatine by Sir Anthony van Dyck, *c.* 1637.

16. Prince Rupert, Count Palatine by Sir Anthony van Dyck, *c.* 1637.

17. King Charles I by Sir Anthony van Dyck, 1636.

Left: 18. William, 1st Earl of Craven, by Sir Anthony van Dyck, 1640.

Below: 19. Powis Castle from the east.

20. Drury House, later known as Craven House.

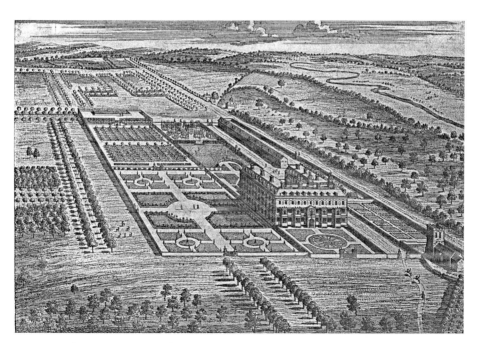

21. View of Hamstead Marshall Park by Kip & Knyff, *c*. 1709.

22. & 23. Melancholy reminders of vanished magnificence: gate piers at Hamstead Marshall. (*Author's collection*)

24. Interior of St Andrew's Church, Shrivenham. (*Author's collection*)

25. Combe Abbey from west, showing William Winde's 1682 wing, and on the right the 1668 wing. (*Author's collection*)

26. King Charles II by
John Riley.

27. Princess Anne
and William, Duke of
Gloucester, studio of Sir
Godfrey Kneller, *c*. 1694.

the cynical and worldly-wise Guistinian, that this was just a ploy to alarm the Austrians. Agreement over the financial side of things was finally reached at the end of September. The King would pay his nephew three years of his pension in advance, a total of £36,000, with the promise of at least another £24,000 if he was successful in his bid. In addition, Charles Louis began negotiations to sell other years of his pension to swell his coffers further. Then there was Craven's money. He now announced his intention, reported Guistinian, of devoting the whole of his fortune to the service of the Palatine house. It was a breathtakingly generous offer even from this most generous of men.[19]

Charles Louis now had a sizeable war chest, certainly if Craven's entire fortune is included. But even so, it was hardly enough to keep a 17,000-strong army in the field for long, and small in comparison with the huge resources of the French state. No one quite knew whether France could be squared; the French ambassador in London, Pompone de Bellièvre, was sounded out informally, and there was talk of obtaining a passport for the Prince Elector. As a matter of fact Richelieu was incensed to find that King Charles was encouraging his nephew to angle for command of the Bernardines, and he redoubled his own secret efforts to come to an agreement with its directors.

It was clear that the Prince Elector's journey to Breisach should be kept as secret as possible, and to this end the King ordered his Secretary of State, Francis Windebank, to instruct Admiral Pennington that, except for the Prince Elector and his party, no persons should be permitted to leave the kingdom until further notice, and furthermore that any letters, even ambassadorial dispatches, should be confiscated. Pennington refused to do this on the grounds that the order had not come directly from the King, and anyway Windebank's instructions were too confused and had not even given the name or the nationality of the person or persons who were to be stopped.[20]

Efforts continued to scrape together the agreed £36,000, while Charles Louis continued to enjoy the pleasures of the chase. Towards the end of September further encouraging letters arrived from Breisach, and on 4 October Charles Louis set out hurriedly for Dover, accompanied by a small group of four or five trusted confidantes, including Fleming and Craven. In his pocket the Prince Elector carried remittances for £10,000 to be drawn on merchants in Lyons and Geneva.[21] The day after his departure, the King, realising the danger, sent a courier after his nephew warning him that he should at all costs avoid visiting the French court.

The plan was to travel incognito, but the first stage of their journey could hardly have been more public. There, riding at anchor in the Downs, was an enormous Spanish armada of some seventy-five ships had arrived a week or so earlier with the intention of relieving the Spanish-controlled port of Dunkirk, currently threatened by the French. A short distance away lay an even larger Dutch fleet of about ninety ships under Admiral Tromp, which was blockading the Spanish fleet to prevent any ships from getting through to Dunkirk. Tromp had attacked the Spanish fleet on its way up the Channel, and the Spanish had taken refuge in the Downs, hoping for assistance from the English. The stand-off was being observed by a small squadron of English ships anchored nearby, under the command of Admiral Pennington. On the Prince Elector's arrival Pennington provided a ship, the optimistically named *Bonaventure*—the same ship that had transported Craven to the United Provinces in 1632. The small party embarked, and as they left the harbour the English flagship fired a salute. It was repeated by the Dutch flagship and then, not to be outdone, the Spanish flagship fired its own salvo.

After this reception, any attempt at travelling incognito was hardly likely to succeed. Still, Charles Louis and his companions crossed to Boulogne and made their way south. Had they but known, it was already too late. The directors of the Bernardines had decided to rebuff approaches from imperialist envoys, but just four days before Charles Louis left London, Richelieu's diplomacy came to fruition. After listening to the persuasive arguments of Guébriant, commander of the Army's French contingent, its directors had finally given in and signed an agreement with the French King. In return for a promise of 1.2 million livres, they had agreed to transfer the entire Army into French service, with all its conquests surrendered to Louis XIII.

Meanwhile, in spite of Charles's half-hearted attempt to stop word getting out of his nephew's journey, the French ambassador in England, Bellièvre, managed to pass a message to his father-in-law Claude de Bullion, the eponymous French Minister of Finance, and the Prince Elector's movements in France were carefully monitored. The small party had got as far as Paris when Craven and Fleming were apprehended by Bullion, who told them that if they proceeded further out of Paris they would receive an affront; that is to say, they would be arrested. Charles Louis hurriedly left the city disguised as Craven's valet and headed for Lyons, under the pretext of following the court; from there, after cashing in his remittances, he planned to proceed to Geneva then north to Breisach. Ominously, on the road to Lyons he was overtaken by Bellièvre's courier, hurrying to alert the authorities ahead to his movements, and on arrival in Moulins, still 100 miles from Lyons, he was arrested by order of Richelieu on the pretext of not having a passport.[22]

Craven and Fleming were allowed to go on their way, but Charles Louis was escorted, with a guard of 100 horse, to the fortress of Vincennes, where he was commanded to speak only in French and forbidden to speak to anyone except in the presence of a guard. News of the arrests soon arrived in the Hague, and Elizabeth raged against the devious conduct of Richelieu, 'that ulcerous priest', and the 'fickle Monsieurs'.

It was probably inevitable that the Most Christian King would win the contest for the Bernardines; Richelieu, after all, had no intention of allowing his plans to be disrupted by a hapless German princeling. The army directors, however, were outraged when they heard of the Prince Elector's arrest. They had undertaken to accept him as their commander; most of them professed themselves his vassals, and they vigorously urged his release.[23] French control of the Bernardines was still uncertain, with many of the army commanders argued in favour of joining the Swedish Army instead.

A few months later, in January, Charles Louis was offered his freedom as long as he gave his word that he would not leave France without permission, and as long as he promised that his intention had not been to employ the Bernardines in any way against the interests of France. He was taken to Paris, where he was treated hospitably at the French court. A few months later there was even talk of allowing Charles Louis to take control of the Bernardines after all, as part of the much-discussed alliance between France and England directed against the Emperor. But, as ever, nothing happened.

The three younger Palatine sons, Maurice, Philip and Edward, were also in Paris, where Elizabeth had sent them to acquire some polish as well as to learn 'manly exercises'. They were a boisterous trio, these three younger Palatines. Their mother had received complaints about them scaring the respectable burghers of the Lange Voorhout by breaking windows and unscrewing the door-knockers of its fine mansions. Maurice, now nineteen, had been bred to be a soldier and had taken part in the siege of Breda. He had been disappointed not to be given a command in the failed attempt to recapture the Palatinate. He had always been close to Rupert; the two of them were always together, so much so that he was known as Rupert's shadow. In Paris he probably attended one of the military academies. Edward, now fourteen, was a more peaceable character, while Philip, aged eleven, was still only a schoolboy. Worried that her three younger sons might be detained too, Elizabeth now wrote urging them to return to the Hague as soon as possible, and to her great relief they were not prevented from leaving France. Maurice left Paris in November to serve as a volunteer in the army of Marshal Baner, but by the spring of 1640 all three sons were back with their mother.

In August Charles Louis was finally allowed to leave France. He had hoped to cross over to England to solicit help from his uncle. But Charles was very keen that his nephew should not come, worried that his presence would destabilise an already fraught situation, and an agitated letter from Secretary Vane suggested that the Prince Elector would be better off going to the camp of the Prince of Orange, although he should trust that the King would leave no stone unturned in achieving restitution of the Palatinate.[24] So Charles Louis made his way back to the Hague, where he remained, hoping impatiently for an opportunity to return to England to ask for help from his uncle, or if he was rebuffed, to seek help from Parliament.

'A purse better furnished than my own'

On his release by the French authorities in January 1640, Craven returned to the Hague. Yet another attempt at reconquest of the Palatinate had failed dismally, and the chances of obtaining further help seemed slight. The Queen of Bohemia's eldest son was detained in Paris, and her second son was still in strictly guarded captivity in faraway Linz. Elizabeth still cherished a hope that her brother might yet come to her aid, but it was an increasingly faint hope.

Craven was to remain in the Hague on and off for most of the next eighteen years. With no prospect of any imminent return to the Palatinate, he took on the role of supporter and financial mainstay of the Palatine family. Soon after he arrived in the Hague he was offered the command of a regiment in the States Army; not one of the English regiments, but instead one of four new regiments being recruited by the States General for purposes unknown.[1] Craven was reluctant to accept, perhaps still hoping that the debacle in France would prick the conscience of the King and spur him on to provide worthwhile help to his sister. Instead, after kicking his heels for a while waiting for a good wind, Craven sailed for England.

He was far from being the only English soldier returning home during these months. Charles I, uncomfortably aware of the dire performance of his army the previous summer against the Scottish Covenanter Army, had been working hard to entice good officers back from the Low Countries and Germany. He was determined to create a sizeable and well-led force with which to confront the Scots a second time, and was offering generous inducements for good officers. Craven certainly had no wish to become involved in Charles's misguided adventures, and once it became clear there was no prospect of further help for the Palatine cause, he did not remain in England for long. He made a brisk tour of his estates, staying for a couple of nights in late February with Brilliana Harley in north Herefordshire, probably en route to see his sister at Powis Castle and to visit his Shropshire estates.[2] The Harleys were staunch Puritans, and it is interesting to find that Craven remained on good terms with even some of the most extreme of the King's opponents. He kept in his possession a letter, a polite request for payment of subsidies dated October 1641, from 'Your very loving friends Warwick, Sele and Saye, Essex, Dover.'[3] All four of these peers were fervent supporters of the Palatine cause, and two of them, the Earl of Warwick and Viscount Saye and Sele, were at the very centre of opposition to the King. When it came to armed conflict between King and Parliament, certainly, Craven's loyalties were unhesitatingly with the King, but among the Puritans support for the Winter Queen, at least for the moment, remained high.

Craven did not remain in England for long. In March he wrote to Constantijn Huygens, secretary to Frederick Henry, Prince of Orange, sounding him out about the chances of obtaining command of one of the English regiments in the States Army. Huygens's reply was favourable; many English officers were returning home and so Craven was in with a good chance, but he would have to be quick.[4] Craven wasted no time; he obtained leave to absent himself from the Short Parliament, due to meet in the middle of April, and returned post-haste to the Hague. His efforts were rewarded; he was duly appointed as colonel of one of the English infantry regiments, and began to prepare for the start of the season's campaign. The regiment's numbers, however, were badly depleted, and so he sent a servant over to England to begin organising the recruitment of new volunteers, 'for without a supply of eighty men I shall bee out of countenance to bring my companie into the field.'[5] The campaign that season was uneventful, with little action other than manoeuvring and skirmishing. In the meantime Craven did what little he could to press for Rupert's release, urging Windebank to speak to the Spanish ambassador on the subject.

In November Craven returned to England, this time in the company of Cave and Honeywood. Much had happened since April. In August the King's weak and undisciplined army had suffered a second disastrous defeat at the hands of the Scottish Covenanters, who had gone on to occupy Newcastle. Charles had been forced to sign a humiliating armistice, and in order to raise funds to pay for the upkeep of the Scottish Army he had been forced to call a new Parliament, known to history as the Long Parliament. As soon as it opened on 3 November, a clique of parliamentarians led by John Pym began to mount a highly effective attack on the King, his policies, and his ministers; on ship-money, monopolies, and the prerogative courts. But Pym's primary target was the Earl of Strafford, whose attempts to bring order to the government and increase its revenues had made him the focus of widespread and virulent hatred. He was now in the Tower of London awaiting his trial for high treason, and there he was joined in December by Archbishop Laud.

Craven put in occasional appearances in the House of Lords; in late December he was appointed to the Committee for the Northern Business, formed to conduct a post mortem on the King's ignominious defeat by the Scots. But, while not busy soliciting for volunteers, he also found time to indulge in more leisurely pursuits, such as having his portrait painted by van Dyck and, not least, lavishing money on building projects. The house to which he turned his attention this time was

Stokesay Castle in Shropshire, let on a long lease to the Baldwin family, wealthy merchants from Ludlow. The current tenant was Sir Samuel Baldwin, MP for Ludlow in the Short and Long Parliaments and a fervent Royalist. In 1640–41, Craven spent just over £530 on the fabric of Stokesay, mainly on a highly elaborate and very charming timber-framed gatehouse, decorated with an exuberant riot of carved angels and dragons. In addition he ordered improvements to the main room of the castle itself, the solar, which was given a new ceiling, overmantel, and panelled walls.

By January 1641, Craven had found a respectable number of volunteers to swell the ranks of his regiment, and on the 20th of that month he obtained permission to transport sixty recruits to the Low Countries. A fortnight later he was given leave to go to his command in Holland, and at the same time he received permission to transport an extra thirty volunteers. In the event however it was not until May that he finally prepared to return to the Hague. By this time London was in a state of uproar: armed mobs roamed the streets, and a desperate need for money had persuaded the King to agree to a marriage between his eldest daughter, Princess Mary, nine years old and very pretty, and the twelve-year-old only son of the Prince of Orange.

The Commons was in the middle of considering a Bill of Attainder against Strafford when Prince William of Orange arrived on 20 April, sumptuously attired and accompanied by a magnificent 400-strong retinue. He was conducted to Whitehall Palace, where it was noted that neither the Queen nor the Princess so much as permitted him a kiss, leading many to doubt whether the marriage would ever actually happen. However, after pressure from the Dutch ambassadors, the wedding did finally take place on Sunday 2 May in the Chapel Royal at Whitehall, after which it was symbolically consummated by the couple lying together in bed in the company of the King and Queen. Charles Louis, who had arrived in England in February despite his uncle's best efforts to dissuade him from coming, had refused to pay the usual courtesy call on the bridegroom and sulked all through the wedding celebrations. Charles had after all led him to expect that the Princess would be his own bride one day.

The wedding was a low-key occasion in a city that seemed increasingly gripped by mass hysteria, and it marked the beginning of a week of high drama. On the following Wednesday, Pym rose in the Commons to reveal the existence of the Army Plot, a loose plan to bring the Army down from York, free Strafford from the Tower, and dissolve Parliament by force. On Friday, wild rumours began to spread that the King and Queen had made a treaty with the French to bring ten regiments over from France; that the Spanish Army was about to invade; even that Papists would set fire to the House of Commons. On the Saturday morning, there were reports that an armed mob was preparing to march on the palace to seize the persons of the King and Queen. They prepared to flee to safety, but the French ambassador persuaded them to stay, assuring the leaders of the mob that the King was ready to give them every satisfaction. On the same day the House of Lords, bullied by the mob and by the Commons, finally passed the Bill of Attainder against Strafford and petitioned the King to sign it. All through that night and the next day Charles vacillated, with the mob outside baying for blood.

On Thursday 6 May, as Craven was preparing to leave the country in time for the start of the season's campaign in Flanders, the House of Lords issued an urgent order shutting the ports following the discovery of the Army Plot. It was rumoured that the ringleaders, Henry Percy, Henry Jermyn, Sir John Suckling, William Davenant, and the Earl of Carnarvon, were attempting to flee to France and Holland. The one person who was to be permitted to leave the kingdom was Sir Thomas Roe, currently kicking his heels at Gravesend waiting to cross to the Hague on his way to the Diet of Ratisbon. Roe was required to produce a list of those travelling with him. Four days later, as Charles gave way and signed the Bill of Attainder against Strafford, Craven too managed to obtain permission from the House of Lords to leave the country, and it was ordered that he and his train should also be allowed passage at the ports. The shutting of the ports was causing chaos and great hardship, with fishermen prevented from putting to sea and merchants petitioning Parliament. On the night of the 10th, 1,000 mariners rioted at the Tower, and three were shot dead.

Roe and his small ambassadorial train of twenty-one had already embarked on the *Hope*, lying off Gravesend, but contrary winds had prevented their departure. On 10 May Craven joined the ship, and with him he brought two servants, a few volunteers for his company, and a falconer and two footmen to ease Rupert's captivity in Linz.[6] That night events took an unexpected turn. As they were still waiting for the wind to turn, boats suddenly appeared alongside the *Hope* and scores of people clambered on board, unannounced and uninvited. The new arrivals included two of the ringleaders of the Army Plot, Carnarvon and Suckling, and dozens of their accomplices, as well as many others not connected with the plot but desperate to get a passage to Holland. There were now over 100 passengers on board, and the newcomers had not brought any victuals. Roe decided to commandeer the roundhouse cabin for himself, leaving everyone else to share the great cabin with the newcomers. Later that night the wind changed and they sailed. The crossing was long, uncomfortable, and hungry, and it was not until towards the end of the month that they finally arrived in the Hague. Roe departed for Ratisbon, after a brief visit to the Queen of Bohemia, and Craven re-joined his regiment. Shortly afterwards Prince William arrived back from London, but without his young bride. Despite his urgings and despite the best efforts of the Dutch ambassadors, he had not been able to persuade the King and Queen to relinquish their daughter, to the considerable irritation of his father.

Roe worked hard for Rupert's release, distributing lavish presents and winning over the new Emperor, who commented that the charm of Roe's conversation would have made him fall passionately in love if Roe had been a beauty of the opposite sex, instead of a gout-ridden sixty-year-old.[7] Roe's persuasiveness secured the desired result; in mid–October, Rupert was at last offered his freedom on condition that he pay homage to the Emperor and that he should undertake never to take up arms against him. Undecided as to whether he should accept, Rupert wrote to his uncle for advice. Charles, well aware that his nephew's help would be invaluable in the event of armed conflict, ordered him to agree to these conditions. So, after three years in captivity, Rupert was at last free. For a time he enjoyed the pleasures of life in the imperial capital, hunting and playing tennis with the Emperor.

Any financial problems were solved when Craven and other friends sent him money, together with handsome garments and a magnificent coach. In November Rupert set off back to the Hague, travelling via Prague to avoid Bavaria. He arrived back at the Wassenaer Hof one evening in early December, lean and weary but in good health. Nobody had expected him back so soon, and Elizabeth, naturally, was overjoyed.

> But what to do with him I know not. He cannot with honour go to the war [in the United Provinces or in Germany], here he will live but idly, and in England no better, for I know the Queen will use all possible means to gain him [for Catholicism].

But whatever worries Elizabeth might have had for Rupert, there was certainly no danger of idleness.

For the 1641 campaign the Prince of Orange had his eye on the town of Gennep, on the River Maas south of Nijmegen, which was garrisoned by Irish troops in Spanish service. The siege was a brief affair.[8] Towards the end of July one of the French colonels in the States Army tried to initiate talks, but the defenders shouted that they were not prepared to surrender to the French. Craven's regiment, when it took over from the French, was more successful, and the garrison surrendered a few days later. Then, after further operations in Flanders, the regiments went into winter quarters and Craven returned to the Hague.

The following January, in 1642, Craven crossed over to England yet again in an attempt to swell the still depleted ranks of his regiment. Towards the end of the month the House of Lords duly empowered him to recruit and transport sixty more volunteers to the United Provinces, and a further thirty went out in March. Craven's latest visit came as the Queen was hastily preparing to leave the country to escort her daughter to the Hague. She had hoped to make the journey the previous July, only to be prevented when Parliament, suspecting with every justification that the real purpose of her journey was to sell the crown jewels in order to buy arms, had forced her to remain in the country. At the beginning of January, Charles had failed in his abortive attempt to arrest a peer and five members of the Commons, including Pym and Hampden, and a few nights later the King, Queen, and their three eldest children had fled precipitously from Whitehall Palace to Hampton

Court. Two days later they moved on to Windsor Castle. The Prince of Orange had made a formal request for Princess Mary to be escorted over to the Hague as soon as possible, and on 7 February the King informed Parliament that he had decided to send his wife and daughter over to the Hague. On the same day Craven obtained leave from the House of Lords to return to his command in Holland, and two days later he visited the royal family at Windsor Castle, where Charles issued a warrant authorising him to accompany the Queen to Holland.[9]

There was something of a sense of panic-stricken haste over the Queen's departure, with Charles anxious to get his wife out of the country before the Commons could change its mind. Later that same day the King, Queen, and Princess Mary made a hurried departure from Windsor on the first stage of the journey to Dover. They left in such haste, complained one courtier, 'that I never heard of the like for persons of such dignity.' For persons of dignity their retinue was quite modest; it included, among others, the Earl of Arundel, Lord Craven, and a number of ladies and maids. The first stop was Greenwich, where the Queen collected as much of her own and her husband's jewellery as she could, as well as the few remaining crown jewels which had not already been seized by Parliament. After bidding farewell to his wife, Charles intended to make straight for Hull to secure the military supplies collected there for his Scottish campaign, but so as not to arouse suspicion he gave out that he intended to spend several weeks hunting, and so he took with him his hunting apparel. The royal party proceeded on to Dover, where they waited a few days while a small fleet of five ships was hurriedly assembled. The Prince of Orange, forewarned, had sent a squadron of fifteen ships commanded by Admiral van Tromp to accompany the Queen and Princess to the United Provinces.

As the royal family were waiting impatiently at Dover for the promised ships to arrive, Rupert, quite unexpectedly, sailed into port. He had come with the stated purpose of thanking his uncle for helping to secure his release, and more discreetly to offer his services should the King require them. Charles was glad to see his nephew but unsure what to do with him. Rupert would be invaluable if and when war came, but Charles shrank from taking up arms and still hoped that a settlement might yet be reached with his rebellious subjects. In the end it was decided that Rupert should return to Holland as an escort for his aunt and cousin. A few days later, on 23 February, Charles bid an emotional farewell to his wife, and Henrietta Maria and Princess Mary embarked on the *Lion*. Though small by royal standards, their retinue, which included six coaches and 120 horses, was still quite substantial. After the small fleet had put to sea Charles rode along the coast for four leagues, keeping abreast of it and waving his hat repeatedly to the ship that carried his wife and daughter to safety.

It was a quicker crossing than Craven's long, uncomfortable passage the previous year, but still not without mishap. Within fifteen hours of its departure from Dover the fleet arrived at Vlissingen, but there a contrary wind sprang up, and at the entrance to the port of Helvoetsluis the ship carrying the Queen's plate capsized and sank before her eyes. When the Queen and Princess finally set foot on Dutch soil, Prince William was waiting for them. His instructions had been to escort the royal ladies by water to Rotterdam, but they preferred—hardly surprisingly—to remain on dry land. Approaching the Hague their procession was met by another containing the Queen of Bohemia with her two youngest daughters, Henrietta and Sophie, and all the quality of the Hague. The two queens climbed into a red velvet state coach, where they sat side by side, with Prince William and his bride opposite. In the back of the coach rode the Prince of Orange, Rupert, Henrietta, and Sophie, the latter chosen from among her sisters because she was closest in age to Princess Mary.

Many years later when she was writing her memoirs, Sophie recalled her surprise at her aunt's appearance. Having only seen flattering portraits of Henrietta Maria by van Dyck, she was expecting to meet a beautiful woman, but was shocked to find that her aunt turned ou to be 'a thin little woman with shrunken arms, and teeth sticking out of her mouth like guns from a fort.' Fortunately, Henrietta Maria commented that Sophie resembled the Princess her daughter, which pleased Sophie so much that after careful inspection she was prepared to concede that her aunt was actually quite handsome, with 'beautiful eyes, a well-shaped nose, and an admirable complexion.' Sophie also overheard some of the English Queen's attendants saying that when she was grown up she would eclipse all her sisters. 'This remark gave me a liking for the whole English nation, so charming is it to be admired when one is young.'[10]

The Queen of Bohemia did her best to make friends with her sister-in-law, although she disapproved of her Catholicism and thought her influence on her husband unhelpful. Their entry into the Hague was marked by fireworks and a salute from eighty cannon, and the Queen was conducted to another conveniently empty mansion, the New Palace in Staedt Straat. Now she turned to the main purpose of her visit, to sell the royal jewels and use the money to buy arms. With the help of friends such as Lord Goring she managed to pawn the jewels, and soon boats loaded with weapons began to sail for English ports, doing their best to evade interception by parliamentarian ships.

For the next year the Hague was to contain three separate courts: the small, temporary court of the Queen of England at the New Palace; the much grander court of the Prince and Princess of Orange, rejoicing in their new status of in-laws of the British royal family; and the sadly down-at-heel establishment of the Queen of Bohemia. Ever since the death of her husband, the walls of Elizabeth's presence and reception chambers had been hung with black velvet, giving them a sombre appearance, as John Evelyn noticed when he came to pay his respects on a visit to the Hague in 1641. But not for nothing had the Queen of Bohemia's court become known as 'the mansion of the muses and graces'. What it lacked in opulence it more than made up for in the charm of its occupants and the sparkle of its guests. Elizabeth adorned her receptions with men of wit and learning; her circle boasted men such as Constantijn Huygens and his son, and religious figures such as John

Dury and Samuel Hartlib. Her most distinguished intimate was the exiled French philosopher René Descartes, who came in 1641 to live at Endegeest, a chateau near Leiden. It became a favourite pursuit for ladies of intellectual pretensions to travel the few miles from the Hague to the sage of Endegeest, and among them was the most intelligent of the Queen of Bohemia's daughters, Princess Elizabeth.

It was only recently that all the Winter Queen's daughters had come to live in the Hague. For some years the nursery palace at Leiden had had just two occupants, Sophie and Gustavus Adolphus, Craven's godson. Their mother used to send for them sometimes to show them off to visitors, and on one occasion a tactless visitor badly shook Sophie's self-esteem. The children had been put through their paces 'as one would a stud of horses', she wrote in her memoirs, when a visitor remarked tactlessly, 'he is very handsome but she is thin and ugly,' and then, as an afterthought, 'I hope she does not understand English.' But Sophie did understand English and was naturally mortified.[11]

The delicate but angelic-looking Gustavus Adolphus had always suffered from epilepsy, and as he grew older the attacks grew longer and more frequent. On 9 January 1641, shortly after his ninth birthday, he died. According to Sophie, an autopsy after her brother's death found a stone the size of a pigeon's egg in his bladder, surrounded by four other jagged ones, and another enormous stone in his kidneys. Towards the end of his life he had been in immense pain, and Sophie felt very angry with the doctors who had been in perpetual attendance. His death meant that she was now alone at Leiden, and to her great joy the nursery was closed down and she came to join her mother at the Hague. To Sophie it all seemed enchanting.

> I was between nine and ten years of age when I came to live at my mother's court at the Hague, and I was lost in an ignorant admiration of all that I beheld. To me it was as the joy of Paradise to see such varying kinds of life and so many people; above all to behold my teachers no more. I was not at all abashed by meeting with three elder sisters, all handsomer and more accomplished than myself, but felt quite pleased that my gaiety and wild spirits should serve to amuse them.[12]

The youngest of a large family, Sophie grew up under the watchful eye of her sisters, petted and teased by her brothers. Pretty, headstrong, and mischievous, she was also the possessor of a sharp tongue:

> Even the Queen took pleasure in me and liked to see me teased, so that I might sharpen my wits in my own defence. I made it my business to tease everyone. Clever people enjoyed the sport while to others I was an object of terror.

Among the men unfortunate enough to become a butt for her wit was Sir Harry Vane, mocked mercilessly because of his long chin. At Rhenen in the summer of 1641—Sophie's first summer of freedom after the closure of the nursery palace—her sisters decided to put on a French play, *Médée* by Corneille, for the entertainment of their mother. Sophie, aged eleven, was vexed when her sisters only allotted her a small part on the grounds that she was too young to learn large numbers of lines. In a fit of pique she decided to learn the whole play by heart, and performed her part with great aplomb, without, however, understanding a word of what she was saying.

The eldest sister was Elizabeth, aged twenty-three, a dark-eyed beauty, often absent-minded and the butt of her youngest sister's lively wit. Perhaps because she had seen little of her mother in early life, relations between the two were distant, particularly because Elizabeth, to her mother's disapproval, was not fond of hunting. She was very learned, wrote Sophie,

> and knew every language and every science under the sun. [...] This great learning, however, by making her rather absent-minded, often became the subject of our mirth. [Elizabeth] had black hair, a dazzling complexion, brown sparkling eyes, a well-shaped forehead, beautiful cherry lips, and a sharp aquiline nose which was rather apt to turn red. At such times she hid herself from the world. I remember that my sister Louise, who was not so sensitive, asked her on one such unlucky occasion to come upstairs to the Queen, as it was the usual hour for visiting her. Princess Elizabeth said, would you have me go with this nose? The other replied, will you wait till you get another?[13]

The second daughter, Louise, was nineteen. Her mother's favourite daughter, she was less beautiful than Elizabeth but in Sophie's opinion of a more amiable disposition, as well as being lively, unaffected, and quicker at repartee. It was always Louise who took the lead in getting up masques and plays. She was a talented painter and became a successful pupil of Honthorst. She cared little for her personal appearance, and looked, according to Sophie, as if her clothes had been thrown upon her. James Harrington, one of the many young Englishmen who haunted the Wassenaer Hof, likened her to a painter who, having failed to paint a horse, threw his brush at the canvas in a rage and thereby succeeded in painting a masterpiece.

Henrietta, the third daughter, was the beauty of the family. Known as Nennie by her mother, she was an attractive blonde girl with soft eyes, a pretty mouth, a well-shaped nose, arched eyebrows, 'hands and arms as perfect as if they had been turned with a lathe', and a complexion of lilies and roses. As to her feet, wrote Sophie, 'they were like those of the rest of the family', which was evidently sufficient praise. Her hobbies were needlework and the making of preserves. She was a gentle, reposeful girl, in contrast to her more assertive sisters.

Although Lord Craven was already a familiar figure at the court of the Queen of Bohemia, it was only now that he became properly acquainted with Elizabeth's younger children, and his role became akin to that of a rich godfather. 'Old Lord Craven', as Sophie referred to him in her memoirs (he would have been in his thirties at this period), was good with children. He was an invaluable friend, she wrote, because 'he possessed a purse better furnished than my own from which to provide presents for my partisans.' On the whole Sophie was fond of him, despite the occasional barbed comment about his lack of common sense, and she regarded him and his eccentricities with a mixture of affection, condescension, and exasperation. 'He needed all these attractions,' she went on, 'to make him agreeable, and to enable us to tease him a little in private.'

> In order to shine in conversation, the good man used to say the oddest things. One day he declared that he was able at pleasure to think of nothing, and, shutting his eyes, said, 'Now I am thinking of nothing'. On another occasion he maintained that French should be spelt in Latin. I told him that for the most part the words in these languages were utterly unlike, and asked him how he would spell '*l'huile*'. He replied, 'With an 'o', because *oglio* is the Latin for oil'; at which we all laughed heartily.[14]

Beautiful, charming, and accomplished though the Palatine princesses were, their marriage prospects were distressingly limited. With sad regularity they were passed over in favour of plainer but less penurious rivals. In the mid–1630s there had been much talk, it is true, of a marriage between Princess Elizabeth and King Wladislaus of Poland, but Elizabeth had refused to convert to Catholicism, and anyway it was clear that Charles I would never have come up with the necessary dowry. In late 1641, it was Louise's turn to be rejected. Five years earlier, Frederick William, son of the Elector of Brandenburg, had visited the Hague and fallen in love with his beautiful cousin. His father, alerted to this danger, recalled his son, and back in Brandenburg the chief minister was thought to have attempted to poison the Prince because of his violent opposition to the threatened Palatine match. In December 1640 the Prince succeeded as Elector of Brandenburg and renewed his approaches, but the affair was forbidden by the Electress Dowager, and the following year the Elector married a plainer but richer alternative, leaving Louise heartbroken.

Such was life at the Wassenaer Hof, a place of stately ritual leavened by masques, plays, and practical jokes. Rhenen, the Palatine summer palace, was a welcome relief from the formality of the Hague. Here the Palatine children could indulge in the outdoor pursuits which they loved—hunting, boating, fishing, and swimming—as well as amateur theatricals. Elizabeth was fond of the theatre, an enthusiasm which was looked upon with disapproval by the consistory of Dutch ministers in the Hague, who tried their utmost to prevent performances by the French troupe of players in the town. Finding that their denunciations from the pulpit had no effect, the ministers went to see the Prince of Orange, who received them coldly and advised them to preach better sermons if they wanted people to forsake the playhouse.

The advent of the Civil War in England split the Palatine family disastrously. In the summer of 1642, Charles Louis was with his uncle at York, but as conflict threatened he refused to help the King, and instead returned to the Hague just as his brothers Rupert and Maurice arrived in England. Roe warned Charles Louis that Rupert's activities—he was accused of extorting money under threat—were damaging the popularity of the Palatine cause in England, rendering Elizabeth an object of suspicion to the Puritans and endangering her pension of £12,000 a year. Charles Louis and his mother had little choice but to publicly denounce Rupert. On 5 October 1642, a declaration was issued by 'the Prince Palsgrave of the Rhine and the Queen his mother, disclaiming and discountenancing Prince Rupert in all his uncivil actions.' Many in Parliament remained sympathetic to the Queen of Bohemia, and she continued to receive her pension, albeit irregularly. But it was generally assumed, quite correctly, that Elizabeth was devoted to her brother's cause, and her letters to England were regularly intercepted. The allowance from England was becoming increasingly unreliable, and when Parliament took over the revenues of tonnage and poundage, the source of her pension, payments ceased altogether. By this time Craven had begun to provide much-needed financial support.

For Craven the ensuing years involved a mixture of campaigning with the States Army, doing his best to keep the court of the Queen of Bohemia from financial ruin, and, judging by the enormous sums of money he drew out through letters of credit during the summer of 1642, also giving discreet financial help to the Royalists. In the first few months after the outbreak of the Civil War there were rumours that Craven had returned to England to fight alongside Prince Rupert. On 26 September, the parliamentarian sergeant Nehemiah Wharton reported that Craven had been present at the Battle of Powick Bridge near Worcester, in which Rupert's cavalry routed the advanced cavalry of the Earl of Essex. 'The chiefs among the Cavaliers,' wrote Wharton, 'were Prince Rupert, who I hear is wounded, Lord Craven and Lord Northampton.' But four days later he corrected himself: 'I wrote that the Earl of Northampton and Lord Craven were with the Prince, but they were not.'[15] In fact, far from fighting in England, Craven was actually on campaign in the lower Rhine Valley, where the States Army was busy skirmishing and manoeuvring against Spanish troops near the town of Orsoy; in November, after the end of the season's campaign, he went to France.

Events in England did sometimes impinge in an unexpected way. In late June, William Murray, one of Charles I's gentlemen of the bedchamber, arrived at the Prince of Orange's camp at Orsoy for secretive discussions, possibly to do with discreet communications between Charles, Henrietta Maria, and the Scottish Covenanters. A man of humble origins who had once been Prince Charles's whipping boy, Murray's high position had not led to a corresponding improvement in his behaviour. 'If I may be allowed to speak frankly,' wrote Huygens to the Princess of Orange, 'this Sr Murray is a strange negotiator, and, in a word, brutal and arrogant like a bedchamberman.' Having acquired a fondness for Spanish wine and tobacco, he became so drunk one evening during a conference with the Prince of Orange that Craven had to take him home and put him to bed.[16]

In 1643, the States Army spent most of the summer in attacks on Spanish forces near the border town of Sas-van-Ghent. It was a diversionary tactic to assist the French Army under the Duc d'Enghien, who was besieging the town of Thionville after his great victory over the Spanish at Roucroy in the Ardennes. Craven seems to have been wounded early on in the campaign; at any rate, he left the Army in the early summer and travelled to Paris to meet his brother John.

In October 1640 John Craven had been elected MP for Tewkesbury, but the election had been contested and subsequently declared void. A faithful Royalist, in March 1641 he had offered to lend the King £1,000 towards military expenses. Lacking either the martial spirit or the robust health of his brother, John decided a few months after the outbreak of the Civil War to join the flow of Royalists seeking safety abroad, and in late February 1643 he obtained a pass from the House of Lords to travel to France with four servants. He remained in England for a few more weeks, and in mid–March he presented the King with his gift of £1,000, for which act of generosity he was rewarded with a barony, taking the title Lord Craven of Ryton. In the middle of April he obtained permission from the House of Lords to transport two 'ambling nags' (that is, horses trained to easy paces) to France, and soon afterwards he left England.[17]

What followed was an adventure which has a flavour not so much of *Don Quixote* as of *The Three Musketeers*. The two brothers met at Saint-Germain-en-Laye, near Paris, but by this time John's health was very poor and William left him under the care of his Swiss servant and maître d'hôtel Pierre Piaget, with a plentiful supply of bills of exchange to ensure John was well cared for. Having made sure his brother was comfortable, he left Saint-Germain-en-Laye and rode southwards towards Bordeaux. The reasons behind his journey remain obscure, though we can make one or two guesses. Whatever his purpose, an English nobleman ambling through the French countryside was only too likely to arouse the suspicion of the authorities. Somewhere in Guyenne, Craven was arrested by order of the Maréchal de Saint-Luc, lieutenant general of Guyenne, and incarcerated in the Chateau Trompette in Bordeaux, one of the three forts which dominated that town. Here he was cross-questioned by M. de Lauson, the intendant of Guyenne, as to the reason for his journey. Craven explained at great length that he had come to France simply to recuperate from his wounds, but his repeated explanations failed to satisfy de Lauson. In despair, Craven wrote to Sir Richard Browne, the English chargé d'affaires at the French court, with a request for help, writing in French to show he had nothing to hide. Could Browne please intervene with the Secretary of State for Protestant Affairs, M. de la Vrillière, to speed his release? After all, wrote Craven, Browne knew better than anyone that he had come to France simply to recover from his wounds.[18]

This may have been true. Or perhaps the real purpose of Craven's visit was to arrange a shipment of arms to England. Despite Mazarin's policy of neutrality towards the conflict in England, a merchantman had left Bordeaux in March loaded with munitions for the royalist commander Lord Hopton, that other devotee of the Winter Queen.[19] Perhaps Craven had intended to arrange another shipment, but if so he kept very quiet about it. Browne, in any case, did as he was asked and interceded with the French authorities, and within a few weeks Craven was released. He returned to Holland, leaving his brother behind at Saint-Germain-en-Laye, tended solicitously by Pierre Piaget.

Whatever Craven's possible involvement in sending munitions to the royalists, his estates were suffering badly as a result of the Civil War. Combe Abbey at least was safe; its occupant, Sir William Craven, was a parliamentary sympathiser and son-in-law of the parliamentary commander Lord Fairfax, and in April 1643 the House of Lords granted the estate a protection order. Craven's estates in Berkshire were not so fortunate. In the same month Caversham House, in a strategic location opposite Reading on the north bank of the Thames, was occupied by the royalist commander Sir Lewis Dyve.[20] Dyve and Prince Rupert were attempting to relieve Reading, besieged by the Earl of Essex, and from Caversham House Dyve sent a soldier named Flower (his nickname, one assumes) to swim across the Thames in order to let the garrison at Reading know that Rupert intended to attack the enemy post at Caversham Bridge, and that the garrison should therefore send barges to collect ammunition and make a sally upon the bridge. But Flower was captured as he climbed out of the water on his return journey, and the scheme was discovered. Towards the end of April, the garrison of Reading finally surrendered after another failed assault by Rupert and the King on Caversham Bridge, and soon afterwards Caversham House too was occupied by the parliamentarians.

In September it was the turn of Hamstead Marshall to be trampled over by the parliamentarians. On the 19th of that month, Essex's wet, hungry, and tired army marched through the park on its way back to London, as the royalist forces under Prince Rupert raced to head them off at Newbury. The parliamentarians had spent three nights in the open after a bloody skirmish at Aldbourne Chase. That night they camped in the fields around Hamstead Marshall and Enborne, and the following day the two armies met a few miles to the east. After a long and inconclusive battle the royalists withdrew, and Essex was able to continue his retreat to London.

With Parliament in increasing need of funds for the war effort, in November 1643 the Committee for the Advance of Money began to assess the estates of known royalists for taxation. The rate was to be anywhere between one twentieth and one half of the value of the property, and Craven's estates were assessed at £2,000. His brother, who had had the temerity to give the King £1,000, had his estates assessed at £3,000. The following March the committee ordered that Craven's assets were to be seized and his goods sold by candle (that is, in an auction whose end would be signalled by the expiration of a candle) at his house in Watling Street.[21] Generally what happened was that the commissioners would make a thorough search of the properties assessed for taxation, melting down silver and taking anything of value. It was a process which could lead to great hardship; in April 1644, John Craven's mother-in-law Lady Penelope Spencer, then living in Drury House, was forced to petition the House of Lords for protection of her goods, protesting that she found herself in danger of being turned out of doors.[22]

The money was slow in coming in, and in May 1645 the committee ordered that further rents and goods should be distrained from Craven's estates to make up the total. Finally, by February 1646 the assessment had been paid in full from Craven's rents and from sales of his goods, and his estates were discharged from sequestration. By and large the commissioners were painstaking in their work, and few royalist sympathisers escaped their attention. Craven's brother-in-law Lord Coventry was assessed at £1,500, and goods and chattels were seized from his house in Westminster to make up the total. Sir Percy Herbert, on the other hand, although a Papist, seems to got off surprisingly lightly to begin with. In February 1646 his estates were assessed at £1,500, but for the moment no proceedings were lauched against him. He did not escape for long, however, and a few years later his estates too were sequestered.

Just now, however, Craven had other preoccupations. On 12 May 1644, Pierre Piaget, who had been looking after John Craven in Paris, died of unknown causes, and all his possessions, including many which belonged to Lord Craven, were peremptorily seized by the justices of the Faubourg Saint-Germain-en-Laye on the orders of the Procurator Fiscal. A few days later, Craven wrote to Sir Richard Browne in Paris listing the items of his which had been in Piaget's possession and begging Browne to do his utmost to recover them. Most important were sealed packets of confidential letters, marked 'not to be opened without my express order', as well as a small red wooden box containing further letters. There were also bills of exchange to the value of almost 10,000 livres, as well as assorted domestic items: silver boxes for keeping miniatures, a camp bed with silver fringe made for Craven's use while in Paris, a long scarf with Spanish colours, and a leather-covered portmanteau belonging to Craven's brother-in-law Sir Robert Townshend. The papers were of considerable importance, so much so that Craven considered Browne would not be safe until he had recovered them.[23]

The wooden box might well have come from the Duke of Richmond, who was with Charles I at his wartime capital of Oxford. Certainly Craven remained in close contact with the royalists, and his activities seem to have extended to the further provision of arms and supplies. In mid–July 1644, the Venetian secretary in England, Gerolamo Agostini, received reports that 'Lord Crever, a very rich English nobleman and devoted friend of the Palatine House' had sailed from France to the royalist-controlled port of Scarborough with a consignment of money, arms, and officers. News of a 'sanguinary battle', Agostini went on, was momentarily expected, 'which will prove of great advantage to the side that is victorious.'[24] The arms were intended for Prince Rupert, who had set out from Oxford in May with the aim of relieving York, under siege from the combined forces of the parliamentarians and the Scots. At the end of June, Rupert arrived outside York and successfully raised the siege. Craven, if the Venetian report is to be believed, had obtained leave from the Prince of Orange to absent himself temporarily from the States Army. In a few short weeks he managed to collect arms, money, and reinforcements and then sailed for Scarborough, having first sent a message to the King in Oxford in early June via Sir Richard Browne in Paris.

The sanguinary battle that Agostini predicted duly took place on 2 July 1644 at Marston Moor, where Rupert, outnumbered by the combined forces of the Scottish Covenanters and two parliamentarian armies, suffered a crushing defeat. In total, about 6,000 men died in the battle, around 4,000 royalist and 2,000 parliamentarian troops. Following his defeat, Rupert moved northwards to meet the Marquis of Montrose in Richmond. He stayed there for two days, sending men to collect Craven's reinforcements from Scarborough before starting to move westwards back towards Preston. For the royalists, Marston Moor was a catastrophe, and in the days after the battle a number of senior officers from York gave up the fight, making their way to Scarborough and thence to the continent. They included the Marquess of Newcastle and his lieutenant-general of foot, Lord Eythin, who was none other than the now ennobled James King, the Scottish soldier whose conduct at Vlotho had been so questionable.

Did Craven really make this lightning dash to Scarborough? It is always possible that Agostini's information was mistaken, though the shrewd Venetian diplomats were seldom wrong. If true, Craven was fortunate that the parliamentarians never got word of it, or his estates would have been sequestered in short order. With his usual boundless energy, Craven managed to re-join his regiment in time for the start of the season's campaign. This time the objective was the town of Sas-van-Ghent. The siege got underway on 27 July. Craven expected the town to fall in a month or six weeks; in the event the siege took forty days, and on 5 September the commander of the garrison capitulated.[25] Craven feared that the Prince of Orange, buoyed by his success, would decide to continue the campaign into the winter months. He was hoping to return to Paris to collect his possessions, which Browne had by now succeeded in recovering, and at the same time to meet the ubiquitous fixer Will Murray, but it looked as though he might be unable to get leave. He wasn't much enamoured with Flanders, he wrote to Browne, 'where both the ayre and all the women in itt are alike infectious.' In the end Craven was in luck; the Prince of Orange was thwarted in his ambitions of continuing his campaign, and Craven was free to make his trip to Paris after all.[26]

The following summer the States Army returned to Flanders, where they succeeded in joining up with the French Army, attacking from the opposite direction. In October the States Army laid siege to the town of Hulst. It was a very wet autumn. Sir Robert Honeywood reported that Craven and his fellow colonel John Cromwell had had a violent dispute over the marching of their regiments, whereupon they had ridden away from the Army as it marched on and had fought a duel on horseback, the result of which had been that Cromwell had been killed and Craven had fled to France. The story reached the ears of a London newsletter, the *City Scout*, which speculated that Craven might open a fencing school in Paris.

> [...] if he turn fencer, and keep a school, it may be, Will Crofts will be his scholar, if Harry Jermine will not tell tales, or fear the man may prove too nimble for him at his own weapon.[27]

But the tale had grown in the retelling. Craven and Cromwell may well have fought a duel, but neither was killed. Craven remained at the siege of Hulst, and both he and Cromwell continued to serve in the States Army for many years to come. Still, the story shows that Craven was no mean swordsman, and it also shows just how easily frayed tempers could lead to drawn swords. Henrietta Maria's retinue of impatient, quarrelling courtiers such as Henry Jermyn were much given to duelling and the settling of old scores. Not that duelling was unknown at the Queen of Bohemia's court either; the following year her equerry, Sir Charles Howard, was forced to flee from the Hague after killing his opponent in a duel.

It does seem that Craven was beginning to tire a little of his life at the Hague. Above all he wished for peace in England; in April 1645, writing to Browne in Paris, he commented on 'the little good news that the kingdom affords, accountinge none good that does not bringe at least the probabilitie of a treatie for peace; without which we must absolutely all be ruined.'[28] In England the parliamentarians seemed to be approaching their final triumph. Bristol had fallen, and to the King, still in Oxford, the future appeared increasingly bleak. The cities of France and the Low Countries were rapidly filling with increasing numbers of royalist exiles, eking out a penurious existence while dreaming of home. Craven, though by no means penurious, was also dreaming of home. In late November 1645, as a long season's campaigning in Flanders was finally drawing to an end, he wrote gloomily to his agent (and secretary to the Duke of Richmond), Thomas Webb, in Oxford.

> [...] it is but now, the 20th of November, that we are returning to Garrison, & if you could do the like & by a good accord meet at London I should far more willingly make that journey than remaayne the suiter [part of the Queen of Bohemia's suite] att the Hage, which for all that I know must eene serve for an assile [asylum] if not a place of requium.[29]

Living the life of an exile and fighting in somebody else's war, while his own country remained in turmoil and the threat of sequestration still loomed threateningly over his estates; it would have been surprising if Craven was not assailed by gloom from time to time. He never deviated from the cause he had chosen as a young man, to devote himself to the Queen of Bohemia and her cause, but perhaps it was not surprising that he occasionally dreamt of home.

'What I have besides in my power shall be at your service'

After the fall of Hulst in 1645, Craven returned to the Hague, where he found the Queen of Bohemia in a state of outrage over the behaviour of her second-but-last son, Prince Edward. For six years Edward, now twenty-one, had been living in Paris, acquiring polished manners and enjoying the revelries and gaieties of the French court. After fighting a duel with an English royalist exile in April 1645, he had talked of joining Rupert and Maurice in England. Nothing had come of this idea, but the following month news leaked out that he had secretly married a wealthy heiress. On 5 May Henry Jermyn wrote to Rupert,

> Your Highness is to know a romance story that concerns you here, in the person of Prince Edward. He is last week married privately to the Princess Anne, the Duke of Nevers's daughter [...] she is very rich, six or seven thousand pounds a year sterling is the least that can fall to her, maybe more: and she is a beautiful young lady.[1]

Beautiful, charming, and high-born, Anne de Gonzague, Princesse de Nevers, was much criticised by Parisian society for throwing herself away on a penniless exile; her elder sister, by contrast, had just married the King of Poland. The reaction of the Queen Regent of France was to order Edward to leave France and return to the Hague immediately. She soon relented, but when news arrived in the Hague the reaction was much more extreme. Anne was a Catholic, and before long it became known that Edward himself had been received into the Catholic Church. The Queen of Bohemia reacted with the same fury and dismay she had shown when Rupert seemed to be close to the same apostasy; she regarded her son's conversion as an unspeakable outrage. She would rather have died, she wrote in distraction to Charles Louis, than see a child of hers abandon the Protestant faith, and she reproached herself bitterly for not sending the boy to England rather than France. The Prince Elector was equally unhappy, but in his case political considerations were to the fore. The possession of a Papist brother would not endear him to the English Parliament, whose good opinion he was taking care to cultivate. In fact, wrote Elizabeth Benger, 'there was not one of Edward's domestic relations to whom his death had not appeared a lighter evil than his apostasy,' and even Princess Elizabeth found philosophy inadequate to console her for the disgrace of her brother.[2]

The episode threw the Queen of Bohemia into a near panic over her youngest son, Philip, who was still in Paris. Desperate to protect him from the pernicious influence of Papists, Elizabeth ordered him to return to the Hague as soon as possible. Charles Louis agreed with his mother that Philip must leave Paris, where 'only atheists and hypocrites' were to be found, and he asked her to dismiss one of Philip's attendants, who was a Catholic. As for Edward, he could surely not really be 'persuaded of the fopperies to which he pretends.'

Elizabeth's alternative plan was that Philip should raise a body of troops for Venetian service, although Charles Louis thought that he was too young for such an enterprise. For the moment Philip returned to the Hague, only to become the central figure in a highly sensational incident of which the details remain murky. Philip, now eighteen, had inherited the Palatine traits of fieriness and impetuosity. Among the circle who frequented the court of the Queen of Bohemia was a certain Jacques de l'Epinay, a French gallant of charming and insinuating manners who was colonel of one of the French regiments in the States Army. De l'Epinay began to spend a great deal of time in the company of Elizabeth and her daughters. Elizabeth enjoyed his company, and so it seems did her second daughter Princess Louise. Elizabeth, unconventional and careless of her reputation as she was, allowed de l'Epinay liberties, even outrageous liberties such as wearing a hat in her presence, which deeply offended most of her children. Charles Louis, on one his visits to his mother's court, saw the Frenchman walking alongside her in the Lange Voorhout with a hat on. Such behaviour was completely beyond the pale, and he had no hesitation in knocking off the impudent man's headgear. Philip for his part demanded that de l'Epinay stay away from the Wassenaer Hof, but de l'Epinay's infuriating reply was that he would cease visiting the Queen when she asked him to stay away. Wild rumours soon spread, including one that de l'Epinay had enjoyed the sexual favours of both the Queen of Bohemia and her daughter Louise.

On the evening of 20 June 1646, Philip, walking through the Hague with one attendant, met the French gallant with three friends close to the Wassenaer Hof. A brawl ensued, only to be frustrated by the arrival of the watch. The following evening, Philip was driving through the streets in a carriage when he caught sight of de l'Epinay strolling back from a dinner at the French embassy. The Prince leapt from his carriage and ran at the Frenchman, brandishing his hunting knife. De l'Epinay just had time to draw his sword before Philip sprang on him, severing his jugular vein. As the Frenchman lay dying, Philip jumped back into his carriage, throwing his hunting knife away, and fled as fast as he could to the Spanish Netherlands.[3]

The Queen of Bohemia was furious with her youngest son, but Philip was warmly supported by most of his brothers and sisters. Charles Louis and Rupert both took his side, as did Princess Elizabeth, who became temporarily estranged from her mother and left the Hague in the months following de l'Epinay's murder. Charles Louis wrote to his mother asking her to pardon Philip, a pardon I would sooner have asked, had it ever entered my mind that he could possibly need any intercession to obtain it. The consideration of his youth, of the affront he received, and of the shame which would all his life have attached to him had he not revenged it, should suffice.[4]

What, however, was Philip to do now? He could not return to the Hague, where the States General had summoned him to stand trial. Elizabeth's fear had always been that her impecunious younger sons would drift into careers unworthy of their station in life, and now her worst fears had been realised. From the Spanish Netherlands Philip crossed over to England, where Charles Louis, with the consent of Parliament, helped him to raise 1,000 men for Venetian service. Craven did what he could to help Philip, providing the hot-headed youth not only with money but also with companionship, in the form of a relative, Captain Craven, to act as a faithful squire. Philip was not happy in Venetian service; he complained to Rupert that his employers were 'unworthy pantaloons'. He soon left the Venetians, and subsequently fought for Spain and then France. Four years later, in February 1650, he was killed in a Spanish attack on a French fortress in the Ardennes.

Back in England, Charles I, after giving himself up to the Scots, was now in the custody of the English Army. Cromwell was keen to conciliate the King and to this end agreed to his wish to see his younger children. Charles had not seen his two youngest, the twelve-year-old Princess Elizabeth and seven-year-old Duke of Gloucester, since leaving London in July 1642, and he had not seen the Duke of York, aged fourteen, since leaving Oxford in 1644. Parliament agreed to a request from Fairfax that the King should be allowed to see them, and on 15 July the three children were escorted to Maidenhead, where Charles was waiting.[5] In the evening they all went to Craven's house at Caversham, where they stayed for two days. For Charles it was a happy interlude: 'here was a gallant court, and his Majesty very cheerful, being attended by many brave gallants.' Cromwell was present at their meeting, and remarked to Sir John Berkeley, with tears in his eyes, that it was the tenderest sight that his eyes had ever beheld. Berkeley passed this on to the King, who seemed, Berkeley reported, 'not to have been well edified with it.'[6]

Berkshire, and more especially the Newbury area, had by this time become something of a hotbed of radicalism, in large part through the efforts of the fiery radical politician Henry Marten, son of the judge Sir Henry Marten. In the summer of 1648, during the Second Civil War, Henry Marten raised an unauthorised cavalry regiment in Berkshire made up of Leveller troops who he encouraged to desert from their own regiments. He had no trouble finding enough men, and the problem of where to find mounts was easily solved by taking horses by force from estates such as Hamstead Marshall, and threatening anyone who resisted. Marten's activities had not been authorised by Parliament, and a few days later the House of Lords ordered that Craven's horses should be returned, considering that he had never borne arms against Parliament. Even so, by the end of August

Marten, 'generalissimo of all the Smock petticoats in his newly erected Empire of Berkshire', had amassed a sizeable regiment. Later in the summer he appeared at a court baron at Hamstead Marshall held by Craven's tenants, and urged them to refrain from paying homage to their landlord, 'claiming that to do so was akin to slavery and a badge of the Norman Conquest.'[7]

Craven's other estates do not appear to have suffered as badly, although Stokesay Castle endured a brief siege in 1646. It escaped serious damage, though the outer walls were pulled down. But years of civil war had had a serious effect everywhere. In January 1649 Craven's agent, Thomas Webb, sent his employer gloomy news of his houses, 'which are like the tymes, ruinous, some of the houses quit fallen doune, many of them falling and all out of repaire.'[8]

In July 1647, John Craven died at Saint-Germain-en-Laye. It was probably a blessed release for a man who had been ill for several years, but a few weeks after his death sorrow turned to consternation when Richard Spencer of Orpington, the deceased's uncle, produced a false will naming himself as executor and residual beneficiary. Spencer, a younger son of the 1st Baron Spencer, had in the past been a man of some wealth, but he had recently lost money in the canal schemes of William Sandys, who had spent vast sums in making the River Avon navigable as far as Stratford. As a result, Spencer was in desperate financial straits. He had written out the altered will himself and then persuaded the dying man to sign it, and luckily for him none of the witnesses present insisted on reading it before appending their names. In law, therefore, the will was perfectly genuine, but most observers agreed that it was quite contrary to the wishes of the deceased. A flurry of urgent correspondence ensued between the Hague, Paris, and England. Thomas Atkinson, the vicar of Stanton Lacy in Shropshire and a close friend of the deceased, wrote in shock to Sir William Craven of Lenchwyke.

> I have been informed touching his [John Craven's] will and I find it so dissonant to his former rational intentions (upon which I am sure none upon earth was more privy than myself) that I cannot but lament afresh that this should go on in his name. He that was acquainted with those variety of humors, which his habituall malady did stir up in him (like so many fluxes and refluxes of the sea) may easily determine in what mood he was in when he gave consent that this should be his last testament.[9]

At the time that the will was signed he had evidently been in a foul mood, and very probably in a state of unspeakable pain; when his cousin Anthony Craven approached his bed after witnessing the will, 'my lord John said to him in anger, take your sword and run it through my body.'

There were some, including even Sir Richard Browne, who considered that the will was genuine and should be respected, but Lord Craven's lawyers in Paris were confident that it could be overturned. In early September, however, Richard Spencer travelled to London to register his will for probate, and Craven countered by appointing lawyers to enter a caveat. Later in the month, Craven's application to have the will overturned came up before the bailiff of Saint-Germain-en-Laye, but a fortnight later the bailiff postponed pronouncing his sentence on the grounds that the matter was of such importance that he needed to consult his colleagues, 'with principal scope to get more money'—or so at least thought Craven's agent de la Garde, who had a healthy disrespect for lawyers' wiles. Spencer in the meantime offered to meet Craven, but he also threatened to take his case to court. After all, given that the will had been properly signed and witnessed he had grounds for hoping that he might just win. Craven replied that there would be no point because the legal costs would use up the entire estate, and Spencer would be better advised to accept a reasonable gratuity. 'I am resolved to keep my interest and right the best I can,' Craven wrote firmly, 'and to part with the less, the more I be pressed or undermined to part with it.'[10]

The court case in Paris ground on. The bailiff agreed that it was very peculiar that the will should include bequests to any children the testator might have in the future if his wife happened to be with child at the time of his death; it was rather an odd stipulation given that he had not seen his wife for eighteen months. Finally, at the end of October, the bailiff declared the will to be null and void on account of the weakness of mind of the testator. He ruled that all the deceased's goods should go to Lord Craven, now deemed to be his brother's heir-at-law and executor, and Spencer was to bring his will along to the bailiff so it could be torn up. Craven honoured most of the numerous bequests in his brother's overturned will, including the establishment of four scholarships—two at Oxford and two at Cambridge—paid for out of the profits from his brother's estate of Causerne in Sussex. Any surplus funds were to be spent on the redemption of English Christian captives in Algiers. Shortly afterwards Craven asked his agents in England to come to a friendly accommodation with Spencer. History does not relate what transpired, but when Spencer returned to England in 1653 after a few years in Brussels he was imprisoned and forced to pay off his debts.

The only other footnote to add to the tale of the forged will is that many years later, in 1670, Sir Anthony Craven of Sparsholt was recorded as collecting money in Caversham parish for the redemption of Englishmen taken by the Turks, perhaps honouring a cause which had been a particular interest of Lord John's.[11]

Lord John had made an unfortunate match, Sir Percy Herbert wrote to his wife; it was a thoroughly bad business, what with the Spencers doing their best to cheat and dishonour the Craven family. Sir Percy was altogether a much more agreeable relative, and Craven always remained close to his sister and brother-in-law. Three years earlier, in September 1644, Sir Percy and his son William, aged twenty-one, had joined the royalist exiles on the continent, and since then father and son had been perambulating around France, Italy, and the Netherlands with a tutor. In October 1647 they arrived in Paris, and at Craven's suggestion Sir Percy enrolled his son in a military academy, where he was to learn riding, dancing, fencing, vaulting, handling a pike and musket, mathematics, and arithmetic. But the best thing about the academy, Sir Percy wrote, was that it had very good discipline.[12] In addition to paying the fees—which amounted to at least 300 pistoles a year—Craven lent a hand by helping to train his nephew in 'manly exercises', that is to say essentials such as fencing and horsemanship.

In an earlier generation, a young English gentleman wishing to learn the art of war would have spent a season or two on campaign as a volunteer with the Prince of Orange or the King of Sweden. But much had changed since those days. After decades of destructive conflict, peace had finally descended on a tired United Provinces and a shattered Germany. For the past four years ambassadors from the Empire, Sweden, France, Spain, and the United Provinces had been meeting in the town of Münster in Westphalia, wrangling over the terms of a treaty. After much delay caused by diplomatic etiquette and jealousies, Spanish and Dutch plenipotentiaries at last signed the Treaty of Münster in January 1648: this established the independence of the United Provinces, bringing to an end the near eighty-year struggle with Spain. It took a little longer for the other combatants to come to an agreement, but on 27 October the plenipotentiaries in Münster signed the Treaty of Westphalia, bringing peace to Germany.

When news of the final ratification of the treaty arrived in the Hague, there were exuberant public celebrations and thanksgivings. The Palatine family rejoiced to find that at long last they had been restored to at least part of their hereditary estates. It would, however, be a sadly diminished inheritance. Elizabeth had agreed to accept the limited settlement which she had angrily rejected in earlier years. Under the terms of the treaty, the Lower Palatinate was restored to its former owners unencumbered with debt, but not the Upper Palatinate, nor the title of First Elector of the Empire. Both of these remained the property of the man in possession, Maximilian of Bavaria. An eighth electorate, the lowest in rank, was instead created for the Palatine family, though with a proviso that if the Bavarian line died out the new electorate would be abolished and the Upper Palatinate returned to the Palatine family. Moreover, the once beautiful Palatinate had suffered desperately since Elizabeth had seen it last. Thirty years of warfare, famine, pestilence, and emigration had turned it into a devastated wasteland whose population had been reduced to one tenth or less of its pre-war figure. Elizabeth never quite realised the true extent of the destruction, continuing to look hopefully to her eldest son for financial relief.

The news from England was more mixed. Royalist uprisings in the past few months had been put down, but in May 1648 a section of the parliamentary fleet revolted and sailed to the United Provinces, where its commanders put it at the disposal of Charles, Prince of Wales. The Prince was at the time still living at Saint-Germain-en-Laye, along with his small retinue of quarrelling, poverty-stricken courtiers, but in June, at the invitation of the young Prince of Orange, he moved to the Hague. His first action as titular admiral of the new royalist fleet was to send for Rupert, now serving in the French Army, to act as his vice-admiral. A brief and inconclusive sortie to the English coast in the summer achieved little except for a few prizes captured in the Thames, and the sailors, mutinous because of the arrears of pay, were mollified by the promise of shares in the prize money.

In October the Prince of Wales appointed Rupert as admiral, and the work of provisioning began in earnest. The Queen of Bohemia pawned some of her jewels, and Craven contributed generously. Back in August, a parliamentarian pamphlet had reported optimistically that Craven had declared that he would not support the Prince of Wales, 'nor by any wayes be instrumental for involving his native country in a more bloody and intestine war.' Perhaps this represented deliberate misrepresentation by Craven's agents in England, who worked hard to prove that he was no enemy of the Commonwealth. By the winter, however, Craven had decided to give generously to provision Rupert's fleet. He wrote to Rupert on 26 January 1649,

> What I have besides in my power shal bee at your service, unless your brother Edward in the mean time disfournish me, now that he has taken an imploy of horse under the Prince of Conti and Monsieur de Longeville who are all at the heads of the Parisiens.[13]

Prince Edward, it seems, had become involved with the brief period of turmoil known as the Fronde, in which much of the nobility, under Conti and Longueville, arrayed themselves against the court. Few shots were ever fired and peace was soon restored, but even so, Craven probably came up with money in the end to help Edward.[14] Further funds for Rupert's fleet meanwhile came from selling the ordnance of the *Antelope* in Rotterdam, and by late January the fleet was ready to sail. Rupert was concerned about the fate of his favourite horse, Black, but Craven promised to look after him as best he could. If he had the resources of Alexander the Great, he wrote, Black 'should have a city erected for to lodge him, at least he shall now be as carefully looked unto, until your Highness be pleased to command him again.'[15] It seems likely that Craven continued to provide help for Rupert's fleet long afterwards. In 1651, when the Prince's battered ships sought shelter in the port of Toulon after a costly encounter with Admiral Blake at Cadiz, their numbers were augmented by a ship from Marseille, the *Speedwell*, owned and commanded by a certain Captain Craven, who renamed his ship *The Loyal Subject*.

Celebrations in the Hague to mark the final ratification of the Treaty of Westphalia were in full swing when news arrived from London that Charles I had been brought under armed guard to Westminster, where he was to be tried for treason. Nobody had expected this. All festivities at the Queen of Bohemia's court were quickly halted, and in London it was reported that Elizabeth was preparing to sail for England to intercede for her brother. But the Commonwealth, fearing her popularity, refused her permission to come to London, and the trial proceeded. Charles Louis, still in England, offered to visit the condemned man, only to have his offer haughtily rejected by a king who distrusted his nephew and wished to spend his last hours alone. In the early afternoon of 30 January 1649, Charles walked out of the banqueting house at Whitehall onto a scaffold draped in black. The execution drew a great groan from the watching crowd.

Two days after the execution of Charles I, the outraged Scottish Covenanter Parliament proclaimed his eldest son King Charles II of Scotland. However, the Covenanters insisted that before their new King was crowned he must undertake to establish Presbyterianism as the national religion. In the hope that Elizabeth would bring her influence to bear on her nephew, they sought an interview with her, but she refused to back any such agreement, preferring instead the scheme put forward by the Marquis of Montrose for an invasion of Scotland.

The death of her brother roused in Elizabeth a passionate fury of indignation, and the anniversary of his martyrdom was kept as a day of mourning forever after at her court. Until now she had maintained a judicious neutrality between Crown and Parliament, but no longer. She became fiercely royalist, cutting off all communication with supporters of Parliament and refusing to give the government of England the title of 'Commonwealth'. As for the Lord Protector, she regarded him as the beast in the Book of Revelations. Her household were strictly forbidden from any contact with the English ambassadors in the Hague. No one associated with them was to be admitted to her court, and anyone who dared to disobey her orders was to be thrown downstairs and kicked out of doors. The consequences for her finances were all too predictable. On 8 May, Parliament declared that her pension of £12,000 a year was suspended, leaving her with no means of support other than Craven's generosity, in a town in which she was already deeply in debt.

Financial difficulties at the Wassenaer Hof became acute, though the merchants of the Hague continued to extend their credit, and the house grew shabbier and shabbier. Elizabeth was forced to disperse her stable, since she could no longer afford to go hunting, and instead she spent her days taking exercise on foot and relearning the art of shooting at the butts. She asked Montrose to find employment for several old servants. Still, some members of the household managed to remain cheerful. 'Our family misfortunes had no power to depress my spirits,' wrote Sophie, 'though we were at times to make even richer repasts than that of Cleopatra, and often had nothing at our court but pearls and diamonds to eat.'[16] Pearls and diamonds could be pawned, of course, and Elizabeth had already pawned some of her jewels to pay for the provisioning of Rupert's ships. But they could also be redeemed, and in December 1649 Craven paid 11,400 livres for that purpose. In the years to come, tragically, they would return to the pawnbrokers, never to be redeemed.

In April 1649, Charles Louis returned to the Hague and to a very frosty interview with his indignant mother, outraged by his behaviour in England. She insisted that he must not visit the parliamentary agent to the States General, and that he must pay his respects to the new Charles II. A family party at Rhenen provided an opportunity. A few months later, Charles Louis made his way to the Palatinate to reclaim, at last, what was left of his patrimony. In early October he arrived in Heidelberg, the town he had left as a child thirty years before. The condition of the Palatinate was tragic, and Heidelberg Castle, once so celebrated for its porphyry halls, its beautiful gardens, and its splendid library, was in ruins. Charles Louis was to spend the rest of his life conscientiously restoring his truncated and shattered lands to prosperity. The Palatinate was so severely depopulated that the Prince Elector, a strict Calvinist, was forced to build Lutheran churches, and even to grant a degree of toleration to Catholics. On arrival he moved into the Commissariat House in Heidelberg town, until part of the ruined castle could be refurbished.

Elizabeth, not realising the true extent of devastation in the Palatinate, fully expected that her son would now begin to pay the jointure which was her due. Charles Louis simply did not have the money to do so, but at least his position enabled him at last, at the age of thirty-one, to take a wife. The following February he duly married Charlotte, sister of the Landgrave of Hesse-Cassel. He also invited his sisters to come and live with him in Heidelberg. By now three of them—Louise, Henrietta, and Sophie—were living in poverty with their mother at the Wassenaer Hof. Sophie, for one, accepted her brother's invitation with enthusiasm, calculating that life might be a little more comfortable, and that she would have a better chance there of finding a husband.

And so the court of the Winter Queen struggled on in increasing penury. The calls on Craven's purse increased exponentially, and at the beginning of 1649 Lewis Ziegler, Craven's secretary, made the first entry in a large ledger in which he scrupulously noted down all his master's payments. It makes fascinating reading.[17] Over the next few years, Craven was to pay out eye-watering sums to sustain the Queen of Bohemia and her family, as well as distributing his means more widely. In December 1649, 11,000 livres went to redeem Elizabeth's jewels, pawned to help pay for the provisioning of Rupert's fleet, followed by 16,000 livres between October 1650 and February 1651 to pay for the upkeep of her court, and 17,000 livres in February 1651 to redeem the Elector's jewels. (14 livres Tournois equated roughly to one pound sterling.)

Regular payments went to most of the Palatine children, too. On the eve of Rupert's departure for Ireland, Craven paid 1,000 livres for a servant for the Prince; on the eve of Sophie's departure for Heidelberg, she received a present of two rings; and in June 1652, Louise received 1,000 livres. There was money for luxuries, as well: 132 livres went on twelve pairs of blue silk stockings (perhaps for the princesses, or for their mother), 340 livres on a silver dish, 175 livres on two Japanese robes, and another 100 livres on an enamelled gold box containing a miniature of Prince Rupert. Prince Philip received regular funds to buy arms, and further payments went to his faithful squire, Captain Craven.

The Margravine of Anspach wrote in her memoirs that an old steward of the Craven family had shown her a bond for £40,000 which Lord Craven had lent to the Queen of Bohemia, and it seems probable that such a bond dated from this period. But the exigencies of the times led to many other calls on his purse. In the months after the King's execution, a flood of more or less indigent royalist soldiers and refugees arrived in the Hague, and Craven's account book records one payment after another to men such as Sir Robert Stone, cupbearer to the Queen of Bohemia and captain of a troop of cavalry in the States Army, and others including Lord Gerard, Sir Edward Brett, and Lieutenant-Colonel Henry Winde (who had fought alongside Craven many years earlier at the siege of Kreutznach and for Charles I in the Civil War). He was now in the service of the States Army and living in Bergen-op-Zoom. Two relatives, Sir Anthony Craven and Robert Craven, future Master of Horse to the Queen of Bohemia, had by now come to live in Zutphen, in the east of the United Provinces, and they too received regular payments. The 6,000 livres which Craven paid to Mr Gibson in Brussels in June 1649 was probably destined for Sir Percy Herbert.

The poor and needy of the Hague seem to have beaten a path to Craven's lodgings; in fact, the soldiers standing guard at his door must have been kept busy fending off unwanted supplicants. Payments went to the orphans of the Hague, and to the deacons of the Kloster Kirche, the French Church, and the Flemish Church to distribute to the poor; 5 livres went to an unnamed woman desperate to return to England, 30 livres to pay for a small dog for a certain Jean Floris, and 1 ducaton to a student from Westphalia. Craven's reputation for generosity spread far and wide, and on occasion begging letters arrived from England. In June 1649, one Thomas Shadman wrote from Peckham,

> If your Honour will now vouchsafe to lend mee 20 l. [...] I shall upon the faith of an honest though poor man, repaye it after one year, at the first demand. I beseech you my good lord, pardon this bold attempt, & save him from perishing, who may live to do your Honour some service, & while he doeth live, will pray the great Remunerator to remember your works of charity.[18]

Craven's literary patronage had not entirely ceased, either. In 1650 John Donne the younger, son of the poet and Dean of St Paul's, dedicated a new edition of his father's poems to his former university friend, who had presumably paid for the printing. The dedication takes the form of a lament over the condition of England, where 'the noise of drums and trumpets [...] have drowned the Muses' harmony':

> In this sad condition those learned sisters are fled over to beg your lordship's protection, who have been so certain a patron both to arts and arms, and who in this general confusion have so entirely preserved your honour, that in your lordship we may still read a most perfect character of what England was in all her pomp and greatness, so that although these poems were formerly written upon several occasions, and to several persons, they now unite themselves, and are become one pyramid to set your lordship's statue upon, where you may stand like armed Apollo the defender of the Muses.[19]

A rather charming image; but Craven's ability to defend the muses, or even to keep the court of the Winter Queen from penury, would soon come to an abrupt halt.

'Barbarous and inhuman rebels'

In the middle of April 1650, the Queen of Bohemia, escorted by Craven and accompanied by her daughters Louise and Sophie, travelled to Breda Castle to meet Charles II, who had arrived from Jersey a few weeks earlier. Lengthy and tortuous negotiations were proceeding between Charles and representatives of the Scottish Covenanters, who had promised him the crown of Scotland on condition that he accept the authority of the Scottish Kirk and Parliament and abandon his support for Montrose. Once the proposed treaty had been signed, Charles intended to sail for Scotland.

The Winter Queen's visit to Breda had another purpose beyond the obvious one of bidding her nephew farewell. Elizabeth cherished a hope of arranging a marriage between Charles and Sophie, who were almost the same age, and Craven had engineered the visit to Breda in the hope of advancing the match. Charles was attracted to his witty, high-spirited cousin. As they had promenaded together along the Lange Voorhout in the Hague the previous year, he had told her that he admired her even more than Mrs Barlow—the assumed name of his mistress Lucy Walter—and that he hoped before long to see her in England. Sophie was wary of her cousin, and her opinion of him had sunk further when she learnt that the real purpose of his frequent visits to the Wassenaer Hof had been to extract money from Lord Craven, at the urging of two of his impoverished courtiers, Lord Gerard and Somerset Fox, who planned to share the money between them.[1] The Queen of Bohemia had been delighted to see her nephew paying attentions to her youngest daughter, but Sophie preferred not to encourage him. When Charles had asked her to take a promenade with him the following evening, she had declined, unromantically pleading a corn as an excuse. Her mother was exasperated, but Sophie reflected in her memoirs that 'the marriages of great kings are not made up by such means'. A staunch royalist, her opinion of Charles sank still further after he signed the Treaty of Breda, abandoning Montrose—who had been planning to raise the Highlands in rebellion—and effectively sending him to his death.

During the visit to Breda, Craven spent long periods closeted with Charles in his withdrawing room and bedchamber, probably arranging the details of a loan; in the end he was to lend over £50,000 to the King. Alongside courtiers such as William

Cavendish, 1st Marquis of Newcastle, and Aubrey de Vere, 20th Earl of Oxford, Craven also waited on the King at table and played bowls with him in the bowling alley. It might have been in the latter place that a famous exchange took place between Craven and Oxford, recounted at a later date by Defoe, in which Oxford made a remark upbraiding Craven, in Defoe's words, 'for being of an upstart nobility'.

Craven's reply was to offer to cap pedigrees with Oxford for a wager. Oxford laughed at the challenge and began reciting the venerable history of the de Vere family, earls of Oxford since 1141. It was a pedigree which would have been hard for anyone to beat, let alone a man whose title was only twenty-three years old, but when Craven's turn came, he described his lineage thus:

> I am William Lord Craven, my father was Lord Mayor of London, and my grandfather was the Lord knows who, wherefore I think my pedigree as good as yours, my lord.

A nice answer and to the point, since Oxford's father had inherited his earldom from a cousin, and his grandfather had consequently had no title either. Very little money had come with the title, as it happened, although Oxford had recently managed to improve his fortunes by marrying a wealthy ten-year-old heiress. Defoe's point, incidentally, was to illustrate that trade was no bar to nobility:

> Sir William Craven, who was Lord Mayor of London, was a wholesale grocer [actually he wasn't, of course—he was a merchant tailor], and raised the family by trade, and yet nobody doubts that the family of Craven is at this day [1726] as truly noble, in all the beauties which adorn noble birth and blood, as can be desired of any family, however ancient, or anciently noble.[2]

The visit to Breda, anyway, was to have most unfortunate consequences for Craven, the result of what appeared at the time to be a thoroughly trivial encounter. Among the many royalist exiles scattered across the towns and cities of the Low Countries were large numbers of soldiers who had left England following Cromwell's victory. Some had found employment in the English regiments of the States Army, but many were poverty-stricken, without employment since the declaration of peace in Germany and the Netherlands. In April 1650, a group of about thirty semi-destitute English officers met in the Breda lodgings of a certain Colonel Drury, and after discussion it was agreed that one of their number, Major Richard Falconer, should draw up a petition begging Charles II for help in paying their arrears of rent. As former officers in the royalist Army they had served his father faithfully, they wrote, but their necessities had grown so great and insupportable that they were forced either to petition or perish.[3]

On the first occasion they tried to present their petition, Charles's secretary, Sir Robert Long, advised them to give it to him instead, 'for that the King had not a pistole to relieve himself'. They continued to press Long, soliciting him daily for three weeks, but to no avail. Finally, the day before Charles was due to leave Breda, two of the officers, Colonel Drury and Captain Brisco, seized their chance and, withdrawing to the other end of the gallery, wrote out a much shorter petition to the same effect and handed it to Charles in person. He put it down on a table unread, but at this point Craven came into the room and Brisco, a former royalist officer who had trailed a pike under Craven in the Netherlands, approached him, 'knowing him to be a lover of soldiers', and asked him to speak to the King on their behalf. Craven replied that he was a servant of the States, not a courtier of Charles II's, and Brisco should present the petition himself. Charles left Breda early the next morning to go to the Prince of Orange's house at Hounslerdijke, and so the petition was never presented.[4]

Little of any use had been achieved at Breda. The Treaty of Breda was soon overtaken by events, and nothing came of Elizabeth's matrimonial scheming. Relations between the Queen of Bohemia and her youngest daughter had deteriorated, and following her return from Breda Sophie decided to accept her eldest brother's invitation to come and live with him in Heidelberg. Elizabeth made no objection. 'I will never keep anybody that has a mind to leave me,' she wrote sniffily, 'for I shall never care for anybody's company that does not care for mine.' Accordingly, in the summer of 1650, the indefatigable Craven set out again from the Hague to escort Sophie to her new home. Two years after the end of the war, the German countryside was still in a state of devastation, plagued by marauding ex-soldiers and starving peasants, and perhaps for this reason the journey was made by water. According to Sophie's own account she begged the loan of a pinnace because she did not wish to put up with the fatigue of a journey by carriage, and she and her entourage were drawn up the Rhine in great comfort.

Charles Louis and his wife came to meet Sophie and her small retinue at Mannheim. Sophie formed an unflattering impression of her new sister-in-law, Charlotte of Hesse-Cassel. The Electress Palatine was undoubtedly handsome, 'very tall with an admirable complexion and most beautiful bust.' Her eyebrows were dyed black, making an odd contrast with her flaxen hair. Sophie innocently praised the carriage they were riding in, but her sister-in-law's grimace told her that this was a sore point. Charlotte complained loudly that her sister had a far better equipage, and that she could have made a much better match if her mother hadn't forced her to marry 'a jealous old man'. It was not long before Sophie concluded that her brother had married a fool. Not that the couple didn't love each other at first; on the contrary, Sophie was alarmed to see them embracing in public. But the warmth did not last, and it was not long before stories arrived at the Hague of how the Electress had thrown a plate at her husband, whereupon he had boxed her ears.

The next of the Winter Queen's children to be married was the lovely, fragile Henrietta. In the autumn of 1650 an offer of marriage arrived from Prince Sigismund Rakoczy, brother of the Prince of Transylvania. Out of a number of possible brides suggested to him he had chosen, on the strength of her portrait, the prettiest but the poorest. Certainly, there was little enough money for any dowry, but Elizabeth suggested that her wedding gift should be a coach to transport her daughter across Europe to her new home. Charles Louis, as head of the family, started to make difficulties, and Henrietta chose this moment to fall ill with smallpox. She recovered, thankfully without any damage to her beautiful complexion, an agreement was reached with the Rakoczy family, and the marriage articles were signed in March 1651. Two months later the marriage took place, a proxy standing in for the Prince, and Henrietta set off in tears towards her new home and a husband she had not yet met, with an entourage of forty-four 'needful attendants' including a court preacher with servant, four maids of honour, a mistress of the robes, a chamberlain with three servants, two ushers with a servant each, and four coachmen. At least, reasoned her mother, she had sensible people around her who would keep her from despair and prevent her from losing her courage, 'as you know is her wont'. The marriage was a great success and Henrietta was very happy; but her happiness was brief. Always delicate, she soon fell ill, and despite visits to the spas of Transylvania she died just five months after her marriage.

The cancellation of the Queen of Bohemia's pension of £12,000 a year had plunged her court into financial chaos. Although the household had been trimmed it was still a considerable establishment. Financial management was never Elizabeth's strong point, and her credit with the tradespeople of the Hague was wearing thin. She fondly imagined that her eldest son, now restored to his domains, would be in a position to start paying the handsome jointure to which she was entitled. On paper she was also the owner of dower palaces in Fridelsheim and Frankenthal, which in theory would make much more desirable residences than her decaying house in the Hague. But Charles Louis, looking out from what was left of Heidelberg Castle on his devastated and depopulated lands, was certainly in no position to pay his mother even a fraction of the £10,000 a year which she was due under the terms of her marriage settlement, let alone to enable her to take up residence in Frankenthal, still occupied by Spanish troops, or Fridelsheim, which was in a state of complete ruin.

At this juncture it suddenly became apparent that Craven, too, was in danger of being thrown into penury. Since the early stages of the Civil War, the Parliamentary Committee for Compounding had been systematically sequestering the estates of royalists who had fought against Parliament. Usually, the owners could choose to compound their estates—that is, to recover them on payment of a hefty fine. As a known royalist sympathiser, Craven had already paid thousands of pounds, but once he had paid in full the threat to his estates had been lifted. Because he had not taken up arms against Parliament he had seemed relatively safe. A number of things, however, had changed in recent years, not least the state of Commonwealth finances. The authorities were in dire need of money to finance a Commonwealth fleet, and they looked greedily at Craven's estates. The trouble was that he had not taken up arms against Parliament, but on 24 August 1649 a parliamentary motion had been passed declaring that all 'who adhere to Charles Stuart, son of the late King' should be regarded as rebels and their estates subject to sequestration. This motion had been put forward by an Irish MP and was intended to apply only to Ireland, but parliamentary spies had noted that Craven had met Charles II on several occasions in the Hague, and conveniently damning evidence of his guilt was supplied by Major Richard Falconer, the officer who had drawn up the petition in Breda the previous year.

Falconer was, it turned out, an agent provocateur working on behalf of the Commonwealth. On his return to England he provided evidence of Craven's supposedly treacherous behaviour to Captain George Bishop, secretary of the Committee for Examinations, the intelligence-gathering wing of the Committee for Compounding, and a man closely involved in ferreting out possible royalist conspirators. The upshot was that on 10 February 1651, Falconer gave evidence in front of the Committee for Compounding sitting in Haberdashers Hall. He claimed that his Breda petition had not been a request for money at all; instead it had been a request to Charles II to allow the petitioners to fight against 'those barbarous and inhuman rebels', the Commonwealth of England. According to Falconer, he had approached Craven with the petition. Craven had read it cheerfully and had advised Falconer to present it to the Queen of Bohemia. Elizabeth had taken it and handed it to the King, after which all of them had retired into a withdrawing chamber. Falconer had seen Craven 'very often and familiar with the said King'. Two other witnesses, Colonel Hugh Reyly and Captain Thomas Kitchingman, also testified that Craven had had lengthy discussions with Charles in Breda, closeted till late with him in his withdrawing chamber, 'there being no man more conversant with the King than he'. He had waited on Charles at table, played bowls with him, and had travelled twice to Rotterdam and the Hague on his behalf.

Reyley also testified that Charles II had given Craven the charge of looking after his mistress Mrs Barlow and of the couple's baby, and that after Charles's departure for Scotland Craven had taken the baby away from its mother, 'for which she went to law with him, and recovered the child back again, as is reported.' Mrs Barlow was of course the assumed name of Lucy Walter, the 'brown, beautiful, bold, but insipid creature' whom Charles had met in the Hague in 1648, and the baby was James, later Duke of Monmouth. James's early years were certainly traumatic, and as a baby he narrowly avoided being abducted by Commonwealth agents. Reyley's story, however, was a complete fabrication, 'inserted but to scandalise the Lord Craven, soe the whole deposition is utterly untrue'.[5] After the sequestration had taken effect, it was clear to Reyley that his life would be in danger if he left England, and so he petitioned Parliament for relief on the grounds that, since his service to the state in witnessing against Craven, he was unable to continue serving in foreign armies, not daring to live abroad. The Committee for Trade and Foreign Affairs considered his petition and duly recommended that he be given £100 in compensation.

Having heard the case, the commissioners were unsure whether they had the authority to order the seizure of Craven's estates, and they referred the matter to the Council of State. Was it or was it not a sequestrable offence for a person living overseas to associate with the King of Scots? The Council of State in turn referred the question to Parliament, which duly considered the matter. The upshot was that on 6 March 1651, Parliament declared that Craven was 'an offender against the Commonwealth of England', and they empowered the commissioners to sequester his estates. A week later, the sequestration committees of Warwickshire, Shropshire, Sussex, Oxfordshire, Middlesex, Herefordshire, Gloucestershire, and London were ordered to seize Craven's estates. Within weeks the Committee for Compounding had begun obtaining valuations of his manors, but even so they received a letter on 30 April ordering them to speed up the process as a matter 'of extraordinary use and concernment to the exigencies of the State'. Over the next year the county committees proceeded to survey all of Craven's properties.[6]

In his absence abroad, Craven had entrusted the management of his estates to his cousin and heir Sir William Craven of Lenchwyke, whose wife Elizabeth was the sister of the Lord General, Lord Fairfax, and to his agent James Pickering, who lived at Hamstead Marshall. Their first action was to draw up an urgent petition to Parliament requesting that the sequestration be suspended while an express was sent to Craven informing him of the turn of events. Their attempt to present the petition was refused, but on 3 July, four months after the sequestration order had been made, Parliament voted that Lord Craven should be summoned to appear before them in two months' time, on 3 September 1651, 'to make answer to all such matters as shall be objected against him on the behalf of the Commonwealth of England'.

While all this was going on the Queen of Bohemia had decided to challenge the power of Parliament to revoke grants made under the Great Seal of England, or at least to challenge its right to withhold the arrears due up to the date of the revocation. In the spring of 1651 she asked her agent in England, Sir Abraham Williams, to send documents supporting her case and then, with Craven's help, she drew up a statement of the grants made to her and the substantial arrears due. Adding up all the allowances granted by her father and brother, the total came to over £100,000. Armed with this lengthly list she approached the States General, then in the middle of treaty negotiations with the English Parliament, asking that it should request the addition of a clause securing the payment of her arrears and petitioning for the continuance of her pension until such time as she received her jointure from the Palatinate.

The States General appointed commissioners to put the Queen of Bohemia's case to Walter Strickland and Oliver St John, the English ambassadors who had arrived in the Hague in March in an attempt to negotiate an alliance between the two Commonwealths. The Hague was a strongly royalist town and the ambassadors went in fear of their lives, only venturing out under armed guard. Given that Elizabeth had forbidden her household from associating with them and had announced that anyone who disobeyed her would be kicked downstairs, it was hardly surprising that they were unsympathetic to her plight. They became even less sympathetic after Elizabeth's son Prince Edward, on a visit from Paris, publicly insulted them in their carriage, causing something of a diplomatic furore. 'You will have heard,' Elizabeth wrote to Charles II, 'of the high business between my son and their pretended ambassadors, whom Ned called by their true names.' The ambassadors complained to the States General, and Edward was forced to make an awkward apology. Still smarting from the insult, they threatened to leave the Hague unless the Prince absented himself from the country, and after a week he agreed to continue his journey to Heidelberg to visit his brother and sisters. For the Winter Queen the incident had put paid to any hope of a favourable hearing, and no one would have been surprised when the ambassadors sent an indignant letter to the States General refusing even to forward her petition to Parliament.

Unaware at first of the threat to his estates, Craven had gone to Heidelberg, attempting as usual to mediate between Elizabeth and her eldest son. He was there in February 1651, and again in April. As soon as news arrived of the proceedings against Craven, Charles Louis wrote to his agent in Holland, Peter de Groot, asking him to request the help of the States General in interceding with the English Parliament. De Groot did as he was asked; in a detailed letter to the States General he pointed out the injustice of the accusations against Craven and of the hasty vote in Parliament in favour of sequestration, and he also emphasised Craven's long service to the United Provinces and how bountifully he had distributed his means in the country.

The response was sympathetic, and the States General sent a letter to Parliament to the effect that due to the exigencies of the times they could not allow Craven, as the senior English colonel in the States Army, to go to London. In consequence of the armies of the Elector of Brandenburg and the Duke of Neuburg being upon their frontiers, they had been obliged to issue an order that all officers in their service should re-join their regiments, 'in obedience to which order the said Lord Craven has come from Germany', and they therefore requested that he might be represented by an attorney.[7] At the same time, Craven sent a brief petition to Parliament protesting his innocence and asking that he be given an opportunity to clear his name. But although this petition was delivered to the Speaker, it was never read. The Queen of Bohemia, too, exerted what influence she had, asking the States General to request the Council of State in Whitehall to reconsider their judgment.

Back in the Hague, Craven addressed a new petition to Parliament, only for the officer entrusted with it to fall sick and die. In October he sent yet another petition, with plenty of signed duplicates this time in case the original disappeared. The accusations against him were utterly unjust, he wrote. He had not travelled to Breda in order to visit Charles II; on the contrary, he had been there in the service of the Prince of Orange. Falconer was the sole witness in the material part of the accusation, that is, the allegation that the petition had contained the words 'barbarous and inhuman rebels', and his testimony was not to be trusted. Was it really credible that he, Craven, would risk his estate by signing such a petition? On the contrary, he had done nothing to offend Parliament, and he respectfully urged its members to reverse the vote declaring him an offender. The vote after all had been taken before formal charges had even been drawn up, giving him no chance at all to mount a defence.

There were many members of Parliament who agreed that an injustice had been committed, and a number who worked hard on Craven's behalf. They included regicides such as Sir Gilbert Pickering and even Craven's troublesome Berkshire neighbour, Colonel Henry Marten. These two, together with James Chaloner, spent many months attempting without success to present Craven's new petition, but it was not until the following June (1652) that it was eventually read in Parliament.[8] By this time new evidence had come to light to support their case. Colonel Drury, one of the two officers who had presented the petition in Breda, had confirmed that it had merely been an appeal for financial aid and had not contained the words 'barbarous and inhuman rebels'. Falconer had proposed that the offending words should be added but the other petitioners had decided against including such uncivil language. Drury even had the first draft of the original petition in his son's exercise book, written in Falconer's own handwriting. Craven's agents presented the fresh information to Parliament in the form of a new petition, but it was never read; instead, on 22 June 1652, Parliament voted by thirty-three votes to thirty-one in favour of proceeding with the sequestration.

Petitions having so far proved useless, Craven's lawyers decided that their only course was to 'resort to the good laws of England for remedy'; to discredit Falconer by proving the falsity of his accusations. If they could demolish his credibility in a court of law, the case against Craven would surely collapse. Accordingly, on 12 July an indictment of perjury was issued against Falconer and delivered to the grand jury at the Guildhall. A date was duly set for the trial and the chief witness for the prosecution, Colonel Drury, was issued with a subpoena. Craven's lawyers, however, hadn't reckoned on the skulduggery of the other side. When the trial opened it was found that Drury had disappeared, and proceedings had to be adjourned until he could be produced. It soon transpired that Captain George Bishop, secretary of the Committee for Examinations, was behind Drury's disappearance. Drury had mentioned to Bishop that he had been issued with a subpoena to give evidence, whereupon Bishop had promptly had him arrested and imprisoned for a week until the grand jury session had ended. The reason for Bishop's action soon became clear. When Craven's estates were put up for sale a few months later, Bishop successfully bid for a large part of them, getting them at a knock-down price.

On 3 August 1652, Parliament approved a bill authorising the sale by the narrow margin of twenty-three to twenty, and the same day a commission was appointed to dispose of his estates. His agents argued that some of Craven's property, including Combe Abbey, worth £2,500 a year, had been entailed and so could not legally be included in the confiscation. But this argument was rejected, and Combe Abbey too was added to the list of property to be sequestered.

Events had moved quickly. At the beginning of September, Craven wrote to William Lenthall, Speaker of the Commons, enclosing a fresh petition in which he offered to pay a substantial fine in return for being allowed to keep his estates. For most owners of delinquent estates, this was the only way of saving their property, and in the end almost all royalists paid up. When Craven's offer was debated, Lord Fairfax urged acceptance. The proposed fine could be considerable and, Fairfax pointed out, Parliament had already received £30,000 out of Craven's rents and personal estate, not to mention the damage done to his woods. Sir William Craven and Sir Edmund Sawyer waited at the door of the House to give assurances that the money could be speedily raised. But as ill luck would have it, as the debate was getting underway the Danish ambassador arrived to take his leave, and after he had left the House voted not to resume the debate. Fairfax's proposal was defeated, and on 29 October Parliament voted by thirty-four votes to thirty that there should be no further debate on Craven's petition. The surveys of his estates were nearing completion, and days were appointed for the sales.

As a whole the sales of delinquents' lands by the Commonwealth represented a huge transfer of land ownership, comparable in scale with the sale of monastic lands in the previous century. The total value of Craven's estates sold in the first few months of 1653 came to almost £250,000. Many of the purchasers, in an early example of parliamentary sleaze, were MPs who had voted for the sale and then bought estates at knock-down prices. According to Craven's agents, nine MPs contracted to buy £5,000 a year of his estate. They included the prominent regicide Lord Grey of Groby, who purchased Combe Abbey using his wife's jointure (apparently for a negligible sum although it was worth £3,000 a year); Sir Michael Livesey, who bought Boddington Manor in Gloucestershire; William Cawley, the member for Midhurst, who purchased Wartling Manor in Sussex; and Thomas Mackworth, the member for Ludlow, who bought Stanton Lacy Manor in Shropshire.

Other purchasers were London merchants or army officers such as Colonel George Joyce, the man who had arrested Charles I, and Colonel Bishop himself—although Bishop in the end withdrew his name after criticism mounted over the injustice of the proceedings. Some buyers probably acted as agents for others, so that the ultimate purchaser is not known. Such was probably the case with Hamstead Marshall Manor, which was bought by a certain William Field and three others.[9]

As for Drury House, it was taken over by the government committee responsible for the sales of delinquent estates, which accordingly became known as the Drury House Trustees. The rooms must have been filled to overflowing with endless volumes of title deeds, valuations, surveys, registers, court rolls, and receipts. The trustees employed as their cook a poor relation of Lord Craven's, one Mrs Latham, who had long lived rent-free in one of the small houses in the courtyard of the main house, and other houses on the site were leased to trustees.[10]

Many purchasers sold on their property straight away, wanting to make sure of their profit in case the sequestration was reversed. Of all Craven's houses, it was Caversham House that had the saddest fate: it was bought for just £1,500 by its housekeeper, Captain George Vaux, who proceeded to strip the house of anything of value, leaving it derelict.[11] It was a melancholy sight for John Evelyn, who rode past in June 1654 and saw the house in ruins and the nearby woods being felled.

It had been an unedifying business, with the entire case against Craven built on false testimony and the chief witness in his defence forcibly prevented from appearing in court. Many within the ranks of the Commonwealth considered that Craven had been wronged, and in the months following the land sales there were rumours that the sequestration was to be reversed as the result of a peace treaty between the Commonwealth and the United Provinces.[12] But the peace treaty was never signed.

On 20 May 1653, too late to prevent the land sales, Falconer's perjury trial finally began. It took place in Westminster Hall before Lord Chief Justice Rolle and other judges of the Upper Bench. The case had become something of a *cause célèbre* and the proceedings attracted large crowds. This time Colonel Drury was not prevented from attending. In court he read out the draft of the original petition. It was, just as he had said, nothing more than a request for relief from penury. Falconer had signed the petition, but once he realised they were not going to get any money out of the King he had vowed to make trouble. 'I will go into England,' he had said, 'and do all the mischief I can.' He had been paid £80 for testifying against Craven. The prosecution had no difficulty in proving that Falconer was an out-and-out rogue. Though he came from a good family and had attended Hart's Hall, Oxford, he had squandered his own inheritance, and then his brother's as well. A few years earlier he had been committed to Aylesbury Gaol under suspicion of felony, robbery, and murder, and since the episode in Breda he had been committed to Newgate on suspicion of felony. He had also once been bound over before the magistrates for drinking a health to the devil on his knees in Petersfield; he had vowed that the family of Falconer should not be extinct before he had done some infamous act; he had often said that Christ was a bastard and the Virgin Mary a whore. Quite apart from all this he was notorious for swearing, perjury, and blasphemy, and he had once attempted to bugger a man. He had even—horror of horrors—'attempted a fact, worse than all these (if worse can be) here forborne to be mentioned'. The mind boggles!

The other side did their best to defend Falconer. Captain Bishop testified, in a long and rambling speech, that Falconer had done the state useful service as a spy. Furthermore, the witnesses for the defence were more trustworthy than those for the prosecution, some of whom were quite unreasonably prejudiced against Falconer for no other reason than because he had assaulted them. Colonel Drury was nothing but a Papist in arms. As for Captain Brisco, he was notorious for selling his companions for 12 stivers a day by the ingenious method of luring them on board ships moored by the quayside in Amsterdam, whereupon they would be clapped below decks and transported to the plantations. To this the prosecution retorted that it was only a Dutchman who said so. More importantly, the defence had failed to produce any evidence that Craven had been in any way associated with the alleged petition. The result of the trial was never really in doubt. After a hearing which lasted five hours, Falconer was duly convicted of perjury and incarcerated in the Upper Bench Prison.

During the period of the trial, Craven's agents issued what amounted to press releases, as well as a pamphlet, *A True and Perfect Narrative of the Several Proceedings in the Case concerning the Lord Craven*, emphasising the iniquity of what had taken place. Bishop countered with his own pamphlet, *The Lord Craven's Case As to the Confiscation of his Estate.*[13] He defended his actions on behalf of the Committee for Examinations and pointed to the flaws in Falconer's perjury trial, adding that the *True and Perfect Narrative* ought more properly to be called an imperfect and deceitful narrative. Most of his own objections, in fact, seemed thoroughly trivial: Drury, for example, had not been imprisoned for five days at all, it had only been for four days, and yes, it might have been true that Falconer had been committed to Newgate, but even honest men were committed falsely. The pamphlet inveighed against Drury, 'a man of no fortune and less reputation,' and Brisco, 'a common cheat, drunkard and an implacable enemy of the commonwealth.' Brisco does seem to have had some very peculiar habits, such as

> [...] baiting mastiff dogs stark naked, without any thing about him or in his hands, and this several times; at one of which a mastiff fastning upon him he bitt off the mastiff's nose, which made the dog cry and run away.

As for Craven, he was 'well known to have very many persons to stickle [lobby] on his behalf,' and despite all that had been said, it was still the case that he had been in close contact with Charles II at Breda.

Something of a propaganda war was fast developing between different factions in Parliament, full of *ad hominem* attacks on the truthfulness of the other side. Craven's supporters countered with the snappily entitled *Reply to a certain pamphlet by an unknown and unknowing author [...] to undeceive those whom that nameless person hath so grossly abused with his falsities, mis-recitals, short recitals and inventions (almost) in every page of his pamphlet*. In outraged tones it complained that the author of *Lord Craven's Case* had used expressions fit only for the disputants of Billingsgate, and it was not surprising that the author had declined to put his name to it. There followed a line-by-line rebuttal of Bishop's allegations. The declaration of August 1649 had only referred to Ireland. The vote of confiscation had been illegal. And Falconer, of course, had been utterly discredited.

It was clear that the process of sequestration had been legally dubious, and there seemed good reason to hope that the order could be annulled. In August 1653, Craven's agents presented yet another petition, urging that the sequestration be reversed now that the sole witness against Craven had been convicted of perjury. In the petition Craven repeated that he had never acted against Parliament; furthermore, the recently dissolved Parliament had twice voted against including his estates in the bill of sale, and the vote had only finally been carried by three votes, there being only forty-seven members present. The following month, after returning from yet another trip to Heidelberg, Craven seems to have paid a short and discreet visit to England to organise his campaign. 'My lord Craven is returned out of Germany,' wrote Sir Robert Stone in an intercepted letter, 'stayed here [in the Hague] for but two nights, and is gone for England.'[14]

In December 1653 the case was reopened again, and in February 1654 Craven petitioned Cromwell, who was sympathetic and referred the matter back to the Committee for Compounding. A partial victory came at the beginning of September when Cromwell ordered that further sales of Craven's property should be stayed—although the vast majority had already gone under the hammer—and that his case should be referred to the new Parliament which was about to assemble. At the request of the Queen of Bohemia, Henry Lawrence, Lord President of the Council of State, used his influence to argue Craven's case. When Parliament opened a few days later Craven's latest petition was referred to a committee, accompanied by another wave of lobbying by both sides in rival newspapers. After hearing a counter-petition by the purchasers of Craven's property, the committee launched into lengthy debate, Craven's counsel giving precedents for unfair judgments being reversed in succeeding parliaments, while the counsel for the purchasers insisted that the Act of Parliament which persuaded them to buy Craven's lands had been valid.

Craven's counsel was the eminent jurist Sir Matthew Hale, who had defended both Strafford and Laud. Speaking in defence of Craven, Hale

> [...] pleaded with that force of argument that the then attorney general [Sir Edmund Prideaux] threatened him for appearing against the government; to whom he answered, 'he was pleading in defence of those laws which they declared they would maintain and preserve; and he was doing his duty to his client, so that he was not to be daunted with threatenings.'

Craven's supporters now brought out yet another pamphlet, *The Lord Craven's Case Briefly Stated*.[15] And so the legal battle and accompanying propaganda war raged on.

'I shall have neither bread, nor meat, nor candles'

The sudden disappearance of most of Craven's income was felt soon enough in the Hague. At the end of May 1653, after noting a few final payments to the Queen of Bohemia and a large bag of 200 ducats provided for Craven's own use, the entries in Ziegler's account book came to an abrupt halt. Instead, Ziegler set about assessing the state of Craven's finances. He drew up three lists: one listing the bonds from Craven's many creditors (worth some 25,000 livres), a second detailing the bonds from Lord John's estate, and a third listing the silver plate in Craven's coffers, with the weight of each piece carefully recorded. Taking all these into account, Craven still had fairly substantial assets, but as a matter of urgency he would have to reduce his expenses. Not least, he would have to reduce the size of his own household, and Ziegler therefore drew up a list of all Craven's valets and domestics, with details of their wages and benefits. There were ten in all, ranging from Benjamin Carter, on 160 livres a year, and Edward Lloyd the cook, on 150 livres a year, to a groom, a driver, and a lackey, all on 60 or 70 livres a year. Some of the servants were on board wages, but all received a new suit of clothes once a year.[1]

In his reduced circumstances Craven would have to retrench drastically, and that meant little or no money to subsidise the court of the Queen of Bohemia. Fortunately, recognising that they had an obligation to support the woman who was still regarded as a heroine by many Protestants, Parliament agreed to grant her a pension of £2,000 a year, a useful sum but small enough compared with the £12,000 a year she had received up until 1649. As for Elizabeth, she was engaged in an increasingly vitriolic argument with her eldest son. She was well aware that his revenues were limited, but she argued that she should at least receive 3,000 rixdollars a month. She had already reduced her household as much as possible, she wrote, but she could not live off air. The other day she had even been without turf for her fires. A steady stream of demands for money travelled from the Hague to Heidelberg, with now and then small and irregular payments coming the other way. Elizabeth Benger in her biography of the Queen of Bohemia loyally likened Charles Louis to one of King Lear's ungrateful daughters, cruelly denying their father a single knight. But she was being unfair to Charles Louis, who after all simply had no money to spare.

The thankless role of go-between fell, needless to say, to Craven, who shuttled regularly between Heidelberg and the Hague trying to persuade Charles Louis to pay his mother her jointure and to allow her to take up residence at Fridelsheim or Frankenthal. Charles Louis countered as before that both houses were in a state of ruin and the cost of restoring them would be prohibitive. Instead, he suggested that she should take up residence in the Otto Heinrich wing at Heidelberg Castle.

Money problems were one thing, but quite apart from this the court at the Wassenaer Hof existed in something of a state of chaos. In 1652, in an attempt to improve the regulation of her household, Elizabeth appointed as her steward Sir Charles Cottrell, former master of ceremonies to Charles I, and Cottrell set to work to improve the running of the household. The 'Orders of the House', penned soon after his arrival, note 'disorders crept into this her Court, in that the most part of the servants and domesticks of both sexes, take the liberty to live therein according to theyr fancy.' As the dinner hour approached, the courtyard would become thronged with a crowd of uninvited and often rowdy visitors, 'quarrelling, fighting, roaring, swearing and storming.' The roasts served up to the Queen were all too often 'bloudy, or burnt on the outside', and other meat 'served half sodden'. As for the cellar, it was subject to 'great abuse'. The regular hours imposed for its opening were ignored, and from the time when the cellar doors were opened it was crowded not only by members of the household, but also by total strangers 'come to demand drinke as if it were a publike Taverne'. The English beer in particular simply vanished. In the 'Sylver Chamber', the Queen's silver was apt to 'straggle abroade,' as did many of the 'pyes, tartes, bunnes, sweetmeates, preserves and fruites' left in the kitchen. In cold weather Elizabeth's waiting men were in the habit of sitting around the fire instead of serving at table. The pages, all of them 'children descended from good and noble houses,' were accustomed to 'prate from one table to another' during meals, 'thwart him who have the direction of the said hall,' rush in and out of the room and even fall to fisticuffs. At night the servants were in the habit of inviting friends round to 'passe away the night' in dicing and card-playing, neglecting moreover to 'lock up diligently the Cheese after every Meale, and keep it from the Cats and rats.' The halbardier on watch in the night-time would often go to sleep on duty and 'let the fyre and Candells goe out before he awake.'[2]

Cottrell tried valiantly to bring some much-needed discipline to the running of the household, as well as acting as a further intermediary between Elizabeth and her eldest son. He had little success, and in the winter of 1653 Craven made yet another journey to Heidelberg in an attempt to secure better terms. Elizabeth's letters to him at this period make melancholy reading. On 7 November she wrote gloomily:

I have received and read both your letters, and find little comfort in them concerning my own particular; it may be my next will tell you I have no more to eat: this is no parable but the certain truth, for there is no money nor credit for any; if this week, if there be none found, I shall have neither meat, nor bread, nor candles, and know my son would have me to be rid of all my jewels because he thinks he doth not deserve so well of me that he should share in them after my death, but that will doe him no good for I will leave to my children what he owes me, which will trouble him more then my jewels be worth [...] I believe he means to starve me out of this place, as they do blocked towns. I know he may do it and has already begun pretty well, but he will have as little comfort as honour by it, for if I be forced by ill usage to go, I shall be very ill company there. All I can desire you to tell him is that for the next week for aught I know I shall neither eat bread, nor flesh, nor have candles.[3]

The poverty of Elizabeth's present life in the Hague was hard to bear, but she was unlikely to find residence in Heidelberg very agreeable either. Charles Louis, perhaps regretting having offered his mother accommodation, waxed lyrical on the disadvantages of the rooms in the Otto Heinrich wing, and on the lack of education and manners of the locals.

I can name few men who are conversible, and the women as little; and what they intimate is still the worst part. Those that are for the French have nothing from them but their cloaths, good letters ill spelled, and the *afféteries* of the Marais, from whence they have all their modes.

As for the pro-Spanish faction, they were 'as dull and impertinent as can be'. Although he painted a grim enough picture, Elizabeth was not deterred, and the result of Craven's shuttle diplomacy was that she agreed with bad grace to move to Heidelberg after all. Perhaps the rooms in the castle would be adequate, though she insisted that she should have two sitting rooms close to her bedroom. However, she was certainly not prepared to travel just yet, when the weather was so atrocious. 'I cannot conceive my son can imagine that I should think of quitting this place this winter,' she wrote to Craven, 'as you have very well represented to him, nor know how to live here neither, but very poorly, and at every day ready to starve this winter, if he send no better means.' She continued to grumble over her son's refusal to restore her jointure houses, especially Fridelsheim, with its fine garden and vineyard.

I confess I did like the place very well. I pray speak of it; if he be just to me, as he should be, he should rather build that up, and Frankenthal.

The latter town had at last been vacated by the French after the Emperor had ceded them Besançon, but the dower house was still in ruins.

In the end Elizabeth never made it to Heidelberg. Her many creditors in the Hague, getting wind of her planned departure, refused to let her leave without a guarantee that their debts would be paid. Elizabeth decided to apply to the English Parliament. She still refused to have any communication with Cromwell, so instead she wrote to the States General. She explained that she had decided to go and live with her son in Heidelberg and begged them to appeal to Cromwell for help in settling her debts. A petition was accordingly sent to the Protector, stressing the desperate state of the tradespeople of the Hague who had continued to give her credit. Elizabeth wrote to her son that she would travel to Heidelberg in the spring, and work began on renovating suitable apartments in the castle. Craven promised to accompany her to Heidelberg, where he had already acquired a substantial house from Charles Louis, as well as the titular office of Master of the Horse to the Elector Palatine.

Parliament had little sympathy for Elizabeth's plight. Not only did it refuse to settle her debts, but it even cancelled the pension of £2,000 per year granted just a year or two earlier. In despair, Elizabeth appealed again to the States General for enough money to satisfy her creditors and allow her to leave the Hague. But the States General, unwilling to offend the Protectorate, turned this request down as well, and Elizabeth was forced to remain in the Hague after all. Ominous cracks were beginning to appear in the walls of the Wassenaer Hof, and the beams showed signs of dry rot; the fine gilded leather wall hangings had become tarnished, and the silk panels were fraying.[4] One by one the Queen's jewels went into pawn in exchange for meat and other necessities, even the great table diamond which had belonged to Henry Prince of Wales and the fine diamond necklace which had been worn by Elizabeth I. The Queen of Bohemia begged her eldest son to redeem these pieces before they were sold by the pawnbroker, but to no avail. Even Elizabeth's own wedding ring went to pawn. She longed to leave the Hague during the hot weather to get away from the dirt of the Wassenaer Hof, and to get some peace too from the creditors who were continually pressing her, but she had no means to do so.

For five years Cottrell struggled to bring a semblance of order to the Winter Queen's undisciplined household. His wages were hopelessly in arrears, but the final straw came when he ordered a carriage from the stables only to find that Margaret Broughton, one of the Queen's maids of honour, had taken the last remaining carriage to do some shopping for her mistress. He left to work instead as an advisor to the young Duke of Gloucester. Margaret Broughton remained, serving her mistress without complaint 'like a spaniel', although in five years she had only received one years' wages.[5]

Even with his now limited means, Craven contrived to help support the household as best he could. Elizabeth wrote optimistically to her eldest son in the summer of 1654:

> I have great need of wine, I have no money to buy it and this I have is my Lord Craven's. I pray send some as quick as you can for all you sent is gone.

Charles Louis did as his demanding mother asked, but the wine he sent did not meet with her approval: 'The last two times he sent me wine that was stark naught,' she complained to Sir Edward Nicholas the following summer.[6] One cannot help feeling a little sorry for Charles Louis, trying his best with limited resources to keep his mother supplied with food and drink. He sent regular supplies of corn, wormwood wine, and cinnamon water.

But wine was far from the only problem. Elizabeth could not in all conscience dismiss servants without giving them their arrears of wages, but she did not have the money to do so. 'My poor servants are almost starved for lack of board wages,' she complained. 'Some days I have not turf, some times candles nor drink.' Aggrieved tradesmen and women appeared with worrying frequency in the Queen's outer chambers to demand payment. There were visits from tavern keepers, 'the Woman of the Spanish Armes', and 'she of "The Golden Head"', as well as a baker, a poulterer, and a chandler. On one occasion, a furious butcher's wife travelled to Heidelberg to demand payment from Charles Louis. By the spring of 1656 Elizabeth had reduced her household to twelve men in livery, but had to beg Charles Louis to send her allowance promptly so she could pay them.

Still, despite the lack of money Elizabeth nevertheless contrived to lead a busy social life. In April 1654 she and Lord Craven travelled to Rotterdam for the christening of the son of Sir Gelyn Quirinson, groom of the bedchamber to Charles II, and his wife Aletta Carey. The Queen of Bohemia stood godmother, and the baby's godfathers were Craven and that amiable old courtier Lord George Goring, now Earl of Norwich.

In 1655, the four English regiments in the States Army were amalgamated into a single unit, which became known as the Holland Regiment. Its command was given to Colonel John Cromwell, a cousin of Oliver Cromwell but a man of strong royalist sympathies; so much so, in fact, that he obtained permission from Charles II to change his name from Cromwell to Williams, 'instead of that which shall be eternally in execration by all Englishmen'.[7] Craven, having relinquished his colonelcy, became involved instead in a series of abortive schemes centred around Prince Rupert, who was tired of inaction and casting around for new employment. Two years earlier there had been discussions with the Scottish Presbyterians over plans for a possible expedition to Scotland led by Rupert, but the Presbyterians insisted that he would have to be accompanied by people who were 'eminent for righteousness'. Craven was one of those who received the Presbyterian stamp of approval, but in the event this scheme, like so many others, came to nothing. In the spring of 1655 a new opportunity for action presented itself, this time in Italy. Warfare between its city states was more or less endemic in this period, and Duke Francis I of Modena, a small state to the east of Milan, was keen to strengthen his army. He invited Rupert to recruit and command a body of troops for defence against the Papal States.

It would be a modest enterprise for a soldier of Rupert's rank and fame, but at least it would give him something to do, and he decided to accept the offer.

Under the terms of the contract he would raise one regiment of cavalry and two of infantry, as well as a body of French troops. He offered the commands of the three regiments to Craven, Charles Gerard, and Sir Edward Massey, and set about recruiting the troops. Over the summer, however, trouble soon reared its head. Recruitment in Germany, still exhausted by the Thirty Years War, was slow, and soon Mazarin began to make difficulties, refusing to allow the proposed French troops to serve under Rupert's command. Then it became apparent that the proposed army was not being raised for defence against the Papal States at all; in fact Duke Francis planned to use it against Spanish-controlled Milan. The whole enterprise seemed increasingly dubious, and when Charles II begged Rupert in July to abandon all other commitments the Prince decided to withdraw from the Modena scheme. Instead he attached himself to the Stuart court, which by now had moved to Cologne.

Charles's desire to have Rupert at his side was prompted by developments in England, where Cromwell's arbitrary rule was coming under increasing strain. Hopes were beginnning to rise for a restoration of the monarchy; various plots were afoot in England, and there was talk of a new campaign against Cromwell based in Scotland. In Charles's court the air was thick with schemes, vigorously canvassed by the 'swordsmen', the faction which clustered around Rupert. This group included men such as Charles Gerard, whose fertile mind brimmed with plans for assassinating the Protector, fomenting risings in England, and making alliances with the Presbyterians in Scotland. Another faction, centred upon Edward Hyde, the Lord Chancellor, argued against such rash undertakings. The shifting arguments at the faction-ridden court were faithfully relayed to John Thurloe, Cromwell's capable spymaster, by Henry Manning, a Commonwealth spy who had arrived in Cologne in January claiming to be a royalist recently released from imprisonment in the Tower.

In July 1655, the Scottish Presbyterian leader Lord Balcarres arrived in Cologne for discussions with Charles II and the swordsmen, who on this occasion included Craven. Manning reported that

> Prince Rupert came on Sunday. The swordsmen endeavour to gain the Presbyterians, the Prince declaring himself a Calvinist as are the rest of his family. The Prince, Wilmot, Gerard, and Balcarres, have had a private meeting with Lord Craven, who appears not in public here because of his pretensions with you.[8]

Craven's involvement in these plots was probably limited to using his many contacts in England to pass on information. His attempts at secrecy were understandable given that he was still fighting hard to have the sequestration of his estates reversed, and he was taking a distinct risk in associating himself with the plotters. A week later, Manning reported that Gerard and Craven had left Cologne and were planning to meet Newcastle, Massey, and others to discuss new plots against the Commonwealth. Thurloe should make sure of having Gerard followed because he planned to assassinate the Protector. 'Remember I have warned you of the Park,' he concluded darkly.[9]

In the end little was to come of all this cloak-and-dagger plotting, in part because Thurloe's formidable intelligence network was highly effective in disrupting such activities. However, it was not long before Manning was unmasked. Edward Hyde was using his own intelligence network to check up on the supposed royalist, and towards the end of the year Manning's correspondence was intercepted at Antwerp and his treachery exposed. On 15 December he was taken to a wood outside Cologne and shot.

At the Wassenaer Hof, Elizabeth managed to subsist thanks to the long-suffering tradesmen of the Hague. Her unused country palace at Rhenen began to decay, its concierge, appointed by Charles Louis, proving to be a drunkard, 'the veriest beast in the world and knave'. Elizabeth's niece, the Princess of Orange, stopped there for a night in November 1655 and told her aunt that 'she had a minde to crie, to see the house so spoiled'.[10] Elizabeth urged her son to sell the house, and ordered the concierge to bring all the furniture and paintings to the Wassenaer Hof. When some of them eventually appeared, she found that even the gold and silver lace from her bed hangings had been stolen.

Things improved a little in the summer of 1655, when Elizabeth's irregular income from the Palatinate was supplemented by 1,000 guilders a month from the States General for one year to enable her to pay off some of her creditors. Elizabeth was never one to be downcast for long, and she continued to write copious and cheery letters to her many correspondents. In March 1655 she wrote to the elderly Lord Finch:

> I did not heare you were dead, wherefore I hope you promise not to die till you let me know it, but you must also stay till I give you leave to dye, which will not be till we meet a shooting somewhere, but where that is, God knows best.[11]

A gossipy letter to Charles II in December gives news of an unnamed countess who was notorious for cheating at cards:

> The peaking countess is now by me, and desires me to say some good of her to you. Good I cannot, but ill I can; for she sinns more Sodome and Gomora like in playing at cards then we did at the maske.[12]

The peaking countess was probably the Countess of Löwenstein, Elizabeth's eccentric childhood friend Elizabeth Dudley, who for many years had been one of her maids of honour. Cheating at cards was evidently rife at the Wassenaer Hof, but perhaps the countess repented; soon afterwards she became increasingly devout, converting to Quakerism and preaching every day in a tub.

Elizabeth's zest for life was undiminished; her letters were full of gossip about plays and fancy-dress balls. Christmas and Kermesse were the festive seasons at the Hague, when the Lange Voorhout was lined with booths and the Wassenaer Hof thronged with merrymakers dancing till five in the morning. The winter of 1655 was distinguished by a ballet arranged to entertain Elizabeth's niece.

> Our Dutch ministers sayde nothing against it in the pulpet, but a little french preacher, Carre, said in his sermon, we had committed as great a sinne as that of Sodom and Gomorra, which sett all the church a-laughing.

Evidently the congregation at the English church was not unduly puritanical, and nor, for that matter, was Elizabeth herself. 'We have gotten a new diversion of little plays after supper,' she wrote. 'I hope the godlie will preach against it also.'

Charles Louis, doing his best to nurse his ruined lands back to some semblance of health, was still unable to pay his mother enough to suit her needs, and she was still complaining vociferously. 'I cannot give my servants their wages,' she wrote despairingly; 'I am forced to sell that little remnant of plate I have.' Most of her jewels had gone now. Rupert, like his mother, was short of money, and like her he had been engaged for many years in a furious argument with Charles Louis. According to long-standing German custom, Rupert was entitled to a handsome appanage, or annuity, from the Palatinate. In 1654 the Elector had managed to scrape together enough to give his brother a limited sum, but relations between the two soon broke down, and Rupert appealed to the Emperor to compel his brother to give him his due. Matters were put on hold with the Emperor's death in April 1657, and Rupert instead appealed to Craven, hoping that an objective third party would succeed where he had failed. Craven travelled to Heidelberg to discuss the matter with the Elector, only to receive the same answer: there was simply no money available.

The finances of the Winter Queen, by contrast, were steadily improving. In 1657, the States General agreed to pay her a pension of 10,000 livres a month; it was a generous sum, about ten times the amount they had granted her two years earlier. Contentment at the Wassenaer Hof, however, was short-lived. The household was very small now; out of Elizabeth's daughters, only Louise had remained with her mother. But early in the morning of 19 December 1657, Louise suddenly disappeared. A frantic search found a letter addressed to her mother announcing that she had been received into the Catholic Church and had decided to flee from the Hague to a secret destination in order to avoid having to take the sacrament on Christmas Day according to the Protestant rite.

Elizabeth was devastated. All her life she had regarded the Catholic Church with horror, and when Edward had converted she had written extravagantly that she wished he had died instead. Earlier she had feared that Rupert too was in danger of conversion, although in the event he had remained true to the faith in which he had been brought up. Her first thought was that, as with Edward's conversion, a secret romance must have lain behind it; indeed, wild rumours to that effect were flying all over the Hague. The following day, a further search revealed letters from the Princess of Hohenzollern which made all clear. Louise had slipped out of the house unnoticed and boarded a boat provided by the Princess. By stages she had made her way to Antwerp, where she intended to enter a convent of Carmelite nuns. Accusations flew back and forth, Elizabeth blaming the Princess of Hohenzollern for what had occurred, the Princess retaliating by spreading rumours that Louise had left home to avoid scandal because she was pregnant, rumours which Louise indignantly denied. Prince Edward, it turned out, had been closely involved in Louise's flight, and in April he arranged for her to travel to Paris, where she stayed in the convent of Chaillot. The following year she took the veil in the convent of Maubuisson, where she continued her painting; although she did not take the religious side of things too seriously, she ultimately became an abbess.

The household at the Wassenaer Hof now consisted of just the Queen of Bohemia and Lord Craven, who after the loss of most of his income had in all probability moved in with her. In later years a belief grew up that there had been a secret marriage between the two, either during these years or else after her return to England. There is, however, not a single contemporary reference to such a marriage, in a period when rumours were rife about secret marriages between Henrietta Maria and Lord Jermyn, and even between Anne of Austria and Cardinal Mazarin. Parliamentary scandal-mongers would have been quick to pounce on any hint that Lord Craven's motives for helping the Queen of Bohemia were more than simply disinterested.

In fact Elizabeth seems to have regarded Craven as not much more than a useful friend, though close enough to be subject to her habitual gentle teasing. Once she kept back some cases of oranges which had been meant for Rupert. 'I believe Lord Craven will tell you how much ado he had to save your part from me,' she wrote to Rupert, 'for I made him believe that I would take one of your cases for my niece and the Prince of Orange. I did it to vex him.'

The apostasy of Louise was soon followed by better news from her youngest sister. Sophie's quest for a husband was showing signs of success. The first serious candidate was the King of Sweden's brother, Adolphus John. Negotiations were quite far advanced when it was realised that the King of Sweden was against the match. For Sophie, it was a relief not to have to marry someone to whom she had conceived a strong aversion. 'He had a disagreeable face,' she wrote in her memoirs, 'with a long pointed chin like a shoehorn.'[13] He was also reputed to have beaten his first wife. But, with the example of her spinster sisters hanging over her, Sophie was determined to agree to the next proposal. So when one came from Duke George William of Brunswick-Lüneberg, 'My answer was not that of a heroine of romance, for I unhesitatingly said "Yes".'[14] George William, however, had only consented to matrimony in return for the promise of a pension. He was enjoying his dissipated bachelor existence in Venice, and so suggested that his brother, Ernest Augustus, should marry Sophie instead; he would be perfectly happy as long as he could keep his pension. Charles Louis took this as an insult. Negotiations stalled, but Sophie told her brother honestly that a good establishment was all she cared for, and that if this was to be secured by marrying the younger brother she would be quite content. So the marriage was agreed. 'In the present condition of our Familie,' wrote Charles Louis to his mother, 'we must be satisfied to take hold of what we can.'[15]

So on 17 October 1658, Sophie was married to Ernest Augustus in the chapel of Heidelberg Castle. Charles Louis wrote to his mother that, owing to the great expense of the wedding, he would be unable to send her much money for the present. Sophie left Heidelberg to join her husband in Hanover. The following year she came to stay with her mother in the Hague, bringing with her her niece Elizabeth Charlotte, or 'Liselotte', the daughter of Charles Louis and his now discarded wife Charlotte of Hesse-Cassel. Charles Louis was now living with his mistress, Louise von Degenfeld, and Sophie, who had grown very attached to her niece, gained Charles Louis's permission to adopt her. Sophie was amused to find that the Queen of Bohemia, who had never much cared for children, became besotted with her granddaughter.

Craven's friends in England, meanwhile, had continued their vigorous lobbying on his behalf. Their case was helped by the fact that Falconer's testimony had by now been discredited. In April 1655, still incarcerated in the Upper Bench Prison, he had made a deathbed confession of his wrongdoing. He had asked for a clergyman to be summoned in the person of an old university friend by the name of James Langley, the minister of St George's Church in Southwark. Falconer confessed that he had given false testimony against Craven; Langley urged him to put his confession in writing, whereupon Falconer asked for ink and paper and wrote down details of how he had perjured himself, and following this Langley gave him communion.

In March 1657 yet another petition by Craven was read in Parliament, and in May the House of Commons at long last resumed its consideration of the case. Craven had retained as his counsel the highly able lawyer Heneage Finch, the future Lord Chancellor and first Earl of Nottingham. Finch had not got far, however, before it was pointed out that there was no counsel present for the purchasers of Craven's estates, and the hearing was postponed once more. It was not until January 1658 that proceedings at last resumed. In his diary the parliamentarian Thomas Burton recorded that

> Finch did open the case, and managed the business with singular dexterity, wit, and applause; and in my opinion it is a case full of equity, and calls loudly on us for justice.

Finch began by calling Langley as a witness of Falconer's confession, and Langley duly told the House how Falconer had made his deathbed confession and had written down full details of how he had perjured himself for lucre and gain. Langley had never seen a man 'shed more tears, or undergo more racks of conscience, or lay himself more open in prayer.'

The case seemed to be going well, but yet again proceedings had to be adjourned when no counsel appeared either for the Commonwealth or the purchasers, and the dissolution of Parliament a few days later brought proceedings to a halt yet again.[16]

Captain Bishop's conduct in securing false testimony against Craven had by this time come under vitriolic attack from another quarter. Bishop had become a Quaker and had returned to his native Bristol, and there he became embroiled in a violent war of words with the Presbyterian minister Ralph Farmer. The original cause of the quarrel was Farmer's outrage at the behaviour of James Naylor, a Quaker who had ridden into Bristol on a donkey in October 1656 in a re-enactment of Christ's entry into Jerusalem. Farmer regarded this as an outrageous blasphemy and, in a pamphlet with the resounding title *Sathan inthron'd in his chair of pestilence*, he denounced both the escapade itself and Bishop's involvement in it. Bishop's conduct in Lord Craven's case attracted Farmer's especial opprobrium; he accused Bishop of bribing Falconer to falsify his statement and of adding lines to it himself.[17] Bishop joined battle with his own pamphlet, *The Throne of Truth exalted over the Powers of Darkness: From whence is judged the mouth of Ralph Farmer, an unclean and bloodthirsty priest of Bristol*. In it Bishop denied all the charges and threw doubt on Falconer's supposed deathbed repentance. He admitted that he had contracted for part of Craven's estate; and what if he had, he asked defiantly. However, out of concern for honest testimony he had withdrawn, and had not bought any part or parcel of the estate. He absolutely denied any suggestion that he had bribed Falconer to give false testimony.

Farmer thundered back with another pamphlet, *The Imposter Dethroned, or the Quakers' Throne of Truth detected to be Satan's seat of lyes, by way of reply to a quaking and railing pamphlet written by Captain Bishop*. The hugger-mugger (i.e. clandestine) sequestration of Craven's estate was tantamount to club law (i.e. government by violence), he wrote. Drury's arrest was a disgrace, and Bishop's defence of his conduct was so inadequate that it was no surprise only a handful of copies of his pamphlet had been printed; that way people would not see the weakness of his arguments. But now Parliament had reopened the case, and Farmer sincerely hoped that it would right the injustice done to Craven before it became the sin of the nation and so 'draw a curse upon the whole for the iniquity of a few'.

Craven, meanwhile, had briefly taken up arms again, this time in Denmark. The Danish King was in urgent need of reinforcements to help defend Copenhagen against the Swedish Army, which in a lightning campaign had captured the whole of Denmark except for its capital. Craven was a veteran of many sieges, but until now always as a besieger rather than as one of the besieged. Now, after the lifting of the Swedish blockade, a Dutch regiment with a sizeable English contingent was hastily dispatched to Copenhagen to support the defenders. In addition to Craven, the regiment included his friend Sir Robert Stone and Stone's nephew Edmund Andros, who had come to the Hague in 1651 after the fall of Guernsey and became apprenticed to Stone. Young and talented, Andros was to become a close associate of Craven, who served as his patron and forwarded his career. The siege of Copenhagen was a desperate affair, with the city walls defended by a scratch force of students and artisans and the outer works held by professional soldiers. In the second week of February 1659, a Swedish assault was successfully repulsed and the siege lifted.

By this time a new Parliament had assembled in London, and in April 1659 Craven secured permission to come and present a new petition in person. The permission came with a proviso that he must attend Parliament within six days of landing; that he must agree to do nothing prejudicial to Parliament while in England; and that after six months he would return to his charge in Holland. In August his new petition was read, but all that was decided was that a committee would investigate how much of his estate had not yet been sold, and that provision might be made for a comfortable subsistence for him. In September his leave to remain was extended until December. It was not until March 1660 that an order was made to stop the felling of woods on his lands, and finally on 6 June, after all the years of argument and lobbying, the House of Lords ordered that he should be restored to the full possession of his estates.[18] His was a special case. For the most part, those who had acquired sequestered estates were allowed to keep them under the terms of the Indemnity and Oblivion Act, but it was recognised that Craven had been the victim of an injustice.

However, the process of regaining possession was not a simple one. Some purchasers refused to give up their property: Elizabeth Vaux, whose husband had been the housekeeper at Caversham House and had proceeded to buy it and strip it for building materials, refused to give up the house and park until issued with an affidavit. Others did relinquish their houses but quietly walked away with much of the contents, and Craven's agents were authorised to make searches for the missing goods and arms. Some of the purchasers did suffer hardship, including the unfortunate Lady Grey, whose late husband had used her jointure to pay for Combe Abbey; on its restoration she was left destitute and was forced to petition Parliament for relief.[19]

The recent history of Craven's London house, Drury House, had been particularly chequered. Part of the building was still occupied by the Drury House Trustees, but in 1656 the lower floors had been leased to the innovative French Mint engineer Pierre Blondeau. In 1651 Blondeau had arrived in London and had managed to interest Cromwell in a technique which he had developed for producing coins with milled edges, making them very difficult to clip or forge. Because his technique used pressing and milling machines instead of the traditional hammered die, his proposals were strenuously opposed by the officials of the Royal Mint; but eventually Blondeau won the argument, and in August and September 1656 the

Council of State voted him sufficient money to pay for the cost of machinery to coin silver bullion to the amount of £2,000, as well as some gold coinage. Blondeau was keen to keep his technique secret and so refused the offer of premises in the Royal Mint. Drury House must have been an obvious alternative, large enough to house his machines and occupied by a committee whose work was largely complete. Blondeau's machines would require a considerable amount of space, and the Drury House Trustees assigned him the kitchen, larder, coach houses, the three large cellars, each of them 60 feet long and 26 feet wide, and any other rooms which were not being used. It was evidently a big operation, probably involving milling machines on the ground floor powered by horses in the cellar. The resulting coins were of superb quality and much prized by numismatists, the obverse featuring Oliver Cromwell garlanded like a Roman emperor.

A year later, Blondeau expanded his operations into the whole of the ground floor, planning to increase coin production to £10,000 per week. Quite how much coinage was minted is not clear, but Cromwell's death in September 1658 removed Blondeau's chief supporter. Production quickly ceased at Drury House, and the Mint reverted to its traditional method of hammered coinage. Blondeau returned to Paris, but after the Restoration Charles II persuaded him to come back to London, appointing him Engineer to the Mint.[20]

The state of Drury House when Craven regained possession is not hard to imagine. Blondeau had presumably dismantled his coining machines to preserve his secrets, but the lower floors of the house must still have resembled a factory, with the upper floors probably still full of records of delinquent estates. A few days before the House of Lords ruled that his estates should be returned to him, Craven secured a warrant to make an inventory of all the papers in Drury House and elsewhere concerning his property.

The Principal Director of Her Court

In the Hague it had been a period of steadily rising hopes, as the prospects for a restoration of the monarchy grew steadily brighter. On 8 May 1660, Parliament proclaimed Charles the rightful King of England. A week later, he arrived in the Hague to wait for the *Royal Charles,* the hastily renamed flagship which was to convey the new King triumphantly back to his country. He was assigned the finest palace in town, the Mauritshuis, and when he arrived Elizabeth was on its steps to greet him.

For eight days the Hague was the scene of wild and joyous celebrations, 'which could not have been more splendid if all the monarchs of Europe had met there.'[1] Cannon thundered so violently that fears were expressed that the ancient walls of the Buitenhof might collapse. The English royal family dined in public daily to the strains of music, and the Queen of Bohemia was always seated on the King's right hand. 'He useth me more like a Mother than an Aunt,' she wrote happily. The town was thronged with English visitors driving around in coaches singing happily; crowds gathered day and night, bonfires blazed, and bells pealed. The Queen of Bohemia kept open house, and her court was always crowded with visitors wishing to kiss the hand of the lady who for so long had been a Protestant heroine. Among those who went to see her was Samuel Pepys, who found her to be 'a very debonaire, but plain lady'.[2] Elizabeth was now sixty-four, and decades of worry, stress, and penury had taken their toll on her once celebrated looks.

On 23 May the wind changed and the royal party left for the port of Scheveningen. Elizabeth dined in state aboard the *Royal Charles* as the King's guest of honour at a final celebratory banquet before the ship sailed; then she returned to the shore by barge with a promise from her nephew that he would send for her just as soon as he was able. Elizabeth greatly looked forward to returning to England, but more urgently she hoped for some relief from her debts. In February she had had to implore her eldest son to advance her some ready money to pay for the expected influx of visitors. She dispatched her agent, Sir Charles Cottrell, to London to plead her case, and together Cottrell and Craven, still in England to oversee the restitution of his estates, did their best to persuade Parliament to pay off her debts. In September their work was rewarded when Parliament voted £10,000 each to all the royal princesses, followed in December by a vote for another £10,000 for the Queen of Bohemia, as a token of the high esteem in which she was held.

Elizabeth was kept abreast of events in England by a network of old friends. There was no shortage of news, much of it gloomy. In September she was shocked to hear that her favourite nephew, Henry Duke of Gloucester, had died quite suddenly of smallpox. In December, her niece Mary, Princess of Orange, succumbed to the same disease. The Princess had returned to England perfectly fit and healthy just three months earlier, but had seldom left Whitehall during that time. In October came startling news of the secret marriage of Elizabeth's nephew, James, Duke of York, to Anne Hyde, daughter of the Chancellor and former maid of honour to the Princess of Orange. Elizabeth firmly refused to believe that such a base marriage could possibly have taken place, telling her eldest son that he should ignore the scandalous rumours. But when Anne's child was born, eight weeks after the marriage, Elizabeth had to confront the awful truth. On 26 November Craven wrote from London:

> For the present, news is that Mrs Hyde is brought to bed of a boy, which she avows to be the duke's, and he married to her: she is owned in her father's family to be the Duchess of York, but not at Whitehall as yet; but it is very sure that the duke has made her his wife. Your majesty knows it is what I have feared long, although you were not of that opinion.[3]

Still, as soon as she learnt that the King had acknowledged Anne Hyde as his brother's wife, Elizabeth followed suit.

Elizabeth waited in vain for the promised invitation from Charles II. She began to toy again with the possibility of moving to Heidelberg, and once again she renewed her demand that Charles Louis should provide suitable accommodation. Once again she met with the same blank refusal, and another series of bad-tempered letters flew between mother and son. Having finally given up the idea of moving to Heidelberg, Elizabeth suggested to her son that he should buy back the house he had sold to Craven a few years earlier, so that he could lend her the sum and so enable her to redeem some of her pawned jewels. Again Charles Louis refused.

The idea of returning to her homeland began to appear more and more attractive. Where, however, would she live if the King still refused to provide apartments for her in one of the royal palaces? Charles had conspicuously failed to send the promised invitation, and Craven had not yet managed to speak to him on her behalf. Henrietta Maria, who had arrived in London from Paris, had promised Craven that she would have a word with the King too, but she had not yet done so, and she was always surrounded by such a throng of courtiers that he never had an opportunity to speak to her. In December he admitted to Elizabeth that 'all things were going very crosse' in London, and he was glad that she was not there. 'Patience is a spetiall vertue in this age,' he wrote apologetically. 'The King has dun nothing for me but putts me off with good words.'[4]

Elizabeth was bitterly disappointed. She considered that by right she should have the annuity to which she was entitled under the terms of her marriage settlement, and that she should be provided with accommodation in one of the royal palaces. 'The Lord Craven has not done very well in my mother's business,' Rupert wrote to his friend Will Legge after a visit to the Hague, adding that Elizabeth did not wish Craven to do anything else in the matter without consulting her first.[5] Months went by and still there was no invitation forthcoming. But Elizabeth's friends in England begged her to come, and her many creditors in the Hague—where she still owed some 200,000 crowns—urged her to go to London while Parliament was sitting, in the hope that her presence would spur it on to agree to pay off her debts. The problem of accommodation was solved when Craven generously offered her the use of Drury House. She would stay there, she decided, though only until she could secure an establishment of her own.

'I believe you will be surprised to finde by this that I am going for England,' she wrote to Charles Louis on 16 May 1661. She did not wish to wait for transport from England, and the States General had agreed to lend her some ships. To begin with she talked of going over on a short visit and then returning to the Hague, 'but I doubt whether the King, her nephew, will permit her to do so,' wrote the French ambassador,

[...] for assuredly she cannot but be very useful to him, being a good creature, of a temper very civil and always equal, one who has never disobliged anybody, and who is thus capable, in her own person, of securing affection for the whole royal family, and one who, although more than a sexagenarian in age, preserves full vigour of body and mind.[6]

On 8 May she carefully made her will and prepared to leave. She had already despatched her luggage and had made her farewells when an urgent letter arrived from Charles II asking her to delay her departure. He thought he had made it clear to her through Prince Rupert, he wrote, that she should not come to England until he sent for her. It was a graceless letter which Elizabeth, though a little flustered, decided to ignore; she had after all already made all her preparations, said her goodbyes, and dispatched all her luggage. She set off for Delft, where her daughter Sophie and granddaughter Liselotte had come to say goodbye, and at the port of Hellevoetsluis she and her retinue of twenty-six embarked on the borrowed ships. Once on board she sat down and penned a reply to her nephew, explaining that his letter had arrived too late for her to change her plans without great embarrassment, and assuring him that she would not stay in England any longer than he wished.

On 26 May Elizabeth arrived at Gravesend and set foot, at long last, in the country she had left almost fifty years before. Lord Craven had taken a week's leave from his duties at the House of Lords in order to welcome his royal guest.[7] Since no preparations had been made for any ceremonial entry into London, she thought it best to slip into the city after dark so as to avoid any embarrassing comment about the poverty of her welcome. From the landing stage a line of coaches bore the Winter Queen and her entourage up Wych Street and into the spacious courtyard of Drury House, by this time cleaned and sumptuously redecorated. Threadbare carpets and unruly servants were finally a thing of the past.

What was it like, this long-vanished house that served as a temporary home for a Queen? An inventory dating from 1669 gives a list of the main rooms. The largest was the Great Dining Room, 36 by 18 feet; other rooms included the 'Queen's Chamber to the garden side', a 'withdrawing room', a 'room behind that's called the oyster room', 'my Lord's cabinet room', a 'gallery with a billiard table', and 'Madame Broughton's room next the court adjoining the gallery'.[8] Elizabeth's faithful maid of honour Margaret Broughton had accompanied her mistress back to England. After the date of this inventory Craven commissioned his godson William Winde, son of his old comrade in arms Lieutenant-Colonel Henry Winde and a former ensign in the States Army, to design a new wing for the mansion. In the following century the building, by now known as Craven House, was divided into tenements, part of it becoming a tavern known as 'The Queen of Bohemia'. By the early eighteenth century, the fabric had become much decayed, and the house was demolished in 1809.

In the end Elizabeth was to remain at Drury House for nine months, with Lord Craven acting in the multiple capacity of Chamberlain, Steward, Comptroller of Household, and Captain of Guards, with his cousin Sir Robert Craven as Master of the Horse. Among the other members of the household were old friends and protégés of Craven's: Andros had already been appointed the Queen of Bohemia's gentleman-in-ordinary, and William Winde became a gentleman usher.

When the Queen of Bohemia arrived in London, the court was in mourning for the infant Duke of Gloucester, the new-born son of Anne Hyde and the Duke of York. There was much comment in court circles about the lack of any formal welcome for the King's aunt. Rumours spread that she had come contrary to his will and this was why she had not been offered apartments in Whitehall or Somerset House, and that she would not stay in England for long. But Charles II, after his initial reluctance, welcomed his aunt, though his generosity still did not extend to offering her accommodation.

Within a month of her arrival, Elizabeth had decided to stay in London for good. She did not intend to remain as a guest in someone else's house, however, even if it was the house of her long-standing friend, and in the absence of any invitation from her nephew she began to cast her eyes around for a suitable mansion to rent. Her first choice was the Earl of Leicester's town house, a large and elegant mansion in Leicester Fields, but when the Earl proved to be less than enthusiastic she agreed to take a lease of Exeter House in the Strand, whose current occupants, the Dutch ambassadors, were thought to be moving out soon.

She intended to move into her new home in August, and in anticipation of the move she decided to send for all of her remaining furniture from the Wassenaer Hof and Rhenen. Great was her indignation, however, when she learnt that, just as the furniture was on the point of being loaded onto a ship in the harbour at Rotterdam, it had been arrested on the orders of Charles Louis, on the pretext that some of it belonged to him. Relations between mother and son plumbed new depths, Elizabeth reviling her eldest son for months to come, while he claimed that he had only intended to delay the passage of the goods for a fortnight in order to check that there was nothing that belonged to him. Eventually the furniture arrived in London, and Elizabeth commented sourly on the poor quality of the pieces from Rhenen, which the 'base castellan' had allowed to go to ruin.

Still, the summer was full of social activity. 'Everie week I march to one place or another with the King,' Elizabeth wrote to Sophie in Hanover.[9] She made frequent visits to the theatre, escorted sometimes by the King, sometimes by Lord Craven. The Duke of Ormonde entertained her at his house in Kensington, and she accepted an invitation to visit Lady Herbert, who had taken a house for the summer at Hampton Court. A correspondent wrote in August,

> The Queen of Bohemia [...] is very much visited by our English ladies, and she is much honoured and beloved by all sorts of people. At her visits she hath six footmen, three coaches, and other attendants very nobly.[10]

Sophie received glowing reports of London's divertissements and hoped for an invitation, writing that her mother would find her very homely compared to the fashionable ladies who visited Drury House every day.

It was rumoured that, as a reward for his loyalty, Craven was planning to ask for the hand of Princess Elizabeth, the Winter Queen's eldest daughter. 'I think I have told you that Lord Craven hath a mind to marry her [Princess Elizabeth], if he can accomplish it,' wrote Samuel Hartlib.[11] Whether or not there was any truth behind the rumour, nothing came of it, and it seems unlikely that the old soldier and the intellectual spinster would have made a good match. A later rumour of course had it that Craven had secretly married the Queen of Bohemia herself during these last months, but this seems improbable. One romance that did blossom at Drury House, however, was between Sir Robert Craven, Elizabeth's Master of the Horse, and her maid of honour, Margaret Broughton. They were married in September 1663 in the Church of St Clement Danes.

In the autumn of 1661, the Genoese ambassador paid a visit to the Winter Queen at Drury House, which he recorded as follows:

> I made the last visit of the evening to the Queen of Bohemia, sister to the late King, and mother to the Prince Palatine [...]. I went thither conducted by the master of the ceremonies, and found her in her cabinet, where she had assembled many ladies, to receive me with the greatest decorum. She sent attendants to welcome me as I alighted from my coach, and at the head of the stairs I was met by Lord Craven, proprietor of the house where she lives and the principal

director of her court. It is incredible the pleasure which her majesty showed at this my office, and the familiar courtesy with which she discoursed with me for a very long time upon the state of the most serene republic [...]. This Princess has learned from nature, and continued through the changes in her fortune, an incomparable goodness; and as people ever turn away from her with profit and applause, she has thus often, by this capital alone, sustained in a most depressed estate the respect due to the dignity of her rank. Now [...] she is restored to some authority, and thus is heightened the lustre of that affable manner with which she wonderfully conciliates the esteem and love of the court.[12]

Time passed and the Dutch ambassadors showed no signs of leaving Exeter House, and Lord Leicester reluctantly agreed that Elizabeth could have the lease of Leicester House after all. A French contemporary wrote that 'le pauvre Milor Craven will be glad to be rid of her, so as not to be altogether eaten up,' although in reality he would surely have been delighted for her to remain as his guest. In the middle of February 1662, she moved with her small household to her new home. The weather was mild, and Elizabeth had recovered from a bad cold with the help, or perhaps more likely the hindrance, of her doctors. They had persuaded her to take medicine which made her 'as sick as a dogge', but she put more faith in the tried and tested method of letting blood.[13] She seemed to have recovered fully, but the business of moving, even in the mild weather, led to a return of her enduring bronchitis, and on 10 February she suffered a haemorrhage from the lungs.

Rupert had recently arrived from Vienna, and she sent him with a message asking the King and the Duke of York to call on her. The following day Charles came, reproaching himself for not doing more to help his aunt. He pressed her to move to apartments in Whitehall Palace, but the longed-for invitation had come too late; by this time she was too ill to move. She received communion, and requested the King to continue paying her pension to her executors so that the last of her creditors in the Hague could be reimbursed. In the early hours of 13 February 1662, propped up in a chair by the fireside in her chamber and with most of her household in attendance, she breathed her last.

Elizabeth's death barely interrupted the gaiety of the court, and in truth few in Restoration London even remembered the exiled Queen who had once inspired such devotion. 'My royal tenant is departed,' wrote Lord Leicester matter-of-factly. 'It seems the fates did not think it fit that I should have the honour, which in truth I never much desyr'd, to be the landlord of a Queene.'

The Queen of Bohemia's funeral took place in the evening of 17 February. Neither the King nor the Duke of York attended; instead, Prince Rupert, the only one of Elizabeth's children in England, was chief mourner. In a solemn, torch-lit procession her body was borne up the Thames from Somerset House to Westminster Bridge, and from there to the abbey. In the funeral service Elizabeth's crown was carried on a cushion by two heralds, supported on either side by Lord Craven and

Sir Robert Craven. The Queen of Bohemia was interred, as she had requested, in Henry VII's Chapel, close to her brother Prince Henry. As the burial service was read, there raged outside 'such a storm of hail, thunder and lightning, as never was seen the like in any man's memorie.'[14]

In her will Elizabeth had named her eldest son as her heir, but she proceeded to leave him absolutely nothing. In truth she had little enough to bequeath. To her eldest daughter, Elizabeth, she left a pair of emerald and pearl earrings, while Edward was to inherit one of her great table diamonds which was attached rather feebly by a ribbon to a bracelet. Sophie was to have the short pearl necklace which her mother had worn regularly for many years. All the remainder of Elizabeth's goods and chattels, including her silver and furniture, as well as any money that she was owed, she bequeathed to Rupert.[15]

What of Lord Craven, left bereft by the death of the woman to whose service he had devoted his life? His response seems to have been to throw himself with characteristic energy into the building projects which he had already put in motion. As soon as his estates had been restored in 1660 he had decided to reconstruct his existing house at Hamstead Marshall in order to create a summer palace for Elizabeth. In the years immediately prior to its sequestration, considerable sums had gone on improvements to the house and gardens—a new chimneypiece here, new plants for the garden there. Perhaps this represented post-war reconstruction after the ravages of the Civil War and the billeting of soldiers, but during the years of sequestration the house had suffered grievously.

The 1660s saw a burgeoning of country house construction in England. Many such houses were commissioned by returning exiles who had become familiar with Dutch architecture and wished to copy the fashionable new style. Craven was among the first of these Restoration architectural patrons, but there was to be nothing Dutch about Hamstead Marshall. Instead, Craven's fanciful plan was to create a version of Heidelberg Castle, to remind the Winter Queen of happier days.

As his architect Craven chose Sir Balthazar Gerbier, whose eldest son, George Gerbier d'Ouvilly, he had commissioned in 1638 as a captain in the ill-fated Palatine Army which was defeated at Vlotho. Gerbier *père* had had a varied career as architect, art agent, diplomat, and, briefly, master of ceremonies for Charles I. Back in the 1630s he had designed York House for the Duke of Buckingham—of which the only remaining part is the Water Gate in Embankment Gardens—and Craven's Drury House has been attributed to him as well. At the Restoration he designed the triumphal arches built to welcome Charles II into London, and on the strength of this he had attempted to regain his old post of master of ceremonies at the royal court, only to be suspended in the face of royal disdain. Elizabeth thoroughly disliked him, writing tartly that 'Gerbier was never esteemed a great man though he pretends gentilitie, being come out of France.' With such pretentions Gerbier seems to have thought architecture beneath him, but in the absence of any other employment he agreed to Craven's request.

Craven decided to appoint his godson, William Winde, as Gerbier's assistant. Although Winde had never designed a building before, Craven must have seen his potential. We know that he had made a study of military architecture in the United Provinces in the 1650s, and no doubt his observations had extended to domestic buildings as well.

Building work at Hamstead Marshall had not even begun when Elizabeth died in February 1662, but Craven went ahead anyway. He decided, so tradition says, that the house would be consecrated to Elizabeth's memory. The ambitious plan of imitating Heidelberg Castle was abandoned, however, and instead Gerbier and Winde drew up plans for an extensive remodelling of the existing mansion. Work started later in 1662, but the exertions of supervising a large building project were too much for the seventy-year-old Gerbier. In the spring of 1663 he died at Hamstead Marshall, either as the result of an accident or perhaps simply through stress. At the time of his death he was owed the considerable sum of £4,000 in wages, suggesting that a good deal of building work had already taken place. He was buried in Hamstead Marshall Church, where a memorial plaque reads,

> Here lyeth the body of Sir Balthasar Gerbier who built a stately pile of Building in the years 1662 to 1665 for the Right Honourable William Earl of Craven at Hamstead Marshall, the greatest part of which was destroyed by fire in the year 1718. He died in the year 1667.

Actually, he died in 1663. William Winde, in any case, stepped smoothly into his shoes; work proceeded without interruption, and construction of the first floor began in July 1664.

The mansion which arose at a leisurely pace—it was not completed for another thirty-five years—seems to have retained a large part of the earlier house, including the central wing with its prominent two-storey bays and mullioned and transomed windows.[16] Gerbier and Winde added a third storey, with a decorative frieze enlivened by swags and blind panels between the windows, and the two long side wings may have been completely rebuilt. The roof was punctuated by long rows of dormer windows, prominent chimneys, and three tall belvedere cupolas.

It is unclear how much of the design was Gerbier's and how much Winde's, but Winde was largely responsible for the interior, for which he employed some of the best contemporary craftsmen, including the mason Edward Pierce and the plasterer Edward Gouge. The collection of forty or so drawings relating to Hamstead Marshall preserved in the Bodleian Library contains only one signed by Gerbier; dated 1662, it shows a pair of highly elaborate gate piers which were never built. The remainder were drawn up by Winde or his subordinates; they include drawings for fine plaster ceilings dating from the 1680s, and another for an extremely grand stable block which was probably never built.[17] Craven is said to have spent a total of £60,000 on the construction of the mansion.

Tragically, the house burnt to the ground in 1718, after fire spread from a burning brazier on the roof. Nothing remains now, except for some melancholy reminders of vanished magnificence in the form of a series of eight elaborate gate piers standing forlornly in the fields, some with sections of garden wall attached. They mark the boundary of the vanished gardens; there were nine originally, but the pair fronting the main entrance were removed in the late eighteenth century to nearby Benham Park. Our only knowledge of the house's aspect comes from an aerial view by Kip and Knyff dating from 1709, which shows the mansion surrounded by elaborate parterre gardens, with a bowling green at the rear and a long range of stabling to one side.

Winde also designed a new mansion for Craven to replace the ruined Caversham House. The new Caversham Lodge, which became the home of Lord Craven's cousin Sir Anthony Craven of Sparsholt, was in a slightly different location to the old house, and Winde created a fine new terraced garden on its Thames side. This house no longer exists either; it was demolished after the family sold the estate in the early eighteenth century.

Craven's other building project, Ashdown House in Berkshire, was no further advanced than Hamstead Marshall at the time of the Queen of Bohemia's death, but here too he continued with his plans. Ashdown House is essentially a hunting lodge in a Dutch style; it would have been too small—before the addition of two later wings, now demolished—to make a satisfactory country house. The architect here too is thought to have been William Winde, though there is no evidence to support this attribution. The house is an improbable-looking structure of great beauty; a tall, square-pile house built of white chalk with sandstone quoins and architraves, three storeys high and with dormer windows at the front and rear. Its roof is surmounted by a balustrade and a cupola which gives access to the roof, allowing visitors to survey the surrounding countryside and watch the progress of the hunt. The house is exactly aligned to the four cardinal points of the compass, and when first built it stood in the centre of a wood, through which four avenues led up to the house, one on each side. Today, only the west avenue remains.

Inside, an enormous staircase, taking up almost a quarter of the entire house, climbs up to the central cupola. Each floor contains one large chamber, with smaller rooms adjoining for servants' accommodation. The building has something in common with the nearby Coleshill House, now demolished, which had been designed by William Winde's Norfolk neighbour Sir Roger Pratt some years earlier. Ashdown House, though, is square in plan and one storey higher, and its windows are characteristically Dutch. History has always maintained that Craven built Ashdown House as a memorial to the Winter Queen, and its Dutch style is therefore completely appropriate. The symmetry of the building (it is almost identical on all four sides), the elegant proportions, the startling whiteness of the walls, the doll's-house-like unreality of it all—together they give the house an air of fragile femininity. It is a moving testimony in stone, the most eloquent testimony that remains, to its builder's obsessive devotion to Elizabeth of Bohemia, whose family portraits still line the walls of the staircase.

'An honour beyond all his gallantries and brave exploits'

For thirty years Lord Craven had devoted himself to the service of the Winter Queen. The remainder of his life—he was to live for another thirty-five years—was in a sense just a postscript to the one great theme which had dominated his life. In fact for the next three and a half decades he was to be as frenetically busy as ever, his days filled with trading ventures and new schemes for colonial settlement; with endless committee meetings and occasional artistic patronage; and, not least, with strenuous battles against the successive disasters of pestilence and fire.

To begin with, he was unsure what to do. Early in 1663 he even contemplated leaving England again and accepting the post of Governor of Jamaica. Certainly the island, captured from the Spanish by Cromwell back in 1655, needed a capable commander in charge of its defence, but the governorship would have been a poor enough reward for his faithful support of the Stuarts. Renewed exile held little appeal, and he declined the offered post.

As soon as he returned to England in 1660, Craven had plunged dutifully into a welter of parliamentary committees: for the reception of the King, for considering precedents for congratulating the Queen on her return to England, for the fens, for the Protestants of Piedmont, and for preventing the exportation of money, to name but a few. In the years following the Restoration he sat on many more; in December 1660 he became a member of the Committee for Foreign Plantations, and later of the Committee for Tangier and the Royal Fishery Company. In fact Craven was to spend much of his time in committees of one sort or another. Pepys commented with typical asperity on the 'confused and ridiculous' meetings of the Fishery Committee which Craven chaired, and he was shocked by Craven's bawdy language—quite out of place, he thought primly, in the rarefied heights of Westminster. The matter under discussion was whether the establishment of a lottery for Virginia would affect the success of a proposed lottery for the fisheries, and Craven argued that it would be a mistake to have two separate lotteries, on the grounds that one would devalue the other. 'For,' he said, using the first analogy that came to mind, 'if I occupy a wench first, you may occupy her again your heart out, you can never have her maidenhead after I have once had it.'[1]

With the return of peace and the Restoration of the Monarchy, England had discovered an enthusiasm for new trading ventures and schemes for colonial settlement. The coffee houses, which were rapidly increasing in popularity, were filled with men promoting joint-stock companies to take advantage of new trading opportunities. At the forefront of this ferment of interest was Prince Rupert, with his wide interests and energetic spirit. As soon as he returned to England in 1660, Rupert wasted no time in promoting trading expeditions to the west coast of Africa, an area which he had visited during his wanderings at sea eight years earlier. In January 1662, a new trading company, 'the Company of Royal Adventurers of England trading into Africa', received its royal charter, with Rupert and Craven among its subscribers. Its primary objective was the search for gold; the charter defined its aims as 'the furtherance of trade, and encouragement in the discovery of the golden mines, and settling of plantations' between the Barbary coast and the Cape of Good Hope. In return the company agreed to render to the King or his successors two elephants whenever he should happen to set foot in the said regions. Success, however, was elusive. The company has been described as 'more reminiscent of an aristocratic treasure-hunt than of an organised business.'[2] It had been founded with insufficient capital, and the returns were minimal. Within a few years it found itself heavily in debt, and its future seemed unpromising.

The same could initially be said of the other venture in which Craven became involved in 1662. In the autumn of that year, a group of eight influential men began lobbying the King for a royal charter allowing them to establish the Province of Carolina, which was to consist of all the territory in the New World between the thirty-first and thirty-sixth parallels—essentially all the land between Virginia and Florida—and extending across America to the South Seas.

The initiative to obtain the Carolina charter came from the Duke of Albemarle, who hoped that a new colony might become a centre for lucrative inter-colonial trade.[3] Albemarle's interest was probably sparked by his cousin Sir John Colleton, a wealthy Barbados sugar planter, and two other men who already had interests in America and the West Indies: Sir William Berkeley, the Governor of Virginia, and Lord Ashley, co-owner of an unprofitable plantation in Barbados and, as it happened, Craven's brother-in-law—Ashley, like Craven's sister Mary, had married into the Coventry family. These four in turn secured the backing of four others: the Earl of Clarendon, who could easily have blocked the scheme if not included; Lord Craven, who had plenty of money to invest; John, Lord Berkeley of Stratton, brother of Sir William Berkeley; and Sir George Carteret, the influential treasurer of the Navy.[4]

On 4 March 1663 Charles II signed a royal charter, making these eight men the Lords Proprietors of the Province of Carolina. Whoever the prime mover behind the charter was, in their original petition to the King the eight petitioners thought it best to stress their zeal for the propagation of the gospel among the heathen. An old story, apocryphal or not, relates how all eight of them appeared before Charles

II in the garden at Hampton Court and presented their petition, full of earnest declarations of their pious intentions. At this,

> [...] the monarch, after looking each in the face for a moment, with a merry twinkle in his eye, burst into loud laughter, in which his audience joined involuntarily. Then, taking up a little shaggy spaniel, with large, meek eyes, and holding it at arms' length before them, he said: 'Good friends, here is a model of piety and sincerity which might be wholesome for you to copy.' Then, tossing the little pet to Clarendon, he said: 'There, Hyde, is a worthy prelate; make him archbishop of the domain that I shall give you.'

With tongue in cheek Charles introduced into the preamble of the charter a statement that the petitioners, 'excited by a laudable and pious zeal for the propagation of the gospel, have begged a certain country in the parts of America not yet cultivated and planted, and only inhabited by some barbarous people who have no knowledge of God.'

The eight Lords Proprietors were given wide-ranging powers equal to those of the Bishop of Durham; legally, in other words, the province would be a palatinate. Its proprietors would be able to make laws, appoint judges, build towns, raise an army, and make war, and they could also grant titles of honour so long as these were not the same as the titles used in England. In exchange they were to pay the King one quarter of any gold and silver found in the province, and a yearly rent of 20 marks. At the first meeting of the Lords Proprietors, on 23 May 1663, it was agreed that each proprietor should begin by contributing £25, and they published their plans for settling the territory. It was to be an agricultural colony in which feudal landlords and their tenants would grow crops such as rice, tobacco, and olives. The Lords Proprietors divided the province into three counties: Albemarle in the north, and Clarendon and Craven in the south. Each county was to contain eight 12,000-acre seigneuries, one for each of the proprietors, and eight baronies granted to a hereditary nobility. The rest of the land was be sold to freeholders.

The first step was to find potential settlers. Initially the proprietors hoped to attract some 3,000 settlers from Virginia and New England. Groups from Virginia had already established one settlement on the Albemarle Sound and another at Cape Fear, and several groups in New England and in London had expressed an interest in obtaining grants from the proprietors. In the event, however, few people came. The proprietors also tried with limited success to encourage settlers to come from Barbados and Bermuda. A group known as the Barbadian Adventurers had expressed an interest in the province, and in 1665 three boatloads of settlers arrived from Barbados and purchased from the Native Americans a tract of land on the Cape Fear River, where they established a new settlement, the Clarendon County Colony. Despite the inducements, however, the new colony failed to attract many settlers; worse, within a short space of time many of the existing settlers packed up and moved to the existing Albemarle settlements or else left for Virginia.

At this juncture the proprietors found themselves with more pressing concerns than the affairs of a distant colony. To begin with, in the spring of 1665 England declared war on the Dutch, and most of the proprietors—Ashley, Albemarle, Berkeley, Carteret, and Craven—found themselves involved in one way or another. Then, as the weather began to warm up in April, cases of plague began to appear among the slum tenements in the parish of St Giles in the Fields, to the north of Westminster. From this centre of infection the plague spread slowly outwards. In the seventeenth century the threat of plague was never far away; the last outbreak in London, from 1640 to 1647, had claimed the lives of over 14,000 people. Since Henry VIII's reign the usual preventative measure had been to shut up the infected houses for forty days, and to prevent anyone either entering or leaving. Some pest houses had been established during the reign of Queen Elizabeth, but most of these had since been converted to other uses. Those remaining were never adequate and were quickly overwhelmed. Now, as cases of plague began to reappear, the Privy Council hastily ordered pest houses to be constructed for the parishes of St Giles in the Fields and St Martin in the Fields.

By July plague was rampant, with deaths reaching over 8,000 a month. From the poor parishes in the suburbs the sickness had begun to establish itself in the City. Those who could afford to do so fled to the country; in late June, Pepys noted 'all the town almost going out of town, the coaches and wagons being all full of people going into the country.'[6] In early July plague had advanced close to the gates of Whitehall Palace, with several houses in fashionable King Street marked with the ominous red cross, and on the 9th a hasty decision was made to move the entire court to the relative safety of Hampton Court. From there the Privy Council drew up an order directing the deputy justices of the peace for Middlesex to remain at their homes in Westminster and the out-parishes, that is, the parishes outside the City.

The City itself, of course, had its own well developed system of government: it was run by the Lord Mayor with the assistance of the aldermen and deputy justices, and most of these officials remained at their posts. The administration of London as a whole, after the sudden flitting of the court and Privy Council, fell largely to two men, the Duke of Albemarle and Lord Craven. Albemarle agreed readily to the King's request that he should remain in London to take over the reins. His prestige was immense, and in the absence of any other authority he acted as a sort of benevolent dictator, maintaining order and keeping a vigilant eye open for plots by republicans attempting to take advantage of the political paralysis. He took up residence at the Cockpit at Whitehall, the town house which he had been granted by Charles II.

As for Lord Craven, although he had been a justice of the peace for Middlesex since the early 1660s, he was under no obligation to remain behind in London. As the plague spread inexorably, virtually all the nobility, gentry, and middle classes—except for those who had been ordered to stay at their posts—fled to the country. An intriguing story in Whitecross's *Anecdotes*—a book of improving tales illustrating biblical passages—describes an encounter said to have inspired Craven's decision to remain in London (with reference to a verse from Psalm 91, 'Surely he shall deliver thee from the noisome pestilence').

> Lord Craven lived in London when that sad calamity, the plague, raged [...]. On the plague growing epidemic, his lordship, to avoid the danger, resolved to go to his seat in the country. His coach and six were accordingly at the door, his baggage already put up, and all things in readiness for the journey. As he was walking through his hall with his hat on, his cane under his arm, and putting on his gloves, in order to step into his carriage, he overheard his negro, who served him as postillion, saying to another servant, 'I suppose, by my lord's quitting London to avoid the plague, that his god lives in the country, and not in town.' The poor negro said this in the simplicity of his heart, as really believing a plurality of gods. The speech, however, struck Lord Craven very sensibly, and made him pause. 'My God,' thought he, 'lives everywhere, and can preserve me in town as well as in the country. I will even stay where I am. The ignorance of that negro has just preached to me a very useful sermon. Lord, pardon this unbelief, and that distrust of thy providence, which made me think of running from thy hand.' He immediately ordered his horses to be taken from the coach, and the baggage to be taken in. He continued in London, was remarkably useful among his sick neighbours, and never caught the infection.[7]

Craven and Albemarle administered the stricken city as best they could through the remaining deputy justices and magistrates, Craven working hard to supervise the shutting up of infected houses and the burial of the dead. While Albemarle's troops, camped out in Hyde Park, busied themselves in rooting out plotters, Craven oversaw the appointment of the searchers for the dead, the watchmen who guarded the doors of infected houses, the nurse-keepers who entered the houses, the bearers who took the infected to the pest houses and by night transported the dead to the plague pits, and the buriers who flung the bodies into the pits. Gruesome jobs all of them, taken only because the alternative was starvation. They were by and large a foul-mouthed and unpleasant crew. According to one observer, the plague victims were more frightened of the nurse-keepers than of the plague itself; many were suspected of killing the people they were supposed to be nursing and robbing their houses.

One of the drivers of the dead carts by the name of Buckingham had a particularly macabre sense of humour. Driving along with his cart loaded up with bodies to take to the plague pits, he would hold up a dead child by the leg and cry out, 'Faggots, faggots, five for sixpence!' Equally ghoulishly, he would leave the bodies of young women fully exposed on the edge of the plague pit. Word of this behaviour soon came to Craven's attention, and in short order Buckingham was taken to the pest house and whipped there in public, then whipped through the fields until his back was bloody, then imprisoned for a year.[8]

For us, looking back from the twenty-first century, the plague year seems a time of unimaginable horror. As the dry, hot summer went by, the Bills of Mortality showed the deaths doubling and doubling again week by week. Ever more houses had red crosses painted on their doors, with the accompanying words 'God have mercy on us!' and the doors guarded by watchmen to make sure no one entered or left. The effect of shutting up infected houses was naturally to increase the deaths, because almost invariably every healthy person shut up with the infected also died. Many streets were entirely deserted, because those who hadn't died had fled, or else kept to their houses out of fear. Silence had fallen over the stricken city; anyone venturing out would hear nothing but the groans and screams of the dying, over the unaccustomed sound of the rapids under London Bridge.

The nobility and gentry, the merchants and shopkeepers had all fled to the country, leaving vast numbers of their servants, apprentices, and journeymen without work, leaving whole families destitute. According to one estimate, 40,000 servants were left homeless. The task of providing relief for the poor was enormous. Craven distributed enormous sums in helping the indigent, and kept his house open to comfort the distressed.[9] According to his contemporary Dr Gumble,

> [Craven] freely chose to venture his life upon a thousand occasions during this afflicted time, in the midst of the infected; provided nurses and physicians for them that were sick, and out of his own purse expended vast sums of money, to supply the necessities of such as were ready to perish: an honour beyond all his gallantries and brave exploits in Germany and elsewhere.[10]

Craven and Albemarle directed that copies of a news sheet with advice on preventing infection should be distributed to the poor. Citizens should live temperately and wash hands and mouth frequently with vinegar and water. If they felt ill they should vomit as soon as possible, then go to bed and sweat it out.

Parliament had been prorogued twice, Charles II intending to summon it to meet in Oxford on 9 October. On the 3rd there were just four members of the House of Lords present when a quorum assembled for yet another prorogation: the Archbishop of Canterbury was appointed Speaker for the day; the others present were the Bishop of London, Albemarle, and Craven, who had just taken his seat in the Lords as an earl. Later that month Pepys went to see Albemarle at the Cockpit, where he found the Duke ensconced with Craven and Sir John Robinson, Lieutenant of the Tower, discussing the transport of coal for the London poor and engaging in light-hearted banter which offended Pepys. 'But Lord!' he wrote, 'to hear the silly talk between these great people.' Pepys by now had moved from the City out to Greenwich with the Navy Office, and perhaps the other three might have been forgiven a little levity in the face of unremitting gloom.

The epidemic reached its height in September, with the bills of mortality peaking at over 8,000 per week. As the weather grew cooler deaths quickly reduced in number, and as autumn turned to winter the fashionable world began to trickle back to London. In early January, the King ordered the Exchequer to move back from Nonsuch to Westminster, and the *Oxford Gazette* reassured worried courtiers that it was perfectly safe to return, pointing out that Craven and his fellow justices of the peace had given orders that all the infected houses were to be well aired and whitewashed, and that the churchyards were to be covered with 2 feet of soil. On 1 February the court returned to Whitehall, and two weeks later the Privy Council issued a series of restrictive plague measures, which only served to show their ignorance of the state of affairs. Burials in churchyards were prohibited; in fact, they had long since ceased because of lack of room. Churchyards were to be covered with twelve inches of unslaked lime; in fact, supplies of lime had run out long ago.

Craven called a meeting of the magistrates to discuss how to respond, and a few days later he wrote a lengthy letter to the Privy Council summarising the measures that had been taken. Burial space was short because the Bishop of London had refused to consecrate any ground unless it was given in perpetuity. If possible the sick had been moved to one or other of the pest houses; otherwise their doors had been marked with a red cross for forty days, with warders set to prevent anyone from leaving or entering, and then the houses had been aired and fumigated for another forty days before anyone else was allowed to enter. There was no lime available, but all bodies had been buried deep. Every morning a raker had gone round with his cart, ringing a bell to summon the inhabitants to bring out their dead, and the streets had been cleaned daily. Most refuse dumps had been removed, as had most beggars.[11]

Craven strongly recommended that the pest houses, which had been completely overwhelmed, should be enlarged. The pest house in Soho had room for only ninety people, and those in Westminster and St Giles for only sixty. He urged that money should be made available for the expansion of the pest houses, since it was unlikely that private charity would be sufficient. 'The middling sort of people' had been largely impoverished by the plague, while the nobility and gentry were unlikely to remain in the city in the event of a fresh outbreak. A Privy Council committee had been appointed to consider the best way of preventing a recurrence of the plague, and when it met in May Craven was added to its numbers. His advice was that the old policy of shutting up infected houses had failed. He had seen the suffering it had caused, and it was only too obvious that it had led to thousands of unnecessary deaths. Instead he repeated his argument for the expansion of the network of pest houses as a way of isolating the sick, with rooms for a physician and surgeon and plague pits for the dead.

The government either could not or would not do anything, so Craven wasted no time in taking action himself. He rented a large plot of land, 3 acres in extent, which became known as Pest House Fields, on the site of what was later to become Golden Square in Soho. Here he built a pest house lazaretto, or isolation hospital, for the parishes of St Clement Danes, St Martin in the Fields, St James's Westminster, and St Paul's Covent Garden. It consisted of thirty-six small houses spaced well apart from one another, and sufficient land to provide a burial ground for the four parishes.

In 1670 Craven purchased the freehold of this site. In 1687 he conveyed Pest House Close to his cousin and heir Sir William Craven, upon trust to maintain the buildings for the relief of the poor in the event of another outbreak of plague. By the early eighteenth century the area had become more densely populated, making it less suitable for an isolation hospital, and the pest house was considered 'a great Prejudice and Nuisance to the Neighbourhood'. In 1736 William, 3rd Baron Craven (1700–39), decided to redevelop his Soho estate, but at the same time he bought 3 acres of land in Bayswater with government funding for use as a pest house in the event of a recurrence of plague. In the nineteenth century, a court case decided that the Bayswater site was no longer needed as a plague hospital, but the Earl of Craven's Pest House Charity still exists as a grant-making body for the benefit of hospitals in the four parishes of St Clement Danes, St Martin in the Fields, St James's Westminster, and St Paul's Covent Garden.

The Great Plague was the last major outbreak of bubonic plague in England. All in all around 80,000 Londoners are thought to have died—a sixth of the city's population. It might have recurred, of course, but for the Great Fire which destroyed most of the City the following autumn. The fire broke out in the early hours of Sunday 2 September, in a bakery in Pudding Lane, a narrow thoroughfare just to the east of London Bridge. Helped by the strong easterly winds, the fire spread too quickly for the customary methods of fire control to work. Usually a team of men would form a human chain along streets leading down to the Thames in order to pass buckets of water up to the site of the fire, and additional water would come from an efficient system of pipes. In addition there were massive fire engines, enormous behemoths pulled by eight horses. But on this occasion the fire engines were unable to move in the crowded streets, while the waterwheels under London Bridge had caught fire and water had ceased to flow through the pipes. If these methods failed to control the blaze, the only alternative was to demolish houses to create a firebreak, and to this end long poles known as fire-hooks were kept in every church tower. As soon as it became apparent that the flames were engulfing the entire street, the Lord Mayor, Sir Thomas Bludworth, was urged to start ordering the pulling down of houses. But Bludworth, indecisive and weak-willed, would not give the order without the consent of the owners.

A few hours later, Samuel Pepys hired a boat to view the fire from the river. He spent an hour looking on with mounting consternation. By this time a whole section of the riverside was in flames. Nobody was attempting to fight the flames; instead, people were frantically trying to save their possessions by flinging them into any boats that were to hand, or if there were none then into the water. Pepys decided he must go to Whitehall to warn the court of the disaster that was unfolding. He landed at Whitehall Steps and was whisked up to see the King and the Duke of York, who were naturally very alarmed by the news. Charles told Pepys to return to the City and order Bludworth to begin pulling down houses immediately. The Duke added that the Life Guards at Whitehall, under the command of the Earl of Craven, would be made available to help fight the fire if the Lord Mayor requested them.

The King and the Duke embarked on the royal barge to assess the situation and were rowed towards the flames. At the front line of the firefighting operations they disembarked. Bludworth had still not ordered any demolitions, nor any help from Craven's guards, and so the King and Duke decided to override his authority. They summoned Sir Richard Browne, a former Lord Mayor (not Craven's old friend from Paris, but another man of the same name), and ordered him to begin pulling down houses. At the same time Charles ordered Craven to take his guards into the City, 'to be more particularly assisting to the Lord Mayor and Magistrates [...] [and] to be helpful by what ways they could in so great a calamity.'[12]

Craven's guards were much needed, because order was rapidly breaking down. The streets were gridlocked, with chaos around the City gates as people tried to flee. Wild rumours circulated that the fire had been deliberately started by Dutchmen, or possibly by Frenchmen. There were rumours of foreigners seen throwing fireballs through the windows of houses, and foreign-owned shops were soon being ransacked and foreigners attacked in the streets. Violence and looting were rampant.

By the following morning the fire had spread alarmingly. Firefighting efforts had so far been patchy and sporadic, and it was painfully obvious to the King that coordinated action was needed. The Duke of Albemarle, Captain-General of the kingdom and Lord Lieutenant of Middlesex, was the obvious man to take charge—but Albemarle was with the English fleet at the Isle of Wight, recovering from the recent battle with the Dutch. Instead, Charles gave the job of overseeing the firefighting to his brother, the Duke of York. James spent most of that day riding up and down the streets of the City with his guards in an attempt to maintain order, rescuing innocent foreigners and encouraging firefighting efforts. Craven, with his detachment of guards, did the same. But as the day wore on mob violence increased, and foreigners feared for their lives.

Because of the continuing strong winds the greatest danger lay on the west side of the City, and the Duke decided to set up a series of command posts in strategic locations around the City's perimeter. There were five posts in all, each under the command of parish constables who were ordered to bring 100 sailors to help with the firefighting. Each team was to be supported by a troop of thirty foot soldiers, together with three courtiers with the authority to order demolitions. The Duke himself concentrated on trying to stop the flames from leaping over the

Fleet River and advancing down the Strand towards Whitehall, and the Council of State ordered the wholesale demolition of houses along the Fleet River up as far as Holborn Bridge. The Duke took responsibility for the stretch from the Fleet Bridge down to the Thames, and Craven, 'next to the Duke the most active in the business', was placed in charge at Holborn Bridge, with responsibility from there down to the Fleet Bridge.

By Monday night the five posts were fully manned, with all available forces marshalled to defend the half-mile length of the Fleet River. The commanders at each post were ordered to give a shilling's reward to any man who stayed at his post and worked hard through the night. All night long men worked frantically trying to douse the flames and pulling down houses along the Fleet, but it was not enough. On Tuesday morning, to general consternation, sparks from the conflagration took hold in Salisbury Court, just behind the Duke of York's position, and he was forced to beat a hasty retreat to Somerset House as the flames began to advance westwards along Fleet Street towards the Temple.

Over at Holborn Bridge, Craven was having more success. He and his men diligently demolished houses along the Fleet River, and by noon on the Tuesday they had managed to extinguish the flames at Holborn Bridge. Craven immediately galloped over to the Cow Lane post at Smithfield, a few streets away to the north-east, where Sir Richard Browne, 'but a weak man in this business', was in danger of being overwhelmed. The Duke of York worked tirelessly from early in the morning until midnight, handling buckets of water, helping to man the pumps, giving orders to blow up houses with gunpowder, and encouraging his men to keep going. Even the King rolled up his sleeves and gave a hand. Since Sunday night the Duke, and no doubt Craven too, had only had two or three hours' sleep. The two of them worked non-stop supervising the firefighting activities and giving encouragement.

As Tuesday wore on the fire spread within the confines of the City, and as night fell flames appeared on the roof of St Paul's Cathedral. Soon the entire roof caught fire, and within an hour the whole building was ablaze, the lead from the roof running in a stream down Ludgate Hill. Over to the west the fire had reached the Temple, and work began on demolishing houses around Somerset House. Already the Exchequer had been evacuated to Nonsuch Palace, and that evening the Queen left Whitehall for the safety of Hampton Court. On the east side of the City the flames had spread alarmingly close to the Tower of London, with its enormous magazine. At all costs the fire had to be stopped there, and engineers from the Royal Ordinance began systematically blowing up houses along Tower Street, while, to avoid any chance of catastrophe, soldiers began the process of moving gunpowder out of the White Tower.

Just before midnight on Tuesday, the wind veered suddenly to the south; then as the night wore on the gales at last began to ease. By six on Wednesday morning the fire had been quenched on both sides of the Strand, and by the afternoon it was clear that the flames had at last been halted and were beginning to die down. The danger now was of a breakdown of order, as wild rumours spread that a foreign army had landed and was marching on London. Panic swept though the crowds of homeless families camped out in Moorfields and other open spaces around the City, and foreigners once again feared for their lives. Their firefighting duties at an end, Craven's guards turned their attention to restoring order.

It was time to assess the magnitude of the disaster. In a little over three days, a sixth of London had been destroyed—some 13,200 houses, and eighty-seven parish churches. The vast majority of the City had gone up in flames, and tens of thousands of people had been left homeless, even though only a handful had lost their lives. But for the change of wind the disaster would in all probability have been much worse. Craven had worked valiantly; in fact, his expertise in fighting fires was to become legendary.

Ambitious plans for building a fine new capital at first went by the board, but by the spring agreement had been reached on how the City was to be rebuilt. An order of the Common Council, approved by the Privy Council at Whitehall on 8 May, laid down in great detail the width of the streets proposed, and the height and materials of all new buildings. On 11 April 1666, Craven was appointed to the Privy Council and to the new Commission of Streets and Highways, whose job was to ensure that the new streets were of the agreed width, and to prevent any sharp practice by landlords surreptitiously trying to move their boundaries.

The new city soon arose, celebrated in poems such as the anonymous *Litterae Consolatoriae, From the Author to the dejected place of his Nativity, the Honourable City of London*. Dedicated to the Lord Mayor, Sir William Turner, it didn't omit to pay due tribute to Craven's hard work.

> All hail, Blest City! Which next age must see
> Head (as Rome once) the worlds chief monarchy [...]
> Away with tears; let's have no more wet eyes;
> Thy lofty roofs already threat the skies [...]
> When to destroy Jove did an angel send,
> He likewise gave an honourable friend,
> Illustrious Craven; whose great Charity
> And virtuous Deeds unto Eternity
> Recorded are in Volumes 'bove the skie.[13]

War, pestilence, fire: the nation had certainly had its share of bad luck over the previous two years. The successive disasters had had a catastrophic effect on trade, and hence on the state of the government coffers. The predictable result was that there was a need for serious cuts in public spending, and in March 1667 a decision was taken—in the face of vigorous protests from Prince Rupert and the Duke of Albemarle—to lay up most of the capital ships of the Royal Navy in the Medway, Harwich, and Portsmouth. The result, given the dire state of Anglo-

Dutch relations, was only too predictable. In early June, a Dutch fleet of seventy ships under Admiral de Ruyter appeared off the Kent coast. With no fleet to oppose them, the Dutch sailed up the Medway; on 12 June they coolly entered Chatham Dockyard, burned five ships, and towed away the *Royal Charles*.

In London there was panic. Albemarle had been sent to Chatham just before the Dutch raid to take charge, but could do nothing to prevent the disaster. The day after the raid Rupert was ordered to Woolwich with a hastily raised regiment of foot, taking Craven with him. Their presence may have deterred another attack, but two weeks later, with de Ruyter preparing to make another attempt to sail up the Thames, Craven received urgent orders to travel post-haste to Gravesend to strengthen the defences there. He took with him William Winde, who had made a study of military architecture in the Netherlands in the 1650s. They hastily ordered fireships, arranged for further ships to be weighted and sunk offshore, and put in hand the enlargement of the fort, adding a new platform onto the old blockhouse. The Dutch Navy continued to prowl around, and towards the end of July a Dutch fleet appeared again at Chatham. An engagement ensued with a small fleet of fireships under the command of the ebullient vice-admiral Sir Edward Spragge, who destroyed some of the Dutch fireships. Two days later Rupert and Craven arrived from the Medway with more ships, and an inconclusive battle followed.[14] There was criticism that the Dutch fleet had managed to escape, but Spragge and Craven both defended themselves vigorously, pointing out that high winds had made it almost impossible to engage the enemy. A few days later a peace treaty brought an end to the conflict, and, to great relief, the Dutch fleet withdrew.

In March 1668 came trouble of a different kind, when disorder broke out among London apprentices who were 'taking the liberty of these holidays [it was Shrove Tuesday] to pull down bawdy houses.'[15] What became known as the Bawdy House Riots began with religiously inspired attacks on brothels. Attacks on brothels were a traditional Shrove Tuesday pastime, but these riots were on a huge scale and had worryingly anti-court overtones. The disorder began in Poplar and continued for three days, causing extreme panic in Whitehall, and all available troops were hastily summoned by beat of drum. The King's Life Guards, commanded by Craven, assembled in Lincoln's Inn Fields. Pepys went there hoping to see the riots, but all he found was the field full of soldiers, 'and my Lord Craven commanding of them, and riding up and down to give orders like a madman.'[16] Evidently he had lost none of his energy.

In April 1667 Craven, keen as ever to support good causes, had agreed to put a substantial amount of money into reviving the Mortlake Tapestry Works, which had been struggling for some years. Founded with great fanfare by James I in 1621, Mortlake's glory days had long passed. During the Civil War production had ceased, but in 1662 Charles II leased the premises to Sir Sackville Crow, promising him an annual grant of £1,000 towards the costs, and for five years Crow continued to run the business, but without, it seems, actually creating many tapestries. By 1667 the tapestry works had fallen victim to government cost-cutting, and in April of that year Crow resigned on the grounds that without continued subsidies he was losing money. What Mortlake needed was a patriotic consortium with deep pockets and a willingness to risk money on artistic patronage. No surprise perhaps that it was Craven who came to the rescue, along with two others: William Ashburnham, cofferer to the royal household, and Thomas Povey, member of the Council for Foreign Plantations. In April 1667, these three signed an agreement undertaking to continue running the Mortlake Tapestry Works at their own expense without the former allowance of £1,000 a year.

In the event the patriotic consortium did not last long. By this time many of the weavers had left Mortlake for the new tapestry works which had opened in Lambeth and Holborn, and perhaps for this reason it proved impossible to restart production. Craven, busy fortifying the Thames against the Dutch, would have had little time just then to devote to a new venture. A few months later, in October 1667, Charles II granted the Mortlake Tapestry Works to the Earl of Sunderland and Henry Brouncker, later Lord Brouncker. In the event these two were no more successful than their predecessors, and a few months later Mortlake came into the hands of Lady Harvey, sister of Ralph Montagu, Master of the Great Wardrobe. Lady Harvey managed to produce some fine tapestries, but in 1674 Montagu himself took over the works and moved some of the weavers to his own workshops in Great Queen Street.[17]

At about the same time Craven became involved in a new venture which did, eventually, produce handsome returns. In 1667 two French fur-traders, Médart Chouart, Sieur des Groseilliers (or 'lord of the gooseberry patch'), and Pierre Radisson, arrived in England with reports of exciting opportunities in the New World. At this period the northern part of North America was still largely in the hands of the French, but the area around the great gulf known as Hudson's Bay, named after the English explorer Henry Hudson, was still largely unexplored. The two adventurers had great plans for opening up the region for fur-trading, but their efforts to interest the authorities in Quebec met with failure. An appeal to the French court in Paris was equally unsuccessful, but in May 1667 Groseilliers was persuaded to travel to England and approach Prince Rupert.

Rupert was excited by the possibilities. He saw the opportunities for fur-trading, but was also gripped by the tantalising prospect of a north-west passage through to the South Seas. When Groseilliers arrived in England he was summoned to the Prince's apartments at Windsor Castle, where he was introduced to a few other men, among them Albemarle and Craven, who might be prepared to put money into the venture. Armed with Rupert's enthusiastic endorsement, Groseilliers travelled to Oxford for a meeting with the King. Charles too was excited, and he instructed his brother to make a ketch, the *Eaglet*, available for the expedition, to be rigged and victualled by the three principal backers, Rupert, Albemarle, and Craven. A second ketch, the *Nonsuch*, captained by an old friend of Groseilliers named Zachary Gillam, was also co-opted for the expedition when it fortuitously turned up in London.

Early in the morning of 3 June 1668, a small skiff containing three visitors left Wapping Old Stairs and rowed out towards the *Nonsuch*, riding at anchor midstream. A salute was fired as Prince Rupert, Lord Craven, and Rupert's secretary James Hayes were piped on deck. They were ceremonially received by Captain Gillam and Monsieur Groseilliers—or 'Mr Gooseberry', as he appears in the instructions for the voyage—and conducted round the vessel, before descending to the captain's cabin where a bottle of madeira was broached and toasts were drunk to the success of the expedition. The visitors then clambered back down into the skiff, to loud cheers from the crew, and returned to dry land. By ten o'clock that night, the *Nonsuch* and the *Eaglet*, both laden with cargoes of assorted tools and trinkets for trade, had weighed anchor and embarked for the New World. Somewhere in the Atlantic the Eaglet, with Radisson on board, lost its mast in a storm and had to turn back, but a month after its departure from London the *Nonsuch* appeared at the icy entrance to Hudson's Strait, and seven days later it arrived in Hudson's Bay. A fort was constructed, a good cargo of furs purchased from the local Native Americans, and the following summer Gillam set sail for England, leaving Groseilliers to make excursions into the interior to persuade the surrounding tribes of the advantages of trading with the English. In October Gillam arrived back in England with a rich cargo of furs and skins, and he reported 'the natives to bee very civill and say Beaver is very plenty.'[18]

It all seemed very promising. A three-masted frigate was commissioned, named the *Prince Rupert*, and Rupert approached the King with a view to obtaining a royal charter of monopoly. The King consented, and on 2 May 1670 a royal charter was granted to eighteen nobles and gentlemen. Rupert became the first governor of the company; the deputy-governor was Sir John Robinson, and other members included Craven, Albemarle, Arlington, Ashley, and the wealthy banker Sir Robert Vyner. These eighteen were incorporated into a joint-stock company, 'The Governor and Company of Merchants-Adventurers trading into Hudson's Bay', into which most put £300. Under the terms of the charter they became the Lords and Proprietors of what became known as 'Rupert's Land', consisting of all the land draining into Hudson's Bay, with the exclusive right to establish settlements and carry on trade. Rupert remained as governor until his death and continued to take an active interest, the company meetings usually held at his house in Spring Gardens. The fur trade increased gradually as the region was developed and a chain of forts built on the shores of the bay, but after a decade the company had lost thirteen ships and had spent £200,000 without much to show for it. Eventually, in 1681, a corner was turned when a cargo of furs was sold for the huge sum of £15,721, and the first dividend was declared in 1684. It was for 50 per cent, a handsome rate of return by any standards, and Craven received a total of £150.[19]

The Company of Royal Adventurers of England trading into Africa had fared much less well. Always under-capitalised, in 1670 it was wound up and replaced by a new company with sounder finances. The new Royal African Company received its Royal Charter on 27 September 1672. This time the principal objects of trade were listed as gold, silver, and, for the first time, slaves. The company was authorised to set up forts and factories, to raise troops and to make war and peace with local chieftains. It took over the assets and liabilities of the Royal Adventurers, and plans were drawn up to raise at least £100,000 by public subscription. About 200 people applied for stock, Craven subscribing for £600, and in just five weeks the company found itself oversubscribed.

As for that other new venture, the Province of Carolina, its prospects had by now undergone a distinct improvement. For much of the 1660s it had looked as though the colony might fail. The proprietors were finding it hard to attract new settlers, and the low point had come when the Barbadians abandoned their colony at Cape Fear. It was Lord Ashley who decided that the project must be reinvigorated, reportedly after a close encounter with death in a carriage accident caused him to consider what legacy he wished to leave to posterity. On 26 April 1669, he convened a meeting of the remaining proprietors and persuaded each of them to contribute £500 towards creating a new settlement at Port Royal, in the south of the province, and a further £200 a year for the next four years. The funds were to be used to finance the fitting out of a fleet to transport settlers out from England. Craven and Albemarle each gave £550 towards the cost of the first ship, the *Carolina*; of the remaining proprietors, Sir Peter Colleton contributed £545, and Lord Ashley and Sir George Carteret both gave £500.

The proprietors decided, as a further inducement to settlers, that the terms offered must be made more attractive, and to this end Ashley's secretary, John Locke, drafted a revised constitution for the province. The resulting Fundamental Constitutions, modelled on James Harrington's influential *Oceana*, incorporated what were regarded as the very best principles of enlightened government. The social order Locke envisaged was to be aristocratic in nature, with property distributed in such a way as to maintain the hierarchy thought essential for an orderly and harmonious society, and to 'avoid erecting a numerous democracy'.[20] Land ownership would be based on a manorial system, with two fifths of the land owned by the proprietors and members of the two proposed orders of nobility, landgraves and caciques. A rent of a penny an acre would be due to the proprietors, who reserved all rights over mines, wrecks, and pearl and whale fishing. Settlements were to be along rivers, but not within 2½ miles of any Native American town.

There would be eight chief offices, one for each of the Lords Proprietors. The eldest proprietor would hold the office of palatine, the other seven acting as admiral, chamberlain, chancellor, constable, chief justice, high steward, and treasurer. At a meeting of the Lords Proprietors on 21 October 1669, the Duke of Albemarle, as the senior of the Lords Proprietors, was elected Palatine, with

Craven as High Constable, with responsibility for matters such as the suppression of piracy and privateering.

In the event Locke's constitution was never adopted, largely because it was too elaborate for a sparsely populated colony, and instead the proprietors issued a series of temporary instructions. But in 1671 they made their first nominations for the province's nobility. Locke was nominated as a landgrave, as was Craven's protégé Sir Edmund Andros, newly married to Mary Craven, younger sister of Sir William Craven of Combe Abbey.

The 'first fleet' consisted of three ships—the *Carolina*, the *Port Royal*, and the *Albemarle*—while other settlers arrived from Barbados. Soon, satisfying reports started to come in from the new settlement at Albemarle Point, and a trickle of English settlers left for the colony, helped by a series of promotional pamphlets directing interested parties to the new Carolina Coffee House which had just opened in Birchin Lane in the City of London. In 1670, settlers from Bermuda founded the settlement of Charles Town on the west bank of the Ashley River.

For many years it was Lord Ashley (from 1672 the Earl of Shaftesbury) who continued to be the driving force behind the promotion of Carolina. After his fall from royal favour in 1674, he was able to spend more time on what had become his pet project, his 'darling'. In that year the proprietors agreed that each of them should contribute £100 a year for the next seven years, and only those who paid in full (of whom there were just three: Shaftesbury, Craven, and Carteret) should have a role in managing the colony.[21] The policy of the proprietors was to encourage the settlers to grow profitable crops such as silk, olives, and wine, and to discourage them from exploring the interior. Ashley's carefully laid plan was to keep the settlers hemmed in by hostile tribes, notably the Westoes, who would deter the Spanish, while the proprietors monopolised the trade and mineral wealth of the interior. It was a policy which had little chance of succeeding, because the settlers too had their eyes on the potential mineral riches inland.

Craven's main responsibilities during these years, however, were military, and much of his time was spent in the delicate task of policing the capital. When it came to disputes between citizens and soldiers—troops were as a rule billeted in inns, taverns, and ale houses, a situation that often led to friction—the Duke of Albemarle invariably relied on Craven's mediation and his influence with the magistrates.[22]

Lord Craven's drums could be heard day and night in the capital as his troops did their best to keep order in the various alarums and excursions that punctuated these years. 'All Hearts fall a-leaping whenever she comes, And beat day and night, like my Lord Craven's drums,' wrote the rakish Earl of Dorset in 1676 in a tribute to an anonymous mistress.[23] During the hysteria surrounding the fictitious Popish Plot in the autumn of 1678, Craven was kept busy arresting suspected troublemakers. When it came to firefighting, he was as energetic as ever. Tradition had it that whenever a fire broke out he was invariably first on the spot, organising the response and preserving order, and it was said that he had managed to train his horse to smell out fires and gallop directly towards them. Major conflagrations were not uncommon; one in Southwark in May 1676 raged for two days and destroyed over 600 houses before it was brought under control, despite the best efforts of Craven, the Duke of Monmouth, and the Lord Mayor.[24]

In 1670, on the death of the Duke of Albemarle, Craven took over command of his regiment, Monck's Regiment of Foot, now renamed the Coldstream Guards after the village where Monck had crossed the Tweed into England in 1660. At the same time Craven succeeded Albemarle as Lord Lieutenant of Middlesex and the Borough of Southwark, and in the same year he was appointed Master of Trinity House, adding to the various other offices he had acquired in recent years, such as High Steward of the University of Cambridge (1667) and Governor of the Charterhouse (1668). In 1677 he joined the Admiralty board. Pepys, in his efforts to improve the quality of the English Navy, soon afterwards proposed that every candidate for the rank of lieutenant should have served at least three years at sea and at least one as a midshipman. It was an eminently sensible proposal which would have created a more professional officer corps, but Rupert, backed up by Craven and the Earl of Ossory, objected on the grounds that service as a midshipman was beneath the quality of a gentleman. They were overruled, and the change went ahead.

Neither Rupert nor Craven felt particularly at home at Charles II's court, though if we are to believe Sophie's account Craven had a talent for engaging the King in light conversation. We are told that he was given the nickname 'Earwig' by Lord Guildford, because of his habit of whispering into the ears of the principal politicians at court. On one occasion Charles II is said to have noticed Craven whispering into the ear of the Earl of Dorset, 'whose high breeding made him a patient listener,' and he asked Dorset what Craven had said. 'Sir,' Dorset replied, 'my Lord Craven did me the honour to whisper, but I did not think it good manners to listen.'[25]

On occasion Craven acted as an intermediary on behalf of Sophie and Charles Louis at the Stuart court. When the question of the possible marriage of Sophie's adopted daughter Liselotte came up in January 1666, Sophie entrusted Craven with a memorandum on the subject to give to Charles II—this despite the fact that Sophie had always had a rather dismissive opinion of her family's faithful servant. When Charles Louis asked Craven to discuss a delicate matter with Charles II, Sophie confessed her surprise that her brother would 'confide serious matters to our milord, who does not have much common sense,' but she acknowledged that he was unswervingly faithful and happy to serve them without any reward—useful for a family with no money.

In 1669, Craven made Sophie a present of orange trees from his house in Heidelberg. Transported to the Bishop's Palace in Osnabruck, they did well in their square tubs, and were still as beautiful as she remembered them from the days when she was a young woman staying at Charles Louis's court at Heidelberg. That autumn Craven sent a portrait of Rupert to Sophie, but she did not think it did justice to his martial appearance. Craven also advised Sophie on paintings, including a series she was keen to commission commemorating Rupert's life, in which she assured Craven that his own exploits would be represented. Later, in 1678, she turned to him in an attempt to persuade Rupert to marry in order to provide an heir for the Palatinate, given that Charles Louis had had no legitimate heirs. But Craven begged to be excused from interfering, unless Sophie could suggest a suitably rich lady willing to marry Rupert. She couldn't, and so there the matter rested.

Of the rest of the Palatine family, Craven also kept up a frequent correspondence with Princess Elizabeth. She wrote to him in 1668 thanking him for a portrait of himself which had found a place in her bedroom beside one of Rupert. On 24 July 1671, she wrote saying how glad she was that Rupert had had his home fitted out so well, but that if he wanted to have good furniture he shouldn't allow dogs in the house. A fortnight later she had changed her mind, asking Craven to tell Rupert that 'she esteems his content more than a clean house and therefore does not wish him to put away his dogs.'

'He would rather be cut to pieces than surrender'

In 1682, Craven's building itch found a new outlet, this time at Combe Abbey. He himself never lived at Combe; following the Restoration the house was occupied by his godson Sir Isaac Gibson, and then from 1680 by Sir William Craven of Appletreewick, the earl's cousin and heir. Although Gibson had built a new west wing in 1668, the house as a whole was badly decayed and in dire need of attention. Once again Craven turned to William Winde, commissioning him to draw up plans to rebuild the west and north wings of the house in a grand Palladian style. From Drury House, where he spent the majority of his time, Craven kept a close eye on the progress of the house and garden at Combe.

Craven's interest in gardening was long-standing. Accounts of his later years invariably mention his friendships with John Evelyn and the naturalist John Ray, but back in 1649, living the life of an exile in the Hague, he had lavished money on his garden at Hamstead Marshall, ordering fruit trees from London and tens of thousands of trees and plants for the garden and park. It is possible too that he can take credit for raising one of our oldest apple varieties, the Wyken Pippin. This variety is traditionally said to have been raised from a pip saved from an apple brought from Holland and planted in the garden of Wyken Hall on the Combe estate in about 1700, and it is easy to imagine Lord Craven having apples sent over from the Netherlands, where he still owned property, and giving instructions that pips from his favourite variety were to be planted at Combe.

On 29 November 1682 Prince Rupert died. He had been in poor health for some time. Two days before his death he had made his will, naming Craven as his executor and bequeathing to him all his goods, chattels, pictures, and other assets, including stock in companies and shares in patents, in trust for Rupert's mistress Margaret Hughes and their daughter Ruperta. Under the terms of the will, Craven also became Ruperta's guardian. Rupert had not been rich, but after selling the gold, silver, and some jewellery, including a pearl necklace which was bought by Nell Gwyn for £4,520, Craven was able to settle a handsome annuity on Ruperta. Items of sentimental value, notably the Queen of Bohemia's picture collection, as well as Rupert's library and other papers, Craven was able to keep, though the library, which consisted of books in French, Italian, Spanish, High Dutch, Low Dutch, and English, was sold by Craven's heirs after his death in 1697.[1]

Rupert's funeral took place at Westminster Abbey on the night of 6 December. In the absence of the King and Duke of York, who by custom did not attend, the role of chief mourner fell to Craven, who followed the Prince's coffin as it was borne in a magnificent and solemn procession from Whitehall Palace to the abbey.

That year, 1682, was one of increasing tension. For the past four years the entire country had teetered on the edge of armed conflict, as Shaftesbury orchestrated attempts to have the Duke of York excluded from the succession. Shaftesbury's Whig circle included two of his fellow-proprietors of Carolina, Sir Peter Colleton and Sir John Archdale, as well as the proprietary secretaries Locke and Wilson. Craven and his fellow proprietor the Earl of Bath, by contrast, were both staunch loyalists. An anonymous newsletter had even named Craven as one of a shadowy and probably fictitious group known as the 'twelve disciples', who were supposedly controlling the affairs of the kingdom in secret and plotting to impose Catholicism.

In March 1681, Charles II had called a Parliament in the safety of Oxford, well away from the London mobs stirred up by Shaftesbury. After posting guards to secure the road to Oxford, Charles placed Craven, a lieutenant-general since 1678, in command of the remaining troops in London and Westminster. If insurrection broke out, he was to quell the riot using all necessary means, 'by killing, slaying or otherwise howsoever destroying those who shall so resist in the disturbance of the public peace.'[2] Fortunately no violence ensued, and in Oxford Charles turned the tables on his opponents by the simple method of proroguing Parliament after just six days. Shaftesbury and his circle had planned to use the Oxford Parliament to seize power by force, but they found themselves outmanoeuvred. Four months later, the Privy Council, to which Craven had been reappointed in March, ordered Shaftesbury's arrest on suspicion of high treason. For four months he was imprisoned in the Tower of London, until in November he was acquitted of plotting to depose the King.

Such was the situation when six of the Lords Proprietors of Carolina met on 21 March 1682 at the Carolina Coffee House, to answer questions from people considering emigrating to the colony. Of the original proprietors, only Craven and Shaftesbury now remained; also present at the meeting were the Earl of Bath (guardian of Sir George Carteret's infant son), Sir John Archdale (a Quaker who had bought John Lord Berkeley's share in 1678 in trust for his infant son), Sir Peter Colleton, and Mr Vivian, acting for Christopher, second Duke of Albemarle. It must have been a tense, not to say incongruous meeting, but it seems to have succeeded in its purpose. The True Protestant Mercury reported that

> [...] there was a great resort of people of all sorts, who came to receive satisfaction in certain particulars, and do find all things so well answer their expectations, that

they intend very speedily, with their Wives and Families, to transport themselves [to Carolina].[3]

In fact there had long been suspicions in government circles that discussions on the colonisation of Carolina were merely a pretext for Whig plotting against the crown. It was, after all, the perfect cover. Under the terms of their charter the proprietors were permitted to raise troops and declare war, to collect funds and hire ships. Government suspicions were confirmed the following year with the discovery of the Rye House Plot, whose organisers apparently intended to use Carolina agents to assassinate the King and Duke and restore the Commonwealth. The plot was allegedly on a huge scale, involving up to 20,000 people, including a number of Scots who had travelled down to London supposedly on Carolina business. The government's response was to arrest all suspected troublemakers, and at the same time to expand the Army. Tangier, problematic ever since its acquisition in 1660, was abandoned, and its formidable garrison summoned back home.

A month after the meeting at the coffee house, Charles II declared martial law in London, banning a Whig feast which Shaftesbury was due to attend and giving Craven orders to use all necessary means to suppress tumultuous assemblies. Still, Carolina business continued uninterrupted; during the next few months the proprietors conducted a flurry of business, sending out a revised version of the Fundamental Constitutions, making land grants, and prohibiting the enslavement of Native Americans. But Shaftesbury, harassed by government agents, was finding life in England increasingly uncomfortable. In September he fled to the safety of the Netherlands, where he died early the following year.

Shaftesbury had long been the motive force behind the development of Carolina, but after a hiatus of a few months the business of recruiting new settlers resumed, this time under the direction of Craven and Archdale. They were an unlikely combination, the Tory loyalist and the Whiggish Quaker, but they worked together conscientiously, and under their leadership the proprietors began a new promotional campaign. Over the next three years a stream of pamphlets appeared extolling the virtues of Carolina; six were published in London, two in Dublin, and a further two in the Netherlands, the latter written in French and directed at French Huguenots, a group of whom had already arrived in Carolina in 1680 to escape Louis XIV's anti-Huguenot pogroms. The pamphlets emphasised the temperate climate, ideal for growing grapes and olives once the land had been improved. At the same time the proprietors issued a revised constitution aimed at bolstering Carolina's appeal to dissenters, and negotiations continued with representatives of the newly formed Scottish Carolina Company, which was granted a county of its own.[4]

The promotional campaign was successful, and between 1682 and 1685 some 500 Presbyterians and Baptists settled in the south of the province, while in 1684 a group of Scottish Presbyterians led by Lord Cardross settled in Port Royal.

The proprietors directed the surveyor general to lay out three counties: Berkeley County, which was to include Charles Town, with Craven County to the north and Colleton County to the south.

In London, meanwhile, tensions continued to mount as the prospect of James's succession grew closer. In October 1684, the King and Duke concentrated four thousand troops at Blackheath and drilled them as a unit. As Charles lay on his deathbed early in 1685, orders went out to the lord lieutenants calling on them to prevent any disorders. At the end of February Charles died, and his brother duly succeeded to the throne. Craven had always been closer to James—martial, serious-minded, and always the Queen of Bohemia's favourite nephew—than to his elder brother. The new King reappointed him to the Privy Council and to the Committee for Trade and Plantations, and in June he was confirmed as a lieutenant-general of the Army.

In June 1686 James ordered the Army to muster on Hounslow Heath, conveniently situated between London and Windsor. But if the aim of the Hounslow camp was to overawe, it was singularly unsuccessful, the camp being treated as a vast fair by the people of London. The following summer the exercise was repeated; this time, Evelyn went out to view the camp and noted 'the commanders profusely vying in the expense and magnificence of their tents.'[5] Whose, one wonders, was the most magnificent? Craven, a lieutenant-general with a princely income, no doubt had a tent of princely magnificence, but whether it surpassed those of other grandees such as the Earl of Feversham, Lord Churchill, or the Duke of Grafton history does not relate.

Craven was now seventy-nine—a very vigorous seventy-nine to be sure, but still seventy-nine. It was intimated to him that the King would be pleased if he resigned his commission as Colonel of the Coldstream Guards, but he replied that 'if they took away his regiment they had as good take away his life, since he had nothing else to divert himself with.'[6] So for the moment he kept his post, and the events of the following year, as the King fled and London descended into chaos, were to show that the post was no sinecure. Craven's levels of energy and stamina would be remarkable even today, but they seem astonishing in an age when few people lived into their seventies.

As James staggered from disaster to disaster in the course of 1688, Craven, as Privy Councillor, Lord Lieutenant of Middlesex, and Colonel of the Coldstream Guards, found himself in the eye of the storm. The beginning of the end for James came in the middle of October, when the Prince of Orange embarked on his invasion of England. He came at the invitation of a group of prominent English peers, who assured him that they were supported by 'all the wise and good men in the nation'.[7] They were not far wrong; there is no doubt that William was seen by most as a liberator. It was the birth of Mary of Modena's son a few months earlier which was the catalyst for opposition. Since the boy was bound to be brought up as a Catholic, the nation was faced with the appalling prospect of being ruled by a dynasty of Catholic kings. A few days before the Prince of Orange set sail, James had held a special council meeting to scotch the rather absurd, if widely believed, allegation that the baby was an impostor smuggled into the bedchamber secretly in a warming pan. Craven was among those who testified that he had been present at the birth, along with scores of others crammed into the poor Queen's bedchamber.

The Prince of Orange had no intention, at that stage, of deposing James and seizing the crown for himself. As his Declaration of 10 October made clear, his aim was much more limited; it was simply to force James to call a free Parliament which would legislate to protect the Anglican ascendancy and thereby secure English support for war against Louis XIV. On 5 November William landed at Torbay and marched to Exeter, where soon a steady stream of people came to pledge their allegiance to their Protestant deliverer.

James decided that the best course of action would be to try and confine the Prince to the south-west of the country, and to this end he advanced with his army to Salisbury, having left enough troops in London to maintain order. As soon as he left the capital, agitators tried to stir up resentment against Mary of Modena by spreading false rumours about her in seditious newsletters: she had assaulted the King and prevented him from coming to terms with the Prince of Orange; she had assaulted her step-daughter Princess Anne, and then, 'like a true virago', she had also beaten Lord Craven, whereupon he had resigned his commission. A few weeks earlier another newsletter had even claimed, a touch improbably, that 'my Lord Craven told the King "He would never be at peace till he had lopped the queen off shorter by the head".' If this was an attempt to create discord between the Queen and the incorruptible commander of her household troops, it was singularly ineffective.[8]

While the English Army mustered near Salisbury, William moved northwards, 'for the King being so much superior to him in horse, it was not advisable to march through the great plains of Dorsetshire and Wiltshire.'[9] So wrote Bishop Burnet. But James's forces, though on paper twice the size of the Prince's, were in fact about as substantial as a house of cards. There were growing signs of disaffection among both officers and men, and James's senior commanders all urged him to come to terms with the Prince. A few days later, on 23 November, James bowed to the inevitable and agreed to return to London, only to find that this was the signal for some of his most senior officers to go over to William; they included his nephew the Duke of Grafton, his son-in-law Prince George of Denmark and, most woundingly of all, his favourite, Lord Churchill. At the same time, news arrived of rebellions in Yorkshire and Nottinghamshire.

On 26 November James arrived back at Whitehall, shaken to the core by the sudden collapse of his army, only to learn that his daughter Princess Anne had fled from her apartments in the Cockpit the previous night. Anne was a fervent Protestant, and 'pretending that the King her father did persecute and use her ill for her religion,' she had made up her mind to flee. James arrived to find Lord Craven busy cross-questioning the sentinels in the gallery to discover how the Princess had contrived to escape unnoticed. She had, it turned out, made her escape down a wooden staircase constructed six months earlier to link her apartments with those of her bosom friend Sarah Churchill. Sarah's doors had been left unguarded, and the two women had fled together with the Princess's mentor, Bishop Compton.

To James, the defection of his daughter seemed an even worse blow than the treachery of the Army. 'God help me!' he exclaimed. 'Even my children have forsaken me!' He abandoned all thoughts of resistance and instead summoned a meeting of peers to advise him on how to proceed. The great council which met on the 27th advised the King to call a free Parliament, to dismiss all Catholics from office, to grant a general pardon, and to appoint commissioners to meet the Prince of Orange. James agreed to all the recommendations. He sent out writs for a Parliament to meet on 15 January, and appointed three trusted commissioners to open negotiations with William.

William, meanwhile, was making his way towards London in a leisurely fashion, finding the time to do a bit of sightseeing en route. Outside Salisbury he visited Wilton House, where he admired the fine van Dycks. Then, on 6 December, he stopped on the way to Hungerford for a tour of Craven's still unfinished mansion of Hamstead Marshall, having heard perhaps that the house had been planned as a summer palace for his great-aunt the Queen of Bohemia.[10] At Hungerford he received the King's commissioners and learnt the terms that James was offering. After discussion with his supporters William set out his own demands. Given the dramatic collapse of royal authority they were not unduly harsh, and it appeared there was a reasonable basis for a settlement which would leave James's title as King intact.

As James's commissioners prepared to return to Whitehall, events in London suddenly took an ominous turn. Over the last few weeks anti-Catholic rioting had been steadily increasing in the capital. But people had begun to hope that the crisis was past; Princess Anne even wrote requesting that the back stairs at the Cockpit should be painted in preparation for her return to Whitehall. But on 4 December, a new declaration by the Prince of Orange appeared on the streets of London. It was full of dark allegations of a build-up of armed Papists in London and Westminster, and of an imminent invasion by French troops. There would be no mercy shown to Papists who were found with weapons in their possession, and all Catholics must be stripped of office.

What nobody knew was that this menacing declaration was actually a forgery. Its appearance at this delicate juncture inflamed an already volatile situation. Attacks on Catholics in London redoubled, and other prominent supporters of the King felt the force of popular anger too; attempts were made to indict Lord Craven and some of his troops on charges of wilful murder and treason during an assault on a Catholic chapel in Clerkenwell in mid–November, during which a number of Protestant youths had been shot by soldiers from the Coldstream

Guards. The charges were eventually dropped, but only after 'powerfull mediations and persuasions'. Many Catholic courtiers fled London, while Catholics in the provinces became targets of spontaneous violence and sought refuge in the capital, thereby inflaming anti-Catholic feeling. Under pressure to do something, the Lord Mayor ordered house-to-house searches in the City to establish just how many Catholics there were, but this ratcheted up the hysteria still further. There was a febrile, dangerous atmosphere, with widespread fear of an imminent Catholic coup.[11]

James felt increasingly alarmed. He had still not heard from his commissioners, but was hoping for good news. When copies of the forged declaration appeared in London, its uncompromising tone came as an enormous shock to him. With London engulfed in a rising tide of anti-Catholic violence, he felt terrifyingly vulnerable. Virtually all his trusted advisers had fled, and he did not know whom to trust. He had very real fears for his own safety and for that of his wife and son. A few days earlier he had sent the six-month-old Prince Charles to Portsmouth with instructions that he should be taken to France, but on the 8th the infant arrived back in London after the Governor of Portsmouth refused James's request. His main concern now was to get his wife and son to safety, and then he planned to slip away after them as soon as he could. On the night of 9 December, the Queen and Prince travelled secretly to Gravesend, where they boarded a boat to take them to France.

The following night, in the early hours of Tuesday 11 December, James himself slipped out of his bedchamber, leaving Craven and the Duke of Northumberland asleep in the antechamber. He descended the backstairs, crossed the privy gardens, and climbed into a small boat at Westminster Stairs. Crossing the Thames to Vauxhall, he rode eastwards towards the Isle of Elmley, where a boat was waiting to take him over the Channel. In a calculated attempt to create chaos, he had instructed Lord Feversham, the commander-in-chief, not to resist the Dutch Army, and he had ordered Lord Dartmouth to send the Navy, such of it as remained loyal, to Ireland. In order to make it impossible to call a legal Parliament he burnt all the parliamentary writs which had not yet been sent out, and as he crossed the Thames he dropped the Great Seal of England into the river. Feversham's response to the King's instructions was to order the Army to be disbanded forthwith without pay, but he omitted to add that the troops should be disarmed. The result was multitudes of armed but penniless soldiers swarming around the south of England, many of whom were Catholics from the feared Irish regiments that James had brought over to overawe his subjects.

With the sudden disappearance of the King, there was an urgent need to maintain some semblance of government before London descended into anarchy. Craven and Northumberland wasted no time in parading the Coldstream and Horse Guards. Meanwhile, the Earl of Rochester, with the support of the Bishop of Ely and Archbishop Sancroft, sent urgent summonses to all the lords temporal and spiritual who were still in London to meet at the Guildhall. Later that morning, twenty-eight peers gathered there and constituted themselves as, in effect, a provisional government. Most urgently, with reports coming in of mobs rampaging through the suburbs, they issued a proclamation forbidding further assaults on private property, and they ordered Lord Craven, as Lord Lieutenant of Middlesex, to summon the militia to prevent any disorder in Westminster or Southwark. But Craven, arriving soon afterwards, told the committee that he had already done just this, and he had also written to the Prince of Orange undertaking to do his utmost to maintain order in London.[12]

There was no agreement among the peers at the Guildhall over how to proceed. Even though the Tory peers were in a majority—eighteen out of the twenty-eight were sympathetic to the King—they were not united, and in the end it was the Whigs who won the argument. After a heated discussion and the rejection of a motion calling for the King's honourable restoration, the peers issued a compromise declaration regretting the King's departure 'by the pernicious counsels of persons ill-affected to our nation and religion', but undertaking to assist the Prince of Orange in restoring order and in attempting to call a Parliament. The provisional government authorised the shutting of the city gates at night and the hanging of chains across the streets between 10 p.m. and 6 a.m. After a wearying night trying to maintain order, Craven added his name to the declaration at seven the following morning.

'No sooner was the King's withdrawing known,' reported one newspaper, 'but the mobile consulted to wreak their vengeance on Papists and Popery.'[13] Panicked Catholics awoke to find that their royal protector had vanished, leaving them defenceless before the violence of the mob. In the course of the day, order broke down in London as rioters attacked the mass-houses, hated symbols of Popish idolatry. As night fell, the streets were filled with 'very great concourses of people' intent on mischief. It was a chaotic and terrifying night of arson, looting, and terror, as the rioters widened their attacks to include the embassies of Catholic nations and the houses of prominent Catholics. That night the rabble were the masters of London, as the mob was taken over by criminal elements. Weld House, owned by Craven's cousin Sir Humphrey Weld and the home of the Spanish ambassador, was sacked and much of its contents looted, while an enormous fire burned in Lincoln's Inn Fields as rioters ransacked and set alight a mass-house. Not since the conflagration of 1666 had the skies above the city been lit up so brightly.

The following morning, the 12th, the peers decided to move from the Guildhall to the Council Chamber at Whitehall. Appalled by the extent of the destruction, they threatened rioters with 'the utmost rigour of law', and deputy lieutenants were empowered to call out the militia. But this had little effect, and by noon disorder had spread to Whitehall, where the peers, with Craven now in attendance, were in conclave. An order was hastily signed authorising Colonels Selwyn and Bagot of the Foot Guards to disperse the mob, if necessary by force. Whitehall was saved, but by the end of the afternoon the mob was threatening St James's Palace, and the peers sent an urgent order for artillery and reinforcements of horse and foot guards. They arrived promptly, but not before some of the rioters had broken into the palace and begun looting the chapel. Cannons were set up in the park and prepared for firing, but after a brisk cavalry charge the mob retreated.[14]

That night a wild panic gripped London, as rumours spread that thousands of soldiers from James's disbanded Irish Army were about to descend on the city and massacre its inhabitants. It was said that they had already burnt Uxbridge and put all its inhabitants to the sword. In what became known as the Irish Fear, the people of London were awoken by a cacophony of trumpets and kettle drums and by shouts of 'rise, arm, arm, the Irish are cutting throats'. In no time over 100,000 Londoners had assembled to defend the city, with candles lit in every window and impromptu barricades formed in the streets. The peers, meeting in the early hours of the morning, soon established that the rumours were without foundation, but to reassure the citizens they ordered the Regiment of Fusiliers to stand at arms. By four in the morning people began to realise that there was nothing to fear, and most returned to bed. The next day, however, the disorder was as bad as ever. By the afternoon it was reported that 'the rabble in Southwark were like to do great mischief without speedy care,' and the trained bands were authorised to disperse the mob, if necessary by firing on them. There was disorder near Charing Cross too, and companies of horse were ordered to guard Whitehall and St James's. By the following afternoon, criminal elements in the mob were starting to attack properties in Bloomsbury, and Craven ordered extra troops of horse to mount guard at night in St James's Square, Leicester Fields, and Southampton Square in Bloomsbury.

The peers worked hard to restore some semblance of order in the country. They issued orders for the payment of troops, they closed the ports so that no Irish soldiers could return to Ireland to stir up trouble there, and they ordered a stop to all foreign posts. All Catholic troops were to be disarmed, and any Jesuits, Popish priests, and other 'eminent offenders against the law' who might be attempting to flee the country were to be arrested. The seamen of Kent set about their task enthusiastically, and on the 12th Lord Jeffreys, the former Lord Chancellor, was discovered on board a ship at Shadwell Dock, disguised as a common seaman and with his bushy eyebrows carefully shaved. He was duly dispatched to the Tower.

The following day came news of the capture of a much more eminent fugitive, in the person of the King himself. James had boarded a ship at Faversham but had turned back to take on extra ballast. Before he could set sail he was apprehended by a band of local fishermen who took him for a Jesuit in flight. His purse was rifled, and he was roundly abused and then taken to an inn, the Arms of England, where he was imprisoned. Here he was recognised, and word was sent to the authorities in London.

After much debate the provisional government authorised four loyalist peers to travel to Faversham to attend the King. After a difficult journey through a countryside still tense with rumours of massacres by Irish troops, the peers met James and begged him to return to London. For his safety the provisional government had sent an escort of 120 guards and fifty grenadiers to accompany him. He agreed to return, and sent a message to the Prince proposing a meeting at St James's Palace on the 17th 'to settle the distracted nation'.

When he arrived back in London on the 16th, James found himself, to his very great surprise, welcomed by cheering crowds who thronged the streets and filled every window and balcony. In a triumphal parade he was escorted back to Whitehall by Craven and his Coldstream Guards. Even an unpopular king was preferable to the anarchy of the last few days. Encouraged by the unexpected show of support, James decided to take up the reins of government again. He summoned the Privy Council, began issuing a series of orders, and discussed with the Protestant bishops the outline of a compromise agreement with the Prince.

For William, however, James's unexpected flight had changed everything. Hitherto all he had aimed for had been a negotiated settlement which would ensure the calling of a new Parliament, but James's disappearance had seemed to signify his rejection of any such settlement. Until now only the most hot-headed among the Whig politicians had advocated that William should seize the throne, but now all of a sudden the throne had for all intents and purposes become vacant, and the crown seemed to be his for the taking. For the Prince therefore, James's reappearance was very inopportune, and he was furious with the peers for bringing him back.

Studiously ignoring James's invitation to meet for talks at St James's Palace, William decided that James must be forced to leave London again, allowing him to claim the throne on the grounds that the King had deserted his people. James must, in short, be deposed. It was agreed that the Prince's guards under Count Solms would first of all take possession of Whitehall Palace, and once this had been achieved the Prince's emissaries would convey a message to the King advising him that 'for his own safety' he should leave Whitehall and go to Ham House.

Shortly after eleven o'clock on the evening of Monday 17 December, Craven's Coldstream Guards, on sentry duty outside Whitehall Palace, heard the tramp of armed men marching up Piccadilly Lane from the west. There were three battalions of them, dressed in the uniforms of the Prince of Orange's Blue Guards, and they were backed up by a squadron of horse. Their commander, Count Solms, sent a detachment to secure St James's Palace, but the main body of guards continued to advance in order of battle, drums beating and matches lit in preparation for firing, towards Whitehall Palace. In front of the palace they halted and deployed in line, and Count Solms rode forward. He announced that his orders were to take command of the posts around Whitehall Palace, and Craven must therefore withdraw his men.

The reply of the stalwart old soldier was that he would rather be cut to pieces than surrender his post without a fight. His guards fell into line and levelled their muskets at the Dutchmen, while he went inside to consult the King, who was on the point of retiring to bed. On his knees Craven begged James's permission to resist, to fulfil the Army's first duty of protecting its anointed sovereign, and to salvage a modicum of its lost honour. James's response was to send for Count Solms and to tell him there must surely have been a mistake. Were his orders not to secure St James's Palace, where James had invited the Prince for talks the following day? The Count produced his orders, which were unambiguously for Whitehall Palace, and withdrew. James argued the matter with Craven for some time. It was outrageous, certainly, but what would be gained by resisting?

At length James told his gallant old servant to withdraw his men. With a bad grace Craven ordered his guards to withdraw, although the command provoked a near mutiny in the ranks. But by eleven o'clock the Coldstreams had withdrawn, humiliated and shamed, to be replaced by the Dutch Guards. The King had become a prisoner in his own palace. Someone asked him whether he would venture to go to bed surrounded by enemies. He replied that they could hardly use him worse than his own subjects had done, 'and, with the apathy of a man stupefied by disasters, went to bed and to sleep.'[15]

Shortly after midnight William's three emissaries, Lords Halifax, Delamere, and Shrewsbury, arrived at the palace and demanded admittance. The Earl of Middleton, the King's gentleman-in-waiting, asked them if they couldn't wait till morning, but they replied that their business would permit no delay. It was now one o'clock in the morning; exhausted by the events of the previous day, James was fast asleep and Middleton had to speak loudly in his ear to wake him up. Sitting up in bed, he listened as the emissaries conveyed the Prince's demand, which was that he must leave London by ten o'clock the following morning and go to Ham House, because the Prince intended to enter London later that day.

James submitted to his nephew's demand. Indeed, he had little choice. He only asked that he might be allowed to go to Rochester instead of Ham, and to this William had no objection. The next day, 18 December, after stressing to the depleted ranks of loyalists around him that he was departing under duress, James left Whitehall. He was not permitted to travel by coach, in case the sight provoked an insurrection. Instead he was taken by barge, under Dutch guard, to Rochester. Later that day the Prince arrived in London.

The Earl of Clarendon described the widespread feeling of outrage at what had just ocurred:

> It is not to be imagined what a damp there was on all sorts of men throughout the town. The treatment the King had met with from the Prince of Orange, and the manner of his being driven, as it were, from Whitehall, with such circumstances, moved compassion even in those who were not very fond of him. Several of the English army, both officers and soldiers, began to murmur.[16]

What had begun as a liberation had ended in a grubby putsch, which was bitterly resented by large sections of the English Army.

> It was said, here was an unnatural thing, to waken the King out of his sleep, in his own palace, and to order him to go out of it, when he was ready to submit to everything [...]. These things began to work on great numbers. And the posting the Dutch guards where the English guards had been, gave a general disgust to the whole English army.[17]

It was an awkward moment. The entire English Army, except for the Coldstream Guards, had been ordered to leave London, and instead the streets of the capital swarmed with 'ill-favoured and ill-accoutred Dutchmen'. The Coldstreams were especially bitter about what had happened. When they were drawn up in Moorfields two days later and ordered to march to Rochester, many of the soldiers threw down their arms and refused the order, thinking they were to be shipped off to Flanders.

Hilaire Belloc regretted that Craven's guards hadn't been allowed to mount a defence of their sovereign. In his biography of James II he wrote:

> It would have been a fine incident in the history of this country if the English guards had been permitted to lay down their lives, as they were willing to do, for their King, and to have fallen under the fire of that superior force of foreign invaders. It would have been a symbolic action only, but it would have been something stamping history honourably for posterity to remember.[18]

It would certainly have made it clear that what had happened was really a *coup d'état*, albeit one with broad popular support.

For the moment James remained in Rochester, where a series of Tory loyalists urged him not to leave the country. As long as he remained he would be a party to any future settlement with the Prince. But James, mindful of his father's fate forty years earlier, feared for his safety in England. He had promised his wife that he would join her and their baby son in Paris, and he had received a warm invitation too from Louis XIV. For a few days he hesitated, but in the early hours of 23 December he slipped out of his lodgings, which had been deliberately left unguarded, boarded a waiting ship and sailed for France.

At a fractious meeting of peers on Christmas Eve, the Tory loyalists fought a rearguard action on behalf of their fugitive King. Rochester and Bishop Turner demanded an enquiry into the circumstances of James's flight, whether it had been undertaken 'freely or by constraint'. Pembroke urged the claims of the infant Prince of Wales; Nottingham and Clarendon argued for talks between the King and Prince; and Craven and Abingdon urged the calling of a Parliament with the writs that had already been sent out. But none of these proposals commanded general support, and in the end the peers agreed on the wording of an address requesting William to assume the direction of government until a convention could be called. William was in effect being invited to become regent until the convention could decide on how to proceed.

When William and Mary were declared joint King and Queen on 6 February 1689, Craven dutifully swore loyalty to them, but not surprisingly he found himself stripped of his various offices. He was replaced as Colonel of the Coldstream Guards by General Talmarsh, and as Lord Lieutenant of Middlesex by the Earl of Clare. However, the revolution did not mark the end of his service to the Stuart family. He shared the widespread concern for the succession to the throne, given that William and Mary had no children and Princess Anne had suffered from a long series of miscarriages. In July Anne gave birth to a boy, Prince William, who was created Duke of Gloucester by his uncle and aunt.

He was a sickly child, and three months later Lord Craven lent Princess Anne his fine house at Kensington Gravel Pits, in the hope that the surrounding air would be beneficial to William's health. The area known as Kensington Gravel Pits lay just to the north of the village of Kensington, straddling both sides of the Uxbridge Road. Craven House was a substantial building with twenty-four hearths, which Lord Craven had bought back in the 1660s from Sir Robert Hyde. It stood in an acre of grounds on the east side of Kensington Church Street, not far from Kensington Palace, which William and Mary had recently purchased and were remodelling as their principal residence in London.[19] Not that Anne's presence in Craven House indicated any closeness between the Princess and her sister and brother-in-law; in fact they were not even on speaking terms, Anne outraged to be kept in a state of relative penury.

Soon after his birth, the infant Duke of Gloucester had begun to suffer from convulsions. After successive wet nurses had come and gone without any improvement in the child's condition, his anxious parents announced a reward for any wet nurse who could cure him. Out of the many applicants Prince George of Denmark selected a robust but alcoholic countrywoman, Mrs Pack, in part 'because of her breasts, which were gigantic'. On seeing her waiting in the anteroom at Hampton Court, he ordered her in to feed his son, whereupon the convulsions immediately ceased. The life of the heir to the throne seemed to depend on Mrs Pack's milk, and she was engaged on the spot. In October 1689 the infant Duke—with Mrs Pack in attendance—was installed in the nursery wing at Craven House, with Mrs Pack in charge of a whole retinue of servants, including two chief nurses, Mrs Atkinson and Mrs Fortress, and assorted nursery maids, footmen, seamstresses, and other attendants. Orders were given that Mrs Pack was never to be contradicted and that she was to be allowed as much food and drink as she wished. The unfortunate result was that her behaviour deteriorated; she never washed and she drank to excess; she was fitter for a pigsty, according to one of the royal doctors, than a royal nursery.[20]

Still, the Duke of Gloucester thrived. He remained at Craven House for the next year, taken for daily rides through the gravel pits in a miniature carriage drawn by Shetland ponies 'scarcely larger than good-sized mastiffs' and guided by Dick Drury, Prince George of Denmark's coachman.[21] Perhaps with the help of these daily constitutionals he recovered, and the following autumn Princess Anne and her husband moved to nearby Campden House, taking their son and Mrs Pack with them. When the news of the infant Duke's recovery spread, Kensington Gravel Pits started to become a fashionable resort for invalids.

Craven spent most of his last years at Drury House, where William Winde had by this time designed a new wing. Leigh Hunt imagined Craven pottering in his garden there, so that 'we may fancy the old soldier busying himself with his flower beds, and Mr Evelyn discoursing on the blessings of peace and privacy.'[22] He continued to disburse money to worthy causes, including £50 towards the rebuilding of St Mary's Church in Kensington in 1694. For a long time he continued to attend company meetings on a regular basis and to carry out his various official duties.

'He had grey hair and lived to a venerable age,' wrote the poet Joseph Perkins in his highly florid Latin elegy published the year after Craven's death, 'and cruel old age came upon him at a slow pace.'[23] He died on 9 April 1697 at Drury House, at the venerable age of eighty-eight years and ten months. He had already bequeathed property in trust to provide for his brother's scholarships at the universities of Oxford and Cambridge. As well as confirming this, in his will he left numerous legacies, including £100 each to Sir Edmond Andros and to his godsons William Winde and Sir Isaac Gibson, and generous sums to his servants. He still owned property in the Netherlands, and this he bequeathed to his cousin Sir Anthony Craven of Sparsholt. But the bulk of his estate passed to his cousin William Craven, eldest son of Sir William Craven of Combe Abbey, who became the 2nd Baron Craven of Hamstead Marshall.[24]

On 20 April, the Earl of Craven was buried in the vault of St Bartholomew's Church at Binley, close to Combe Abbey. Sadly the church contains no memorial plaque to his memory. Perhaps to his young heir he seemed a forgotten figure from the distant past. His exploits in battle with the great Gustavus, his devotion to the Queen of Bohemia, his support for her family, even his exertions in the catastrophes of the Great Plague and the Great Fire—all were now just a distant memory. He has an incomparable memorial, of course, in the form of Ashdown House, that beautiful monument to his devotion to the Winter Queen. But if one were to choose an epitaph for this good, brave, generous man, perhaps it would echo those words from St Matthew's Gospel: 'Well done, thou good and faithful servant.'

Endnotes

Introduction

1 Quiller-Couch, Sir Arthur, 'The Tempest', *Q Anthology* (London: J. M. Dent, 1948), p. 286.
2 Baker, L. M., *The Letters of Elizabeth, Queen of Bohemia* (London: The Bodley Head, 1953), p. 19.
3 Chesterfield, Philip Dormer Stanhope, 4th Earl of, *The works of Lord Chesterfield, including letters to his son, etc.* (New York: Harper, 1838), p. 579.
4 Wilson, H. Schütz, *Studies in History, Legend and Literature* (London: Griffith & Farran, 1884), p. 159.

Chapter 1. The Lady Elizabeth

1 Oman, Carola, *The Winter Queen: Elizabeth of Bohemia* (London: Phoenix Press, 2000), p. 36.
2 Green, Mary Ann Everett, *Elizabeth Electress Palatine and Queen of Bohemia* (London: Methuen, 1909), pp. 51-4.
3 Oman, p. 94.
4 *Ibid.*, p. 118.
5 *Ibid.*, p. 122.
6 *Ibid.*, p. 125.
7 *Ibid.*, p. 127.
8 Green, p. 90.
9 *Ibid.*, p. 140.
10 Raleigh, Sir Walter, 'A Discourse touching a Marriage between Prince Henry of England, and a Daughter of Savoy', in *The Works of Sir Walter Raleigh, Kt.*, vol. 1 (London: R. Dodsley, 1751), p. 278.

Chapter 2. Triumph and Disaster

1 Green, p. 121.
2 *Ibid.*, p. 133.
3 *Ibid.*
4 *Ibid.*, p. 151.
5 CSPD, 22/29 January 1620, Chamberlain to Carleton.
6 Oman, p. 212.
7 *Ibid.*, pp. 212-3.

8 *Ibid.*, p. 215.
9 Green, p. 154.
10 *Ibid.*, p. 156.
11 Oman, pp. 221-2.
12 Green, p. 167.

Chapter 3. The Queen of Hearts

1 Oman, p. 247.
2 Trevelyan, George Macaulay, *England under the Stuarts* (London: Methuen, 1965), p. 191.
3 The houses at Kneuterdijk 22 have long since been demolished. By the time Elizabeth finally left in 1661 they were in a dilapidated state, and were replaced soon afterwards by a baroque mansion also known as the Wassenaer Hof, standing on what had been the forecourt of the old house.
4 Oman, p. 252.
5 Green, p. 179.
6 Blaze de Bury, the Baroness, *Memoirs of the Princess Palatine, Princess of Bohemia* (London: Richard Bentley, 1853), p. 84.
7 Green, p. 212.
8 Oman, p. 256.
9 Green, p. 199.
10 *Ibid.*, pp. 193-4.
11 *Ibid.*, p. 192.
12 Nichols, J. B., *Progresses, Processions and Magnificent Festivities of James I*, vol. 3 (London: John Nichols, 1828), p. 751.
13 Oman, p. 265.
14 *Ibid.*, p. 273.
15 *Ibid.*, p. 274.
16 Birch, *Court and Times of James the First*, vol. 2 (London: H. Colburn, 1848), p. 359.
17 Green, p. 218.
18 Oman, p. 278.
19 Sophia, Electress of Hanover, *Memoirs*, trans. by H. Forester (London: R. Bentley & Son, 1888), p. 3.
20 *Ibid.*, pp. 5-6.

Chapter 4. The Gentleman Volunteer

1 Craven Papers, vol. 74, Bodleian Library.
2 See his will, PROB 11/132/147 and 153, Wills from Prerogative Court of Canterbury.
3 Stone, Lawrence, *The Crisis of the Aristocracy, 1558–1641* (Oxford: Clarendon, 1965), p. 629; Marston, John, 'What You Will', in *Old Plays, Being a Continuation of Dodsley's Collection*, vol. 2, by Charles Wentworth Dilke (London: Forgotten Books, 2012), p. 212.
4 Stone, Lawrence, *The Crisis of the Aristocracy, 1558–1641* (Oxford: Clarendon, 1965), p. 607.
5 Stater, 'Sheffield, Edmund, first Earl of Mulgrave, 1565–1646', *Oxford Dictionary of National Biography* (Oxford: Oxford University Press, 2004).
6 Bald, R. C., *Donne and the Drurys* (Cambridge: Cambridge University Press, 1959), p. 105.
7 Nichols, J. B., *Progresses, Processions and Magnificent Festivities of James I*, vol. 4 (London: John Nichols, 1828), p. 805.
8 PRO 30/53/7/33, Herbert Papers.

9   Aubrey, John, *Aubrey's Brief Lives* (New Hampshire: David R. Godine, 1999), p. 181.

10   Gosse, Edmund, *Life and letters of John Donne*, vol. 2 (London: W. Heinemann, 1899), p. 320.

11   Birch, *Court and Times of James the First*, vol. 2, p. 422.

12   *Ibid.*

13   *Ibid.*, p. 461.

14   Chambers, R., ed., *The Book of Days: A Miscellany of Popular Antiquities*, vol. 1 (London, 1869), p. 493.

15   Manning, Roger, *Swordsmen, the Martial Ethos in the Three Kingdoms* (Oxford: Oxford University Press, 2003), p. 125.

16   *Ibid.*, p. 130.

17   Birch, *Court and Times of James the First*, vol. 2, p. 471.

18   CSPD, 31 July and 4 Aug 1624.

19   Colvin, Howard, *A Biographical Dictionary of British Architects, 1600–1840*, 4th ed. (London: John Murray, 1978), p. 248.

20   CSPD, 24 July 1624.

21   Craven Papers, vol. 74, Bodleian Library.

22   'The Life and Death of Colonel Harwood', *The Harleian Miscellany: a collection of scarce, entertaining and curious tracts*, vol. 4 (London: White & Co., 1809), p. 271.

23   Howell, James, *Epistolae Ho-Elianae: Familiar Letters, Domestic and Foreign* (London: R. Ware, 1765), pp. 264-5.

24   Birch, *Court and Times of Charles the First*, vol. 1, p. 201.

25   Nichols, *Progresses, Processions and Magnificent Festivities of James I*, vol. 4, p. 1007.

26   Birch, *Court and Times of Charles the First*, vol. 1, p. 209.

27   Pepys, Samuel, *Diaries* (London: Bell, 1983), 26 August 1666.

28   Blayney, Glenn H., 'Convention, Plot and Structure in *The Broken Heart*', *Modern Philology*, 56 (August 1958), pp. 1-9.

29   Hore, J. P., *The History of Newmarket and the Annals of the Turf*, vol. 2 (London: A. H. Baily & Co., 1886), p. 14.

30   Stone, p. 497.

31   *Ibid.*, p. 105.

32   *Report on the Manuscripts of the Family of Gawdy* (London: RCHM, 1885), p. 123.

33   Aretin, J. von, *Beyträge zur Geschichte und Literatur*, vol. 7 (Munich, 1806), p. 179.

Chapter 5. 'Cartropes shall not detain me longer in this place'

1   SP 84/134 f. 215.

2   Craven Papers, vol. 74, Bodleian Library.

3   Boulenger, Jaques, *The Seventeenth Century* (London: William Heinemann, 1920), p. 80.

4   CSPD, 3 December 1628.

5   Craven Papers, vol. 281, Bodleian Library.

6   Craven Papers, vol. 74, 31 July 1629, Bodleian Library.

7   Prynne, William, *Hidden works of darkenes brought to publike light* (London: Thomas Brudenell, 1645), p. 212.

8   Schreiber, Ray, *First Carlisle: Sir James Hay, First Earl of Carlisle as Courtier, Diplomat and Entrepreneur, 1580–1636* (Philadelphia: American Philosophical Society, 1984), p. 84; CSPD, Doncaster to Carlisle, 17 February 1629.

9   CSPD, Craven to Boswell, 8 May 1629.

10   Craven Papers, vol. 74, Bodleian Library.

11   Markham, Clements, *The Fighting Veres* (London: Sampson, 1888), p. 436; Dalton, Charles, *Life and Times of General Sir Edward Cecil, viscount Wimbledon, colonel of an English*

regiment in the Dutch service, 1605–1631, and one of his Majesty's most honourable Privy Council 1628–1638 (London: Sampson Low, 1885), p. 292.

12 Spelman, Sir Henry, *The History and Fate of Sacrilege* (London: J. Hartley, 1698), p. 237.

13 Aretin, p. 197.

14 Dalton, p. 293.

15 *Ibid.*, p. 297.

16 CSPD, Laud to King, 6 September 1628; Blakiston, Herbert E. D., *Trinity College* (London: Routledge, 1998), p. 112.

17 SP 84/140/45.

18 Malcolm, Noel, ed., *The Correspondence of Thomas Hobbes*, vol. 1 (Oxford: Clarendon Press, 1994), p. 7.

19 Craven Papers, vol. 74, 17 October and 7 November 1629, Bodleian Library.

20 *Report on the Manuscripts of Lord Montagu of Beaulieu* (London: RCHM, 1900), p. 113.

21 Sprunger, Keith L., *Dutch Protestantism: A History of English and Scottish Churches of the Netherlands in the Sixteenth and Seventeenth Century* (Leiden, 1982), p. 144.

22 Chambers, E. K., ed., 'Notes to poems hitherto uncollected', *The Poems of John Donne* (London: Lawrence & Bullen, 1896). These lines appeared first in a volume of notes and queries with a note stating that 'this curious poem, never before printed, was written by the famous Dr Donne in the year 1630 and sent to Rome to William Lord Craven.' However, in 1630 Donne himself was an infirm divine who had long since done with secular poetry, and the editor of the 1896 edition of Donne's poetry noted that it was much more probable that the lines had been written by his son.

23 Oman, p. 309.

24 Green, p. 277.

Chapter 6. In which our hero's bravery impresses the Great Gustavus

1 Benger, Elizabeth, *Memoirs of Elizabeth Stuart, Queen of Bohemia, Daughter of King James the First, including sketches of the state of society in Holland and Germany in the 17th Century*, vol. 2 (London: Longman, 1825), p. 278.

2 CSPD, 3 July 1631.

3 Add. MS 78201, Evelyn Papers, Craven to Sir Isaac Wake; Dalton, 314; SP 84/144/f.83, Vane to Dorchester, 4 September 1631, 'My Lord Vere's relation of the victorie of the holanders against the spaniards upon the rivers of the low countries'.

4 Meautys to Lord St Albans, 11 Oct 1631, in *The Works of Francis Bacon, Lord Chancellor of England*, vol. 3 (Philadelphia: Carey & Hart, 1842), p. 170.

5 Oman, p. 314.

6 Birch, *Court and Times of Charles the First*, vol. 2, p. 138.

7 *Report on the Manuscripts of the Family of Gawdy*, p. 136.

8 Cornwallis Bacon, Jane Lady, *Private Correspondence of Jane Lady Cornwallis Bacon* (London: S. & J. Bentley, 1842), p. 241.

9 CSP Venice, 28 November 1631.

10 Birch, *Court and Times of Charles the First*, vol. 2, p. 148.

11 CSP Venice, 12 December 1631 and 26 March 1632.

12 *Seventh Report of the Royal Commission on Historic Manuscripts* (London: Eyre & Spottiswoode, 1879), p. 548.

13 Oman, p. 314.

14 Pursell, Brennan C., *The Winter King: Frederick V of the Palatinate and the Coming of the Thirty Years War* (Aldershot: Ashgate, 2003), p. 271.

15 Harte, Revd. Walter MA, *The History of Gustavus Adolphus King of Sweden Surnamed The Great*, vol. 2 (London: John Joseph Stockdale, 1807), p. 174.

16 Rushworth, John, *Historical Collections of Private Passages of State: Volume 2, 1629–38* (London: D. Briowne, 1721), p. 176; Watts, William, *The Swedish Intelligencer* (London, 1632), p. 81; Harte, *The History of Gustavus Adolphus King of Sweden Surnamed The Great*, vol. 2, p. 175.

17 CSP Venice, 26 March 1632.

18 SP 84/146 f.138, Craven to Vane, 18 March 1632, quoted in Green, p. 291.

19 *Ibid.*

20 SP 81/38/116.

21 Harte, *The History of Gustavus Adolphus King of Sweden Surnamed The Great*, vol. 2, p. 192.

22 SP 81/38/124.

23 Munro, Robert, *Munro, his Expedition with the Worthy Scots Regiment called Mac-Keys* (London, 1637), p. 101.

24 Harte, Revd. Walter MA, *The History of Gustavus Adolphus King of Sweden Surnamed The Great*, vol. 1 (London: John Joseph Stockdale, 1807), p. 241.

25 SP 81/38/124.

26 Frederick to Elizabeth, 29 May 1632, *Correspondence of Elizabeth, Queen of Bohemia*, vol. 2, ed. Nadine Akkerman (Oxford: Oxford University Press, 2011), p. 95.

27 Markham, p. 442; Hexham, Henry, *A Journall of the Taking in of Venlo [...] the Memorable Siege of Mastricht* (Delft, 1633), pp. 26-7.

28 Markham, p. 445.

29 Wedgwood, C. V., *The Thirty Years War* (London: Cape, 1944), p. 332; Aretin, p. 270.

30 Green, p. 301.

31 Oman, p. 321.

Chapter 7. Back in England

1 CSPD, 4 June 1633, Goring to Windebank.

2 PRO 30/53/7/15, Herbert Papers.

3 *Collections Historical and Archaeological Relating to Montgomeryshire and its Borders*, vol. 20 (London, 1943)

4 Fullerton, Lady Georgiana, *The Life of Elizabeth Lady Falkland 1585–1635* (London, 1883), p. 176.

5 Brydges, Sir Egerton, *Collins's Peerage of England*, vol. 5 (London: F. C. & J. Rivington, 1812), p. 454.

6 Granger, James, *A Biographical history of England, from Egbert the King to the Revolution*, vol. 2, 5th ed. (London: W. Baynes & Son, 1824), p. 318.

7 V.b.110, Folger Manuscript, Folger Shakespeare Library, pp. 88-90.

8 'Biography of Colonel Harwood', *The Harleian Miscellany: a collection of scarce, entertaining and curious tracts*, vol. 5 (London: White & Co., 1809), p. 199.

10 *Joe Miller's Jests* (1739), p. 15, quoted in the *Otago Witness*, 11 September 1890.

11 Peacey, Jason, *Politicians and Pamphleteers: Propaganda During the English Civil Wars and Interregnum* (Aldershot: Ashgate, 2004), p. 740.

12 Green, p. 323.

13 CSP Venice, 26 November 1636.

14 CSP Venice, 7 December 1635.

15 CSP Venice, 14 December 1635.

16 Strafford, Earl of, *The Earl of Strafforde's Letters and Dispatches*, vol. 1 (London: W. Bowyer, 1739), p. 490.

17 CSP Venice, 21 December 1635.

18 CSPD, Windebank to Scudamore, 27 December 1635.

19 CSP Venice, 4 January 1636.

20 CSPD, 1 January 1636.

21 CSP Venice, 22 February 1636.

22 CSPD, Roe to Elisabeth, 1 May 1636.

23 Roe to Elisabeth, 30 July 1636; Akkerman, p. 490.

24 CSP Venice, Correr to Doge, 4 April 1636.

25 Ferencz to Elizabeth, 11 August 1636; Akkerman, p. 498.

26 Roe to Elizabeth, 1 August 1636; Akkerman, p. 502.

27 CSPD, 12 August 1636.

28 Blakiston, p. 112.

29 Heisler, R., 'Robert Fludd: A Picture in Need of Expansion', *Hermetic Journal*, 1989, p. 143.

30 Morrah, Patrick, *Prince Rupert of the Rhine* (London: Constable, 1976), p. 44.

31 Wood, Anthony à, *History and Antiquities of Oxford*, vol. 2 (Oxford: Clarendon Press, 1796), p. 412.

32 CSP Venice, 5 December 1636.

33 Green, p. 324.

34 Boothby, Richard, *A Brief Discovery or Description of the most famous island of Madagascar* (London, 1646), p. 22.

35 Bromley, Sir G., *Collection of Original Royal Letters* (London: John Stockdale, 1787), p. 96; Green, p. 336; Gawdy, p. 162; CSP Venice, 13 February 1637.

36 Nathaniel Hobart to Sir Ralph Verney, 6 Feb 1636–37, Verney, Sir Ralph, *Verney Papers* (London: Camden Society, 1853).

37 Leicester, Countess of, *Correspondence of Dorothy Sidney Percy, Countess of Leicester* (Farnham: Ashgate, 2010), p. 100.

38 Hannay, Margaret P., *Mary Sidney, Lady Wroth* (Farnham: Ashgate, 2010), p. 276.

39 CSP Venice, Venetian ambassador to the Hague to the Doge and Senate, 12 February 1637.

40 CSP Venice, 20 February 1637.

41 *Ibid.*, 27 March 1637.

42 *Ibid.*

43 Roe to Elizabeth, 18 May 1637; Akkerman, p. 596.

44 CSP Venice, 9 July 1637.

45 *Ibid.*, 1 May 1637.

46 Benger, p. 334.

47 Wilson, Peter H., *Europe's Tragedy: A History of the Thirty Years War* (London: Allen Lane, 2009), p. 322; Murdoch, Steve, *Scotland and the Thirty Years War, 1618–1648* (London: Brill, 2001), pp. 6, 20.

48 Gatty, Charles T., *Mary Davies and the Manor of Ebury*, vol. 2 (London: Cassell, 1921), p. 157.

49 CSPD, 28 August 1637; Gardiner, Samuel R., ed., *Documents relating to the Proceedings against William Prynne*, Camden Society, vol. 1 (London, 1877), p. 80.

50 Manuscripts of Capt. F. C. Loder-Symonds; *Victoria County History of Berkshire*, vol. 4 (London, 1924), p. 539; Pevsner, Nikolaus, *Buildings of England. Berkshire* (London: Penguin, 1966), p. 515.

Chapter 8. In which our hero is captured in Germany then apprehended in Paris

1 Green, p. 325.

2 Manning, *Swordsmen, the Martial Ethos in the Three Kingdoms*, pp. 116, 128.

3 CSP Venice, 6 November 1637.

4   *Ibid.*, 14 May 1638.

5   *Ibid*, 21 May 1638.

6   Wilson, Peter H., p. 594.

7   CSP Venice, 12 June 1638.

8   Manning, Roger, *An Apprenticeship in Arms: The Origins of the British Army 1585–1702* (Oxford: Oxford University Press, 2006), p. 107; Guthrie, William P., *The Later Thirty Years War: from the Battle of Wittstock to the Treaty of Westphalia* (London: Greenwood Press, 2003), p. 73.

9   PRO 30/53/7/22, Herbert Papers.

10   CSP Venice, 16 July 1638.

11   *Ibid.*, 1 October 1638.

12   Murdoch, p. 6.

13   CSP Venice, 27 November 1638.

14   *Report on the Manuscripts of Lord Montagu of Beaulieu*, p. 123.

15   CSP Venice, 5 August 1639.

16   Wotton, Sir Henry, *Reliquiae Wottonianae; or, a collection of lives, letters and poems*, 3rd ed. (London: T. Roycroft, 1672), p. 480.

17   CSP Venice, 19 August 1639.

18   *Ibid.*, 9 September 1639.

19   *Ibid.*, 30 September and 14 October 1639.

20   CSPD, Pennington to Windebank, 4 October 1639.

21   CSP Venice, 7 October and 14 Oct 1639.

22   Gardiner, Samuel R., ed., *Documents relating to the Proceedings against William Prynne*, Camden Society, vol. 9 (London, 1877), p. 64; CSP Venice, 30 October 1639; Gerbier to Elizabeth, 1 and 8 November 1639, Akkerman, pp. 843, 846.

23   CSP Venice, 9 December 1639.

24   CSPD, 14 May 1640.

Chapter 9: 'A purse better furnished than my own'

1   J. Bouillon to Sir William Boswell, 9 January 1640, *Manuscripts of the Earl of Cowper* (London: RCHM, 1889), p. 249.

2   *Manuscripts of the Duke of Portland* (London: RCHM, 1891), p. 60.

3   Craven Papers, vol. 282, Bodleian Library.

4   Huygens to Craven, 21 March 1640; Worp, Dr J. A., ed., *De Briefwisseling van Constantijn Huygens 1608–1634* ('s-Gravenhage: Martinus Nijhoff, 1911).

5   SP 84/156 f. 29, Craven to Vane, 17/27 Apr 1640.

6   Strachan, Michael, *Sir Thomas Roe 1581–1644* (Salisbury: Russell, 1989), p. 253.

7   *Ibid.*, p. 258.

8   Huygens to Princess of Orange, 20 July 1641, Worp; Cannon, Richard, *History of the Third Regiment of Foot, or the Buffs* (London: Longman Orme, 1839), p. 106.

9   CSPD, 9 February 1642.

10   Sophia, Electress of Hanover, p. 9.

11   *Ibid.*, p. 8.

12   *Ibid.*, p. 9.

13   *Ibid.*, p. 14.

14   *Ibid.*, p. 26.

15   CSPD, 26 and 30 September 1642.

16   Huygens to Princess of Orange, 25 June 1642, Worp.

17   *House of Lords Journal*, 24 February and 17 April 1643.

18   Add MS 78190, Evelyn Papers, Craven to Browne, 22 July 1643.

19   CSP Venice, 27 March 1643.
20   'Biographical memoirs of Sir Lewis Dyve', *Gentleman's Magazine*, 99(1829), p. 205.
21   CSPD, Committee for the Advance of Money.
22   House of Lords Journal, 6 April 1644.
23   Add. MS 78190, Evelyn Papers, Lord Craven to Sir Richard Browne; Add MS 78205 ff. 37–47, 85, Evelyn Papers.
24   CSP Venice, 15 July 1644.
25   Guthrie, p. 180.
26   Add MS 78190 f. 12, Evelyn Papers, Lord Craven to Sir Richard Browne, 15 August 1644.
27   CSPD, Honeywood to Vane, 7 October 1645; *City Scout*, 7 to 14 Oct 1645.
28   Add. MS 78190 f. 15, Evelyn Papers.
29   Add. MS 78205 f. 25, Evelyn Papers.

Chapter 10. 'What I have besides in my power shall be at your service'

1   Scott, Eva, *Rupert Prince Palatine* (Westminster: Constable & Co., 1899), p. 209.
2   Benger, p. 379.
3   Oman, p. 566.
4   Scott, p. 211.
5   Gardiner, Samuel R., ed., *Documents relating to the Proceedings against William Prynne*, Camden Society, vol. 6 (London, 1877).
6   Godwin, William, *History of the Commonwealth of England: From the Death of Charles I to the Protectorate* (London: Nabu Press, 2010), p. 361.
7   Durston, Chris, 'Henry Marten and the High Shoon of Berkshire', *Berkshire Archaeological Journal*, vol. 70.
8   Add. MS 63743, f. 1, Craven Papers, British Library.
9   Craven Papers, vol. 306, Bodleian Library.
10 *Ibid.*
11 Wing, W., 'Lecture on Old Caversham', reprinted from *Reading Mercury and County Paper*, 12 November 1894.
12 PRO 30/53/7, Herbert Paper.s
13 *Report on the Manuscripts of J. Eliot Hodgkin* (London: RCHM, 1897), p. 110.
14 Craven Papers, vol. 79, Bodleian Library.
15 Morrah, Patrick, *Prince Rupert of the Rhine* (London: Constable, 1976), p. 236.
16 Sophia, Electress of Hanover, p. 43.
17 Craven Papers, vol. 80, Bodleian Library.
18 Craven Papers, vol. 282, Bodleian Library.
19 Donne, John, *The Poetical Works of Dr John Donne* (Boston: Little, Brown & Co., 1855), p. 1.

Chapter 11. 'Barbarous and inhuman rebels'

1   Sophia, Electress of Hanover, p. 23.
2   Defoe, Daniel, *The Complete English Tradesman* (London, 1727), p. 378.
3   Howell, Thomas Bayley, and William Cobbett, *A Complete Collection of State Trials and Proceedings for High Treason and other Crimes and Misdemeanors*, vol. 5 (London, 1816), p. 353.
4   *Ibid.*, pp. 323–66.
5   *Ibid.*; Craven Papers, vol. 152, Bodleian Library.
6   Cases before the Committee, Calendar of Committee for Compounding, December 1646.
7   States General to Parliament, 25 July and 4 August 1651, *Manuscripts of the Duke of*

Portland, vol. 1, N.X., 59; *House of Commons Journal*, 22 August 1651.

8 *A True and Perfect Narrative of the several proceedings in the case concerning the Lord Craven* (London, 1653), p. 9.

9 Calendar of Committee for Compounding, December 1646; Thirsk, Joan, *The Rural Economy of England* (London: Hambledon Press, 1984), p. 85.

10 Calendar of Committee for Compounding, 4 August 1653; Bald, p. 120.

11 Howell, p. 344.

12 Thomas Harley to Sir Robert Harley, 7 May 1653; *Manuscripts of the Duke of Portland*, p. 200.

13 Feola, Maryann, *George Bishop: Seventeenth-Century Soldier Turned Quaker* (New York: William Sessions, 1996), p. 37.

14 Sir Robert Stone to Sir Walter Vane, Thurloe Papers, vol. 3, 19 September 1653.

15 Peacey, Jason, *Print and Public Politics in the English Revolution* (Cambridge University Press, 2013), p. 326.

Chapter 12. 'I shall have neither bread, nor meat, nor candles'

1 Craven Papers, vol. 80, Bodleian Library.

2 Oman, p. 416.

3 Green, p. 379.

4 Oman, p. 375.

5 *Ibid.*, p. 421.

6 Baker, pp. 211, 239.

7 Cannon, p. 114.

8 CSPD, Manning to Thurloe, 10/20 July 1655.

9 A letter of intelligence, CSPD, 28 July 1655.

10 Oman, p. 418.

11 Baker, p. 231.

12 Queen of Bohemia to Charles II, Thurloe Papers, vol. 1, 27 Dec 1655.

13 Sophia, Electress of Hanover, p. 52.

14 *Ibid.*, p. 56.

15 Oman, p. 406.

16 Burton, Thomas, *Diaries of Thomas Burton* (London: H. Colburn, 1828), 23 January 1658; *House of Commons Journal*, 23 January 1658.

17 Ralph Farmer, *Sathan inthron'd in his chair of pestilence* (London, 1657)

18 *House of Lords Journal*, 6 June 1660.

19 *House of Lords Journal*, 4 June, 26 June, and 24 August 1660.

20 Henfry, Henry William, *Numismata Cromwelliana* (London: John Russell Smith, 1877), p. 114; Lesson, A. Marvin, *Summary of the Cromwell Coinage* (London: British Numismatic Society, 1966), pp. 163, 165, 172; CSPD, 3 December 1656; CSPD, vol. 23, February 1652.

Chapter 13. The Principal Director of her Court

1 Oman, p. 434.

2 Pepys, 17 May 1660.

3 Green, p. 400.

4 Oman, p. 439.

5 Rupert to Will Legge, *Manuscripts of the Earl of Dartmouth* (London: RCHM, 1887), 24 April 1661.

6 Green, p. 403.

7 *House of Lords Journal*, 15 May 1661.

8 Craven Papers, vol. 144, Bodleian Library.

9 Oman, p. 447.

10 *Gentleman's Magazine*, 1832, p. 74.

11 Add. MS 32498, Correspondence from Hartlib to Worthington, 4 June 1661.

12 Oman, p. 450.

13 *Ibid.*, p. 454.

14 *Ibid.*, p. 456.

15 *Wills from Doctors' Commons*, Camden Society, vol. 83 (London, 1863), p. 109.

16 Stokes, Penelope, *Craven Country: The Story of Hamstead Marshall* (Newbury, 1996), pp. 31-32.

17 Gough Papers.

Chapter 14. 'An honour beyond all his gallantries and brave exploits'

1 Pepys, 18 November 1664.

2 Davies, K. G., *The Royal African Company* (London: Longman, Green & Co., 1957), p. 41.

3 Roper, L. H., *Conceiving Carolina: Proprietors, Planters and Plots, 1662–1729* (New York: Palgrave Macmillan, 2004), p. 16.

4 See Ver Steeg, Clarence L., *The Formative Years* (London: Hill & Wang, 1964); Waterhouse, Richard, *A New World Gentry* (Charleston: History Press, 2005).

5 Mann, Henry, *The Land We Live In; or The Story of Our Country* (New York: The Christian Herald, 1896), p. 86.

6 Pepys, 21 June 1665.

7 Spurgeon, Charles H., 'Whitecross's Anecdotes', *The Treasury of David*, vol. 4 (London, 1875), p. 241.

8 Bell, Walter George, *The Great Plague in London* (London: John Bell, 1924), p. 185.

9 Skinner, *The Life of General Monk* (London, 1724), p. 365.

10 Waldie, Adam, *Waldie's Select Circulating Library*, vol. 15, part 1 (Philadelphia, 1832), p. 26.

11 Stowe MS 152 f. 112, British Library, 'Lord Craven notes for the prevention of the plague, 1666'.

12 Tinniswood, Adrian, *By Permission of Heaven: The Story of the Great Fire of London* (London: Jonathan Cape, 2003), p. 55.

13 Anon, *Literae consolatoriae, from the author to the dejected place of his nativity, the honourable city of London* (London, 1669).

14 CSPD, 27 July 1667.

15 Pepys, 24 March 1668.

16 *Ibid.*

17 Thomson, William, *A History of Tapestry from the Earliest Times until the Present Day* (London: Hodder & Stoughton, 1930), p. 300; CSPD, 22 April 1667.

18 Wilson, Beckles, *The Great Company* (Toronto: The Copp Clark Company, 1905), p. 37.

19 Morrah, p. 385.

20 'The Fundamental Constitutions of Carolina', 1 March 1669, in *America's Founding Charters*, ed. Wakelyn (Westport, CT: Greenwood, 2006), p. 222.

21 CSP Colonial, 6 May 1674.

22 CSPD, undated papers 1670.

23 Bullen, H., ed., *Musa Proterva: Love Poems of the Restoration* (London, 1889), p. 36.

24 *Gentleman's Magazine*, vol. 13, p. 359.

25 Waldie, p. 26.

Chapter 15. 'He would rather be cut to pieces than surrender'

1   Alston, R. C., *Inventory of Sale Catalogues of named and attributed owners of books*, vol. 1 (privately printed, 2010) p. 97.

2   CSPD, 9 March 1681.

3   Roper, p. 72.

4   Sirmans, M. Eugene, 'Politics in Colonial South Carolina: The Failure of Proprietary Reform 1682–1694', *The William and Mary Quarterly*, Third Series, vol. 23, no. 1.

5   Evelyn, John, *Diaries* (Oxford: Clarendon Press, 2000), 12 June 1687.

6   Granger, p. 182.

7   Burnet, Bishop, *Bishop Burnet's History of the Reign of King James the Second* (Oxford: Oxford University Press, 1852), p. 344.

8   Strickland, Agnes and Elizabeth, *Lives of the Queens of England from the Norman Conquest*, vol. 6 (London, 1840–49), p. 253.

9   Burnet, p. 503.

10   Clarendon, Henry Hyde, Earl of, *The Correspondence of Henry Hyde, Earl of Clarendon and his brother Laurence Hyde, Earl of Rochester*, ed. Samuel Weller Singer, vol. 2 (London, 1828), p. 218.

11   For the events of these months, see Beddard, Robert, *A Kingdom without a King* (Oxford: Phaidon, 1988), pp. 17-65.

12   *Ibid.*, p. 38.

13   *Ibid.*, p. 41.

14   Webb, Stephen Saunders, *Lord Churchill's Coup: The Anglo-American Empire and the Glorious Revolution* (New York: Knopf, 1995), p. 162.

15   Macaulay, Thomas Babington, *History of England*, vol. 2 (Philadelphia: Porter & Coates, 2008), p. 603.

16   Clarendon, p. 231.

17   Burnet, p. 413.

18   Belloc, Hilaire, *James the Second* (London: Faber & Gwyer, 1928), p. 229.

19   Sheppard, F. H. W., ed., *Survey of London: vol. 37, Northern Kensington* (London: London Council, 1973).

20   Gathorne-Hardy, Jonathan, *The Rise and Fall of the British Nanny* (London: Hodder & Stoughton, 1972), pp. 36-38.

21   Strickland, p. 233.

22   Hunt, Leigh, *The Town: Its Memorable Characters and Events* (London: Gibbons & Co., 1893), p. 264.

23   Perkins, Joseph, *Elegus in obitum [...] Gulielmi Comitis de Craven*, etc. (London, 1697).

24   PROB 11/437/296, Wills from Prerogative Court of Canterbury.

Bibliography

Primary Sources

Bodleian Library, Oxford
—Craven Papers
—Gough Papers

British Library
—Correspondence from Hartlib to Worthington
—Craven Papers
—Evelyn Papers
—Thurloe Papers

The National Archives
—Herbert Papers
—Wills from Prerogative Court of Canterbury

Historical Manuscripts Commission
—*Manuscripts of Capt. F. C. Loder-Symonds* (London: RCHM, 1892)
—*Manuscripts of the Duke of Portland* (London: RCHM, 1891)
—*Manuscripts of the Earl of Cowper* (London: RCHM, 1889)
—*Manuscripts of the Earl of Dartmouth* (London: RCHM, 1887)
—*Report on the Manuscripts of J. Eliot Hodgkin* (London: RCHM, 1897)
—*Report on the Manuscripts of Lord Montagu of Beaulieu* (London: RCHM, 1900)
—*Report on the Manuscripts of the Family of Gawdy* (London: RCHM, 1885)
—*Seventh Report of the Royal Commission on Historic Manuscripts* (London: Eyre &
 Spottiswoode, 1879)

House of Commons Journal Archives
House of Lords Journal Archives

Folger Shakespeare Library, Washington, DC

Press

Gentleman's Magazine

Printed Sources

Akkerman, Nadine, ed., *Correspondence of Elizabeth, Queen of Bohemia*, vol. 2 (Oxford: Oxford University Press, 2011)

Anon, *Literae consolatoriae, from the author to the dejected place of his nativity, the honourable city of London* (London, 1669)

'A Reply to a Certain Pamphlet written by an Unknowing and Unknown Author' (London: R. White, 1653)

Aretin, J. von, *Beyträge zur Geschichte und Literatur*, vol. 7 (Munich, 1806)

A True and Perfect Narrative of the several proceedings in the case concerning the Lord Craven (London, 1653)

Aubrey, John, *Aubrey's Brief Lives* (New Hampshire: David R. Godine, 1999)

Bacon, Francis, *The Works of Francis Bacon, Lord Chancellor of England*, vol. 3 (Philadelphia: Carey & Hart, 1842)

Baker, L. M., *The Letters of Elizabeth Queen of Bohemia* (London: The Bodley Head, 1953)

Bald, R. C., *Donne and the Drurys* (Cambridge: Cambridge University Press, 1959)

Beddard, Robert, *A Kingdom Without a King: the Journal of the Provisional Government in the Revolution of 1688* (Oxford: Phaidon, 1988)

Bell, Walter George, *The Great Plague in London* (London: John Bell, 1924)

Belloc, Hilaire, *James the Second* (London: Faber & Gwyer, 1928)

Benger, Elizabeth, *Memoirs of Elizabeth Stuart, Queen of Bohemia, Daughter of King James the First, including sketches of the state of society in Holland and Germany in the 17th Century*, vol. 2 (London: Longman, 1825)

Birch, Thomas, *Court and Times of Charles the First*, vol. 1 and 2 (London: H. Colburn, 1848)

—*Court and Times of James the First*, vol. 2 (London: H. Colburn, 1848).

Bishop, George, *The Throne of Truth exalted over the Powers of Darkness* (London, 1957)

Blakiston, Herbert E. D., *Trinity College* (London: Routledge, 1998)

Blayney, Glenn H., 'Convention, Plot and Structure in The Broken Heart', *Modern Philology*, 56 (August 1958)

Blaze de Bury, the Baroness, *Memoirs of the Princess Palatine, Princess of Bohemia* (London: Richard Bentley, 1853)

Boulenger, Jaques, *The Seventeenth Century* (London: William Heinemann, 1920)

Bromley, Sir G., *Collection of Original Royal Letters* (London: John Stockdale, 1787)

Brydges, Sir Egerton, *Collins's Peerage of England*, vol. 5 (London: F. C. & J. Rivington, 1812)

Buchan, Alice, *A Stuart Portrait: being a brief study of a Stuart princess* (London: Peter Davies, 1934)

Bullen, H., ed., *Musa Proterva: Love Poems of the Restoration* (London, 1889)

Burnet, Bishop, *Bishop Burnet's History of the Reign of King James the Second* (Oxford: Oxford University Press, 1852)

Burton, Thomas, *Diaries of Thomas Burton* (London: H. Colburn, 1828)

Calendar of State Colonial Series, America and West Indies, ed. W. Noel Sainsbury (London: HMSO, 1880)

Calendar of State Papers Domestic, James I, ed. Mary Anne Everett Green (London: HMSO, 1859)

Calendar of State Papers Domestic, James II, ed. E. K. Timings (London: HMSO, 1960)

Calendar of State Papers relating to English Affairs in Venice, ed. Allen B. Hinds (London: HMSO, 1923)

Calendar of the Proceedings for the Committee for Compounding, 1643–1660, ed. Mary Anne Everett Green (London: HMSO, 1892)

Cannon, Richard, *History of the Third Regiment of Foot, or the Buffs* (London: Longman Orme, 1839)

Chambers, E. K., ed., 'Notes to poems hitherto uncollected', *The Poems of John Donne* (London:

Lawrence & Bullen, 1896)

Chambers, R., ed., *The Book of Days: A Miscellany of Popular Antiquities*, vol. 1 (London, 1869)

Chesterfield, Philip Dormer Stanhope, 4th Earl of, *The works of Lord Chesterfield, including his letters to his son*, etc. (New York: Harper & Brothers, 1838)

Clarendon, Henry Hyde, Earl of, *The Correspondence of Henry Hyde, Earl of Clarendon and his brother Laurence Hyde, Earl of Rochester*, ed. Samuel Weller Singer, vol. 2 (London, 1828)

Collections Historical and Archaeological Relating to Montgomeryshire and its Borders, vol. 20 (London, 1943)

Colvin, Howard, *A Biographical Dictionary of British Architects, 1600–1840*, 4th ed. (London: John Murray, 1978)

Cornwallis Bacon, Jane Lady, *Private Correspondence of Jane Lady Cornwallis Bacon* (London: S. & J. Bentley, 1842)

Dalton, Charles, *Life and Times of General Sir Edward Cecil, viscount Wimbledon, colonel of an English regiment in the Dutch service, 1605–1631, and one of his Majesty's most honourable Privy Council 1628–1638* (London: Sampson Low, 1885)

Davies, K. G., *The Royal African Company* (London: Longman, Green & Co., 1957)

Defoe, Daniel, *The Complete English Tradesman* (London, 1727)

Donne, John, *The Poetical Works of Dr John Donne* (Boston: Little, Brown & Co., 1855)

Durston, Chris, 'Henry Marten and the High Shoon of Berkshire', *Berkshire Archaeological Journal*, vol. 70

Evleyn, John, *Diaries* (Oxford: Clarendon Press, 2000)

Farmer, Ralph, *Sathan inthron'd in his chair of pestilence* (London, 1657)

—*The Imposter Dethroned, or the Quakers' Throne of Truth detected to be Satan's seat of lyes* (London: 1658)

Feola, Maryann, *George Bishop: Seventeenth-Century Soldier Turned Quaker* (New York: William Sessions, 1996)

Finet, Sir John, *Ceremonies of Charles I: the note books of John Finet, 1628–1641*, ed. A. J. Loomie (New York: Fordham University Press, 1987)

Fullerton, Lady Georgiana, *The Life of Elizabeth Lady Falkland 1585–1635* (London, 1883)

Gardiner, Samuel R., ed., *Documents relating to the Proceedings against William Prynne*, Camden Society, vols. 1, 6, and 9 (London, 1877)

Gathorne-Hardy, Jonathan, *The Rise and Fall of the British Nanny* (London: Hodder & Stoughton, 1972)

Gatty, Charles T., *Mary Davies and the Manor of Ebury*, vol. 2 (London: Cassell, 1921)

Godwin, William, *History of the Commonwealth of England: From the Death of Charles I to the Protectorate* (London: Nabu Press, 2010)

Gosse, Edmund, *Life and letters of John Donne*, vol. 2 (London: W. Heinemann, 1899)

Granger, James, *A Biographical history of England, from Egbert the King to the Revolution*, vol. 2, 5th ed. (London: W. Baynes & Son, 1824)

Green, Mary Ann Everett, *Elizabeth, Electress Palatine and Queen of Bohemia* (London: Methuen, 1909)

Guthrie, William P., *The Later Thirty Years War: from the Battle of Wittstock to the Treaty of Westphalia* (London: Greenwood Press, 2003)

Hannay, Margaret P., *Mary Sidney, Lady Wroth* (Farnham: Ashgate, 2010)

The Harleian Miscellany: a collection of scarce, entertaining and curious tracts, vols. 4 and 5 (London: White & Co., 1809)

Harte, Revd. Walter MA, *The History of Gustavus Adolphus King of Sweden Surnamed The Great*, vols. 1 and 2 (London: John Joseph Stockdale, 1807)

Heisler, R., 'Robert Fludd: A Picture in Need of Expansion', *Hermetic Journal*, 1989

Henfry, Henry William, *Numismata Cromwelliana* (London: John Russell Smith, 1877)

Hexham, Henry, *A Journall of the Taking in of Venlo [...] the Memorable Siege of Mastricht*

(Delft, 1633)

Hore, J. P., *The History of Newmarket and the Annals of the Turf*, vol. 2 (London: A. H. Baily & Co., 1886)

Howell, James, *Epistolae Ho-Elianae: Familiar Letters, Domestic and Foreign* (London: R. Ware, 1765)

Howell, Thomas Bayley, and William Cobbett, *A Complete Collection of State Trials and Proceedings for High Treason and other Crimes and Misdemeanors*, vol. 5 (London, 1816)

Hunt, Leigh, *The Town: Its Memorable Characters and Events* (London: Gibbons & Co., 1893)

Kitson, Frank, *Prince Rupert: Portrait of a Soldier* (London: Constable, 1994)

Leicester, Countess of, *Correspondence of Dorothy Sidney Percy, Countess of Leicester* (Farnham: Ashgate, 2010)

Lesson, A. Marvin, *Summary of the Cromwell Coinage* (London: British Numismatic Society, 1966)

Macaulay, Thomas Babington, *History of England*, vol. 2 (Philadelphia: Porter & Coates, 2008)

Malcolm, Noel, ed., *The Correspondence of Thomas Hobbes*, vol. 1 (Oxford: Clarendon Press, 1994)

Mann, Henry, *The Land We Live In; or The Story of Our Country* (New York: The Christian Herald, 1896)

Manning, Roger, *Swordsmen, the Martial Ethos in the Three Kingdoms* (Oxford: Oxford University Press, 2003)

—*An Apprenticeship in Arms: The Origins of the British Army 1585–1702* (Oxford: Oxford University Press, 2006)

Markham, Clements, *The Fighting Veres* (London: Sampson, 1888)

Marshall, Rosalind K., *The Winter Queen: The Life of Elizabeth of Bohemia* (Edinburgh: Scottish National Portrait Gallery, 1998)

Marston, John, 'What You Will', in *Old Plays, Being a Continuation of Dodsley's Collection*, vol. 2, by Charles Wentworth Dilke (London: Forgotten Books, 2012)

McLellan, Ian William, 'Herbert, Percy, second Baron Powis (1598–1667)', *Oxford Dictionary of National Biography* (Oxford: Oxford University Press, 2004)

Morrah, Patrick, *Prince Rupert of the Rhine* (London: Constable, 1976)

Munro, Robert, *Munro, his Expedition with the Worthy Scots Regiment called Mac-Keys* (London, 1637)

Murdoch, Steve, *Scotland and the Thirty Years War, 1618–1648* (London: Brill, 2001)

Nichols, J. B., *Progresses, Processions and Magnificent Festivities of James I*, vols. 3 and 4 (London: John Nichols, 1828)

Oman, Carola, *The Winter Queen: Elizabeth of Bohemia* (London: Phoenix Press, 2000)

Peacey, Jason, *Politicians and Pamphleteers: Propaganda During the English Civil Wars and Interregnum* (Aldershot: Ashgate, 2004)

—*Print and Public Politics in the English Revolution* (Cambridge University Press, 2013)

Pepys, Samuel, *Diaries* (London: Bell, 1983)

Perkins, Joseph, *Elegus in obitum [...] Gulielmi Comitis de Craven*, etc. (London, 1697)

Pevsner, Nikolaus, *Buildings of England. Berkshire* (London: Penguin, 1966)

Prynne, William, *Hidden works of darkenes brought to publike light* (London: Thomas Brudenell, 1645)

Pursell, Brennan C., *The Winter King: Frederick V of the Palatinate and the Coming of the Thirty Years War* (Aldershot: Ashgate, 2003)

Quiller-Couch, Sir Arthur, *Q Anthology, a selection of the prose and verse of Sir Arthur Quiller Couch* (London: J. M. Dent & Sons, 1948)

Raleigh, Sir Walter, Kt., *The Works of Sir Walter Raleigh, Kt.*, vol. 1 (London: R. Dodsley, 1751)

Roper, L. H., *Conceiving Carolina: Proprietors, Planters and Plots, 1662–1729* (New York: Palgrave Macmillan, 2004)

Rushworth, John, *Historical Collections of Private Passages of State: Volume 2, 1629–38* (London: D. Briowne, 1721)

Schreiber, Ray, *First Carlisle: Sir James Hay, First Earl of Carlisle as Courtier, Diplomat and Entrepreneur, 1580–1636* (Philadelphia: American Philosophical Society, 1984)

Scott, Eva, *Rupert Prince Palatine* (Westminster: Constable & Co., 1899)

Sheppard, F. H. W., ed., *Survey of London: vol. 37, Northern Kensington* (London: London Council, 1973)

Sirmans, M. Eugene, 'Politics in Colonial South Carolina: The Failure of Proprietary Reform 1682–1694', *The William and Mary Quarterly,* Third Series, vol. 23, no. 1.

Skinner, *The Life of General Monk* (London, 1724)

Smuts, R. Malcolm, 'Craven, William, Earl of Craven', *Oxford Dictionary of National Biography* (Oxford: Oxford University Press, 2004)

Sophia, Electress of Hanover, *Memoirs*, trans. by H. Forester (London: R. Bentley & Son, 1888)

Spelman, Sir Henry, *The History and Fate of Sacrilege* (London: J. Hartley, 1698)

Sprunger, Keith L., *Dutch Protestantism: A History of English and Scottish Churches of the Netherlands in the Sixteenth and Seventeenth Century* (Leiden, 1982)

Stater, 'Sheffield, Edmund, first Earl of Mulgrave, 1565–1646', *Oxford Dictionary of National Biography* (Oxford: Oxford University Press, 2004)

Stokes, Penelope, *Craven Country: The Story of Hamstead Marshall* (Newbury, 1996)

Stone, Lawrence, *The Crisis of the Aristocracy, 1558–1641* (Oxford: Clarendon, 1965)

Strachan, Michael, *Sir Thomas Roe 1581–1644* (Salisbury: Russell, 1989)

Strafford, Earl of, *The Earl of Strafforde's Letters and Dispatches*, vol. 1 (London: W. Bowyer, 1739)

Strickland, Agnes and Elizabeth, *Lives of the Queens of England from the Norman Conquest*, vol. 6 (London, 1840–49)

Thirsk, Joan, *The Rural Economy of England* (London: Hambledon Press, 1984)

Thomson, William, *A History of Tapestry from the Earliest Times until the Present Day* (London: Hodder & Stoughton, 1930)

Thurloe, John, *A Collection of the State Papers of John Thurloe* (London, 1742)

Tinniswood, Adrian, *By Permission of Heaven: The Story of the Great Fire of London* (London: Jonathan Cape, 2003)

Trevelyan, George Macaulay, *England Under the Stuarts* (London: Methuen, 1965)

Verney, Sir Ralph, *Verney Papers* (London: Camden Society, 1853)

Ver Steeg, Clarence L., *The Formative Years* (London: Hill & Wang, 1964)

Wakelyn, Jon, ed., *America's Founding Charters: Primary Documents in Colonial and Revolutionary Governance* (Westport: Greensood Press, 2006)

Waldie, Adam, *Waldie's Select Circulating Library*, vol. 15, part 1 (Philadelphia, 1832)

Waterhouse, Richard, *A New World Gentry* (Charleston: History Press, 2005)

Watts, William, *The Swedish Intelligencer* (London, 1632)

Webb, Stephen Saunders, *Lord Churchill's Coup: The Anglo-American Empire and the Glorious Revolution* (New York: Knopf, 1995)

Wedgwood, C. V., *The Thirty Years War* (London: Cape, 1944)

Weiss, John Gustav, 'Lord Craven und die Familie des Winterkönigs', in *Zeitschrift für die Geschichte des Oberrheins*, n. 43 (Karlsruhe: Badische Historische Commission, 1930)

Willson, Beckles, *The Great Company: being a History of the Honourable Company of Merchant Adventurers trading into Hudson's Bay* (London: Smith, 1900)

Wills from Doctors' Commons, Camden Society, vol. 83 (London, 1863)

Wilson, Beckles, *The Great Company* (Toronto: The Copp Clark Company, 1905)

Wilson, Derek, *All The King's Women: Love, Sex and Politics in the Life of Charles II* (London: Hutchinson, 2003)

Wilson, H. Schütz, *Studies in History, Legend and Literature* (London: Griffith & Farran, 1884)

Wilson, Peter H., *Europe's Tragedy: A History of the Thirty Years War* (London: Allen Lane, 2009)

Wing, W., 'Lecture on Old Caversham', reprinted from *Reading Mercury and County Paper*, 12 November 1894

Wood, Anthony à, *History and Antiquities of Oxford*, vol. 2 (Oxford: Clarendon Press, 1796)

Worden, Blair, *The English Civil Wars 1640–1660* (London: Weidenfeld & Nicolson, 2009)

Worp, Dr J. A., ed., *De Briefwisseling van Constantijn Huygens 1608–1634* ('s-Gravenhage: Martinus Nijhoff, 1911)

Wotton, Sir Henry, *Reliquiae Wottonianae; or, a collection of lives, letters and poems*, 3rd ed. (London: T. Roycroft, 1672)

Yates, Francis, *The Rosicrucian Enlightenment* (London: Routledge & Kegan Paul, 1972)